Faithful
Attraction

Other Tor books by Andrew M. Greeley

All About Women
Angel Fire
The Final Planet
God Game

Faithful Attraction

Andrew M. Greeley

TOR

A TOM DOHERTY ASSOCIATES BOOK

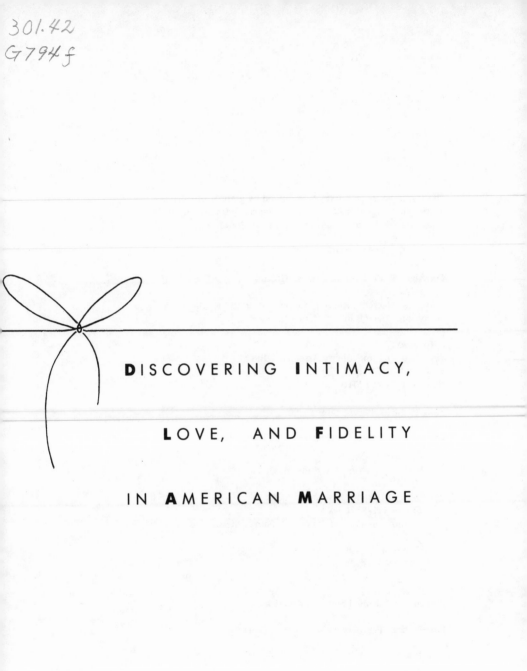

DISCOVERING INTIMACY,

LOVE, AND FIDELITY

IN AMERICAN MARRIAGE

NEW YORK

The *Psychology Today* survey was funded by grants from "The Home Show" and "Inside Edition." The second phase of the study was funded by an advance from Tor Books.

FAITHFUL ATTRACTION

A Tor Book
Published by Tom Doherty Associates, Inc.
49 West 24th Street
New York, N.Y. 10010

BOOK DESIGN BY JUDITH A. STAGNITTO

Library of Congress Cataloging-in-Publication Data

Greeley, Andrew M.
    Faithful attraction / Andrew M. Greeley.
        p.   cm.
    "A Tom Doherty Associates Books."
    ISBN 0-312-85109-X
    1. Marriage—United States.   2. Family life surveys—
United States.   I. Title.
    HQ728.G64   1991
    306.81'0973—dc20   90-48779
                                                  CIP

Printed in the United States of America

First Edition: February 1991

0 9 8 7 6 5 4 3 2 1

For George Harris, whose idea it was

Contents

Faithful
Attraction

1. How the Study Came to Be

This chapter describes the background and the history of the project on which the book is based. It argues that even before the data analyzed in this study were collected, there was some reason to doubt that marriage was in as unsatisfactory a condition as the mass media Conventional Wisdom would have led one to believe. Moreover, it considers the possibility that women might be the victims of the social changes celebrated as a "Sexual Revolution." The chapter may be skipped by the reader who wishes to dig into the findings which are reported in subsequent chapters. On the other hand, those who wish to know more about how and why the study was done and the predispositions with which the author began it will demand such a chapter (not unreasonably). So here it is.

THE DECLINE OF MARRIAGE?

We social scientists often engage in the (harmless) posture of pretending that we sit in our isolated think tanks, play with ideas and theories, derive hypotheses from our theories, and then seek data to test the hypotheses—either from original data collection or from existing data sets.

This posture is required for publication of our articles (which in turn wins us promotion and tenure) and is generally an innocent fiction. In fact, the quest for truth is a much more complicated and spontaneous affair. We follow hunches, instincts, guesses, sudden ideas, preconscious insights, and occasionally voices in the night (in our dreams). The theories are always there, usually in background mode, shaping our preconscious romps through social reality and gently pointing the direction in which our creativity rushes.

Occasionally it is helpful to try to trace the origins of a project and its development as a spontaneous surge of the preconscious (or the creative intuition if you will). In this study of marital intimacy and fidelity, it may even be necessary, so that the reader will understand the direction from which I'm coming.

The project started with my reading a *Newsweek* cover story in August 1987 about the decline and alleged revival of marriage in America. It was a more sophisticated essay than many others on the same subject. Contemporary marriage, it was argued, is caught in the counterpressures of two-job families, the decline of the extended family, geographic and occupational mobility, greater demands on emotional intimacy, the weakening of old community ties, and the erosion of old moral values. Divorces are increasing; cohabitation without marriage is increasing; the age at marriage is increasing; the number of never-married people is increasing; approval of premarital sex is increasing; half the marriages in the country will eventually end in divorce; half the young people in America will not grow up in the traditional family of husband, wife, and children. Etc. Etc. Etc.

I had read this sort of article often before and had not taken it too seriously, for reasons I'll outline in the next section. However, a quote from my fellow sociologist Norval Glenn stopped me cold. The proportion of married people who said they were very happy had declined from the early years of the General Social Survey (GSS) to its later years. Marriage, Glenn observed, seemed to be responding less effectively to human needs in our hedonistic culture than it once had (Glenn and Weaver 1988).

Since I have great respect for Glenn as a scholar and a friend, I did not begrudge him his purple prose—which sounded more like the enthusiasm of Robert Bellah than the sober conclusion of a survey researcher. Quite apart, however, from my own suspicion about judgments concerning "hedonism," I was impressed by the apparent decline of the happiness of married people. What, I wondered, was going on?

FALLACIES ABOUT CHANGE

Through thirty years of sociological work, I have learned to be skeptical of the rapid-social-change scenarios which the mass media present and which many of my sociological colleagues seem ready to accept in fields other than their own specialties. This skepticism is neither principled nor dogmatic, but empirical. I believe that serious social change is happening only when I see convincing evidence of it. Much of the heralded social change is supported only by private opinions and guesses and dubious data. Until someone shows me solid data, I don't believe that anything has changed very much.

Much of the babble about social change in the popular media suffers from one or a combination of three fallacies: The first is the Future Shock fallacy. Based on the work of Toffler (1971), this approach argues that the enormous changes in the speed of transportation and communication (jets, TV, computers) have so changed the ambience in which we humans live that all our old norms and communities and anchors have been called into question. Generally, this approach begs the question: it assumes what is to be proven, namely that norms and communities and stabilities are indeed affected by dramatic changes in technologies. One must prove that, for example, jet travel does weaken the bonds between husband and wife instead of assuming as inevitable such a weakening.

I derive from this the following rule: no social change is to be considered inevitable as a consequence of other social changes unless it is proven in fact to be such a consequence.

The second fallacy about social change is the "rise and fall" fallacy. The mass media require paradigms to interpret social reality "on the fly"; that is, to prepare news stories on deadline. The "secularization" paradigm assumes the decline of religion. Its flip side, the "resacralization" (or return to religion) paradigm, assumes that there can be a "surge" or rise of religion. Thus for the last twenty years journalists have hassled me as a sociologist of religion about evidence they find for a "return to religion." For the last ten years they have also desperately sought evidence or opinion on the "rise of the religious (or Fundamentalist) right."

The week before I wrote this chapter I received calls about "a religious return among Baby Boomers" and the possible increase of "Fundamentalists" in the nineties.

Both paradigms assume a cycle. I routinely (and routinely in vain) point out that just as there is no evidence for a decline of religion in America, there is no evidence of a "religious revival." Religious behavior correlates with age: it declines from the middle teens to the middle twenties and then increases to the middle forties when it is not significantly different from the behavior of previous cohorts. Baby Boomers are no more likely on the average, and no less likely, to drift back to that from which they drifted away earlier in life.

Moreover, I say to those who are concerned with the "rise of the Moral Majority"[1] that Fundamentalism has always been part of American life. The "First Great Awakening" was in 1744. For as long as we have survey data, the Fundamentalist component of American religion has been about 22% of the population. There is no evidence that it has increased in size during the last twenty years. The "rise" of Fundamentalism is merely the discovery by the New York–based national media of something that has always been there.

I confess that this experience with journalists on the aspect of sociology I know best has made me dubious about all their scenarios. Even before I read the *Newsweek* article in the summer of 1987, I assumed that the parallel scenario of "Sexual Revolution" and "new sexual conservatisms because of AIDS" was equally dubious—though I could hardly deny the increase in the divorce rate.

This brings us to the third fallacy, the "rate" fallacy. Rates are measures of human behavior—how many teenagers per hundred, for example, have experimented with drugs. They are not causes of behavior. They do not have an energy or a reality of their own which affects behavior. Yet often they are used in journalistic reports as though they were independent forces which cause social change instead of measures of change. The teenage drug-

---

[1] A phrase in which there are three fallacies—"rise," "majority," and "moral."

usage rate is not a force which will inevitably and invariably cause younger men and women to use drugs when they become teens. Media articles or commentary about rates often seems to imply that the only thing rates can do is increase. If 15% of adolescents experiment with drugs this year as opposed to 10% last year, then surely 20% or maybe even 27.5% will experiment with drugs next year.

There is, however, no inherent reason why rates cannot go down as well as up. A younger generation of teenagers may use drugs less than their predecessors (which is in fact what has happened), thus depressing the rate.

If divorce rates, cohabitation rates, never-married rates, number-of-children rates, and age-at-marriage rates all continue to change, then eventually no one will be married and there won't be any more children—suggestions which seem to be implied by much of the mass media commentary on marriage.

Yet any reading of the literature on the history of the family[2] shows that demographic rates can vary remarkably over time. Thus in Ireland before the Great Famine, age at marriage was low, birth rates were high, and illegitimacy was high. After the Famine, all the rates changed. With the first sign of prosperity in modern Ireland in the 1960s, the rates all changed again. In more remote eras, these crucial demographic rates bounce up and down, usually in response to economic conditions. Andrew Cherlin's work (1981) demonstrated that age at marriage and number of children have been relatively constant in the United States in this century, save for the years during and after the Second World War. The larger families and the younger age at marriage in the forties and fifties are the exception, and not the long-range trend from which the present rates are a deviation.

Thus my predispositions are to assume that a change in patterns of marital and premarital behaviors are the result of technological and economic factors which enable men and women to do what they would have rather liked to do anyway.

Research by Robert Michael, then director of the National Opinion Research Center (NORC) and now dean of the School of Public Policy Studies at the University of Chicago, seemed to

---

[2] Research on family structure—size, age at marriage, number of children, illegitimacy, death of spouse, remarriage, etc.—from local community records in ages past, especially in France and Britain (Wrigley 1969, Demos 1970, Laslett 1971, 1972, Shorter 1977).

confirm this predisposition. In the late 1970s, Michael (1988) constructed an elaborate econometric model which assumed that the increase in divorces was a result of the development of the birth control pill and the resultant freedom of women to take advantage of employment opportunities. This model predicted a leveling off of the divorce rate in the 1980s, once the impact of the Pill had worked its way through the "system." Reality fit the curve of Michael's projection: divorce rates did indeed level off precisely when he predicted they would. A conclusion from this ingenious research exercise was that more effective fertility control enabled women to escape from marriages in which they had previously been trapped or in which they would have been trapped if they had not gained some economic independence.

Culture had changed because technology had made the culture change possible. It seemed to me that the new technology of the Pill could account for everything else that has been labeled "Sexual Revolution." It was easier—and safer—to engage in behavior which had never been unattractive.

Moreover, speculating on Michael's research, I reflected that an increase in the divorce rate need not mean that there was more frustration and less satisfaction in marriage. It might just as plausibly mean that it was now easier for those who were unhappy to leave their marriage, with the result that the average level of happiness inside marriage had gone up—or at least had remained the same.

Let us assume a hypothetical population of marriages in which half are relatively satisfactory and the other half not and which the divorce rate is 10%. A survey would reveal that 55% of the respondents report that their marriage was very happy. Then let us say that divorce becomes easier, and that more of the other 45% choose to divorce, so that the divorce rate rises to 20%. Assuming no change in the level of marital happiness in the population, one would discover in the second survey that 63% of the married population said that they were very happy. The divorce rate would have gone up and so would the proportion of those remaining married who said that they were very happy—and the level of marital dissatisfaction would not have changed in the population.

I'm not saying that this is what in fact has happened. I'm saying, rather, that one cannot assume in the absence of proof that this has not happened.

Let's take another scenario into consideration. Let us suppose that in the first example the actual level of satisfaction among the ever married increases at the same time, for reasons that are unrelated to the changes which make divorce easier. *Thus* the proportion ever married who are very happy rises from 55% to 60%. If the divorce rate is 20%, the proportion of those currently married who are "very happy" will be 75%—half again as high as it was before the two orthogonal changes took place. Again, I don't say that this is what has happened in the United States. I don't know, and neither does anyone else. I am saying that such a possibility cannot be ruled out in the absence of any evidence other than the fact of the increasing divorce rate.

The satisfaction of those who remain married is a matter for empirical investigation, not for a priori assumptions based on the divorce rate. That is, in the absence of data about those who remained married, there is no a priori reason to conclude that an increase in divorce indicates an increase in frustration and un-happiness among those who remain married.

Not only did the divorce rate level off in the early and middle eighties, so too did the rate of those who had never married, the average age at marriage, and even approval of premarital sex. As I argue later, this leveling off does not seem to fit the scenario of a reaction to AIDS. Rather, the stabilization of rates seems more readily explicable according to the same model as that which Michael had developed for the rise in divorce rates: the effect of safe and easy fertility control working its way through the social "system."

Michael in other research (Willis and Michael 1988) also es-tablished that most cohabitation is not an escape from marriage but a preparation for marriage.

Thus my assumptions in the summer of 1987: I was not dis-posed to be convinced that there had been a "decline" or a "re-vival" in marriage. Rather I suspected that improved methods of fertility control would account for most if not all the changes which had occurred in sexual and marital behavior. Marriage was in a lot less trouble, I assumed, then the popular media analyses suggested that it was.

I suspected that the usual proclivities to view with alarm or to celebrate social change revealed more about those who took such positions than they did about the actual condition of marriages in America. "Conservatives" warned of the end of marriage and the family unless there was a return to the old morality. "Liberals" celebrated the new freedom and enthusiastically announced that half the marriages would end in divorce and that more than half of the children in the country would not grow up in "traditional" family environments. "Reactionary" church persons denounced materialism and consumerism and selfishness (and narcissism, if they knew the word). "Progressive" church persons warned that the churches would have to keep up with changing patterns of morality and intimacy.

Most such posturing, it seemed to me at the time, was a replay of positions taken repeatedly before by the same observers and their ancestors. There was nothing new under the sun. The more things changed, the more they remained the same. Certainly, a change in technology had made possible some changes in behavior, but the "New Permissiveness" and the "Sexual Revolution," as moral philosophies, sounded much like the old "Playboy Philosophy" in new garb. They were, I suspected, often nothing more than a new excuse which enabled men to justify attempts to "score" with women without any sense of responsibility for their victims.

Obviously I am attempting more here than to describe my state of mind in the summer of 1987 on the alleged decline of marriage. I am also trying to persuade the reader to concede for the sake of the argument, if nothing else, that the evidence to support the thesis of a dramatic decline in marriage was less than conclusive. Most people married. Most people were still married to their first spouse. Most divorced people remarried. Most cohabitations were a preparation for marriage. The decline of marriage—almost a dogma in the paradigms of mass media Conventional Wisdom—was arguably an artifact of the three fallacies I have listed in previous paragraphs.

Given the lack of evidence to the contrary, the descriptions of marriage that emerged from our *Love and Marriage* study are not so surprising after all. Yet I will admit that I was surprised by the dramatic difference between the Conventional Wisdom about marriage and the empirical data.

In the summer of 1987, however, I faced a challenge to my skepticism. If Norval Glenn's speculation based on data was valid, then there had been not only a technological change created by the birth control pill, but a substantial cultural change that seemed independent of the Pill: marriage was not working as well as it used to.

MARRIAGES LESS HAPPY?

Professor Glenn graciously made available at my request a pre-publication copy of his yet unpublished paper (Glenn and Weaver 1988)—and like the true scholar that he is, welcomed the dialogue which ensued.

The dependent variable—the one being measured—in his analysis was a response to the simple "happiness" question, which has become a staple measure of psychological well being in the survey research fraternity.[3] Clearly that measure had declined for women since the early 1970s. However, the next measure in the GSS questionnaire—on happiness of the respondent's marriage[4]—displayed no change between the early seventies and the middle eighties for either men or women. Moreover, another measure of satisfaction with family life also showed no decline. Women were less personally happy, it seemed, but not less happy with either marriage or family.

The decline in personal happiness was limited to married mothers under forty who were caught in cross pressures between home and work. They were satisfied with their jobs and with their marriage and family, but their personal happiness had eroded because of the difficulties of balancing both dimensions of life. (I return to this issue in Chapter 20.)

The solution was apparently trivial. Everyone knew that younger working mothers were caught in such pressures. One hardly needed intricate survey analysis to establish that fact, though it was perhaps useful to have the number pinned down precisely. Marriage, however, was not failing to make women happy. Society was failing to provide ways in which younger women could balance career and family.

[3] "Taken all together, how would you say things are these days—would you say that you are very happy, pretty happy, or not too happy?"
[4] "Taking things all together, how would you describe your marriage? Would you say that your marriage is very happy, pretty happy, or not too happy?"

While I was working on this analysis I read Lenore Weitzman's book *The Divorce Revolution* (1987), a study of the California "no-fault" divorce legislation. A feminist and a liberal, Weitzman assumed (as did most feminists and liberals) that such legislation would benefit women. To her consternation she discovered that in fact it hurt women: in the year after a divorce women experience a 72% decline in the standard of living, while their former husbands experience a 42% rise in their standard of living. Weitzman concluded her study with the observation that, until there is gender equality in society, gender-neutral legislation will in fact discriminate against women. Thus women need to be given special legal protection, a position which is a reversal of her previous feminist attitude.[5]

I agreed with Weitzman's conviction that "easy" divorce legislation would not be repealed, but I began to consider more seriously the possibility that in the midst of all the progress of feminism in the seventies and eighties there were many women who were suffering severe cross pressures and even being exploited and victimized by men on the pretext of the "New Permissiveness."[6]

I sent my response to the Glenn article off to the *Journal of Marriage and Family*. After considerable nit-picking, it was turned down—approved for publication but without a high enough priority so that it actually would be published. An article which suggested that perhaps marriage was not failing after all, but that younger women were caught in cross pressures, was not deemed worth publishing.[7] You win some and you lose some in the academic publishing game, but I was troubled by the decision of the editors of the journal whose field was marriage and family

---

[5] She does not add, perhaps because it is not pertinent to her work, that this policy position is not unlike that of some of those who opposed the Equal Rights Amendment.

[6] For the record, I endorse all the goals of feminism (including the ordination of women as priests, and eventually as bishops, and even as Pope in the Catholic Church) if not all the stands of the Feminist movement. I believe that the goal of an authentic feminism ought not to be the masculinization of women (there is already too much male aggression in the world) but the feminization of men—the creation of freedom for men to develop the more tender aspects of their personality. Moreover, I believe that society ought to be restructured so that the conflict between motherhood and career is eliminated. Nevertheless, I believe that Feminism as a movement has been callously insensitive to those women who are paying the costs in exploitation and victimization, in pressure and frustration, in loneliness and poverty, for the greater freedom of women in general.

[7] Glenn himself had no objections. Quite the contrary, he seemed pleased with the dialogue that his article had occasioned.

that dialogue with an already published article on the decline of marriage was not appropriate.

A MONOGAMOUS PEOPLE

The article was eventually published in *Sociology and Social Research* (1989). By then my interest in the condition of marriage had been increased considerably by a battery of questions included in the 1988 General Social Survey about the AIDS problem. One of the questions asked how many sexual partners the respondent had had in the past year. The reponse was that 86% of all sexually active Americans and 96% of married Americans had had only one sexual partner during the previous year. Ninety-six out of every hundred married Americans were claiming marital fidelity in the past year. Moreover, a similar study from England reported virtually the same finding (British Market Research Bureau Ltd., 1987). Promiscuity (defined without implications of moral judgment as having more than one sexual partner) was prevalent only among the young and the unmarried. Of the respondents between twenty-five and thirty, three-quarters were monogamous, as were more than four-fifths of every older age cohort. Only among those twenty-four and under did promiscuity approach average behavior (44% for men and 39% for women).

This first hint of the fidelity epidemic did not seem to be attributable to fear of AIDS (i.e., knowing someone who had died of AIDS did not significantly alter the proportions of monogamous and faithful respondents).

Robert Michael, Tom Smith, and I wrote an article describing these findings, and since we considered them important data for those concerned with the AIDS epidemic, shipped the article off to *Science*. It was promptly rejected without comment. *Scientific American* also rejected it with the blunt remark that they simply did not believe our findings. The article was eventually published in *Society* (Greeley, Michael, and Smith 1990).

The dogmatism—I almost wrote "arrogant dogmatism"—behind this response is one of the more unattractive aspects of American science. Any research which seems to challenge the Conventional Wisdom is dismissed out of hand with almost no attention paid to the analysis involved. In this case the Conventional Wisdom was not previous research—no one had studied monogamy or marital fidelity in the United States before—but the conventional paradigms of the mass media.

Were our respondents lying? How did the distinguished editors know that? If they were lying, who was lying and how much? Why would English respondents lie the same way? What evidence did we have that they were telling the truth? Why would the nonmarried respondents report such high levels of monogamy? What moral code demanded that unmarried men and women report high levels of sexual restraint? Why did marriage add only about twenty-five percentage points to the monogamy rates of the unmarried?

In the 1989 GSS we added a question about the number of sexual partners in the course of a lifetime. We defined "chastity" as having no more sexual partners since the eighteenth birthday than one has had marriage partners. It is a minimum estimate of marital fidelity, since the partners other than the spouse may have been partners before the marriage (Smith 1990). By this standard, 48% of married Americans are chaste, 65% of the women, 30% of the men. Chastity rates for men do not vary with age. They do for women, but even among women under forty, 45% are chaste. Moreover, among these younger women who were not chaste, the average number of sexual partners in addition to marital partners is one.

The NORC/Kinsey study of 1970 indicated that at the time, 28% of the men and 78% of the women were chaste at the time of their marriage (in the sense that they had had sexual intercourse only with their future spouse). These numbers suggest change only among women in the last twenty years and also indicate that most sexual experimentation takes place before marriage.[8]

The picture which emerged from these analyses was of sexual experimentation before marriage and of moderately high (and perhaps very high) levels of fidelity after marriage. The only

[8] An intractable problem in this kind of research is that while fidelity rates for men and women are the same as are reports of the frequency of sexual intercourse, there are striking differences between men and women in the number of sexual partners reported in the course of a lifetime and among those who are not married. One gender or the other (or possibly both) is exaggerating. See Smith (1988) for a discussion of this problem. Note, however, that on matters of marital fidelity there are no gender-related differences.

change in two decades seemed to be an increase in experimentation before marriage by young women. However, nearly half of young women and a third of young men had only one sexual partner after their eighteenth birthday.

Taken together, these findings did not seem to suggest a picture of an institution in deep trouble. Even if a quarter of our married respondents were lying—a gratuitous assumption if there ever were one—still, over 70% of them would have been monogamous and hence faithful during the previous year. Even if they were only as monogamous as unmarried people (who surely would have no reason to deceive), three out of five would be faithful. Fidelity in marriage even in that unlikely scenario would still be the norm.[9]

I suppose that if I had not encountered the dogmatism of scholars who rejected findings out of hand even though they have no research data of their own to refute such findings, I might have lost some interest in the subject. But scholars who take their paradigms from the mass media and from such efforts as the Hite Reports infuriate me. Hence when T. George Harris, then the editor of *Psychology Today*, proposed a study of fidelity in marriage, I leaped at the invitation. No one had ever studied the subject before. It was high time.

THE   PERSISTENCE
OF   ROMANCE?

Harris also suggested a related theme: the persistence and importance of romantic love in marriage. He noted that one of the basic themes of my novels is the renewal of romance, the rebirth of love, the chance of a second (and third and fourth and fifth) chance. While tough-minded marriage counselors and educators and church persons normally dismiss romantic love, my impres-

---

[9] In a later chapter I examine in greater detail the theory that our respondents are not telling the truth about their sexual behavior. For the moment it is worth noting that those who rejected our findings on these grounds are basing their rejection on testimony about extramarital sex from individuals to whom they have spoken—conducted their own informal survey, in other words.

How do they know that *their* respondents are not lying?

sion is that it is only the periodic renewal of romantic love which sustains many marriages.[10]

Perhaps Roger Staubach, quarterback for the Dallas Cowboys back in the days when they were America's team, uttered the classic statement of this position when he said that he fell in love at least as often as did his colleague Broadway Joe Namath of the New York Jets (remember them?); but he always fell in love with the same woman.

Sweet? Romantic? Saccharine? Unrealistic?

Merely a paradigm for research.

There is not a complete overlap between the novelist in my head and the sociologist. I had not thought about the possibility of research on romance.

But when George Harris suggested it, I thought it was a great idea.[11]

---

[10]Theologically I believe these renewal interludes are sacraments—hints of the nature of God's relation to us.

[11]I will not take seriously the ad hominem put-down that a priest is unable to analyze survey data about marriage unless and until someone demonstrates that I mishandle the data in a way that a married researcher would not.

2. Ground Rules

This chapter lays out the ground rules for the rest of the book—what the book is about and what it is not about. This chapter may be skipped by those readers who are ready to accept on faith the accuracy of the rest of the book. However, many of them, I suspect, will want to return to this chapter to discover the rules of the game.

THE STORY TO BE TOLD

This is a report on fidelity and intimacy in American marriage based on the first national probability sample study ever attempted of love and intimacy among married Americans. The typical finding of the study, as hinted by the title, is that fidelity is common in American marriage, even epidemic. Indeed it might be called pandemic rather than epidemic.

Marriage in America is in better condition than most married Americans think it is. That statement is not an Irish bull, though it may sound like one. Nor is it a paradox. It is statistical fact based on a phenomenon called *pluralistic ignorance*—most respondents are ignorant of what most other respondents reply. In this case, most Americans think that most other Americans are not as happily married as they themselves are.

On the subject of marital fidelity, two-thirds say they are more concerned about fidelity than most people—in other words, *most* say they are more concerned about fidelity than most people, a classic manifestation of pluralistic ignorance.[12] Three-quarters of Americans agree strongly that fidelity is essential for a happy marriage, and nine out of ten say that they have been faithful to one another, but only a quarter agree that most married people are faithful to one another, yet another example of pluralistic ignorance.

Thus there is every reason to believe that the typical respondent in the survey being analyzed would deny the truth of the picture that the very same respondent has helped to create with his/her self-description.

Thus this report is likely to be quite controversial and even find itself denounced by those who would insist that, while it may be describing their own marriage accurately, it is not a valid description of marriage in general.

What can I tell you?

Because of the controversial nature of findings that everyone knows cannot be true (except of course in their own case), it seems appropriate to define at the beginning what this book is and what it is not. Every word in the first sentence of this chapter thus becomes important.

S O C I A L S C I E N C E , N O T E T H I C S

The goal of this volume is to report social science data and not to present ethical, philosophical, or ideological assertions. Like everyone else, I have ethical and philosophical orientations on the subject of marriage. I am in favor of marriage, fidelity, romance, and even sexual abandon in married love (easy enough for someone who doesn't have to practice it). But I do not need

[12] A phenomenon not unlike that reported at Lake Wobegon where all the women are strong, all the men are good looking and all the children are "above average." Later in the present work we will report that the average respondent thinks his/her relationship with the children in the family is "better than average."

empirical data to support these orientations. I would not oppose marital fidelity if nine out of ten Americans were unfaithful to their spouse. Nor is my conviction that it is ethically desirable behavior reinforced by the fact that it turns out also to be popular behavior. Ethical and philosophical positions are not derived from survey research.

I am also opposed to the exploitation and victimization of women, a position which cannot be weakened or enhanced by survey findings. However, when the evidence reported in this book demonstrates that many women have been the losers in the changes of sexual behavior during the past quarter century, I am not disposed to hide my dismay that the Feminist movement has paid so little attention to this victimization.

Because this book is an exercise in empirical sociology, not ethics or philosophy, it does not follow that there are no ethical or philosophical conclusions which may be drawn from it. In the concluding chapter I engage in my own reflections, which I emphasize now do not follow inevitably from my social science findings (no philosophical or ethical conclusions ever follow inevitably from science).

ANALYSIS, NOT PRESCRIPTIONS

I intend this book to be neither an outline of social policy prescriptions nor a "how-to-do-it" manual for married people. The reader will search in vain for a solution to the problem of the declining happiness of married mothers or for a set of hints on how to revive a dull marriage. I am not trying to lay down rules and regulations, guidelines or helpful suggestions for anyone. It may be that rules and suggestions can be derived from my analysis, but I will not do the deriving. Thus it would appear from the data that the joint shower or bath is an inexpensive, effective, and popular sexual turn-on for many married people. It would also appear that undressing for one's spouse has a considerable erotic payoff, especially for women. The reader ought not to conclude that I am recommending such behaviors for anyone not presently engaged in them as a normal part of marital intimacy.

Such amusements do not seem to do much harm to those who perform them, but it does not follow that you should head for the shower with your spouse yourself, much less that you must do so.

M A R R I E D   P E O P L E,
N O T   E V E R Y O N E

This book is about married men and women only. I intend no slight to unmarried parents (usually mothers), the never married, the divorced and not remarried, those cohabiting without marriage, gays or lesbians. However, since 54% of Americans over eighteen are presently married (approximately 104 million people), four-fifths of them to their first spouse,[13] and since there has never been a national probability sample survey of them, it does not seem inappropriate for this particular exercise to concentrate on married people. The notion that marriage is gradually fading away to be replaced by alternative life-styles will be discussed in the next chapter. It is enough in this chapter to be content with the observation that marriage still seems popular with a substantial segment of American adults.

A   P R O B A B I L I T Y   S A M P L E

I will analyze data from a number of different sources in this report—most notably from two surveys done for *Psychology Today* in the winter of 1989–1990 by the Gallup organization (Gallup/ *Love and Marriage I* and *II* or sometimes merely *Love and Marriage*), and two surveys of the annual General Social Survey directed by NORC (NORC/GSS). In addition I will on some occasions use the

[13] Figures are taken from *General Social Survey*, 1985 to 1989 (Davis and Smith, 1972–1989). Regarding nonmarried people, 11% of all Americans over eighteen are widows or widowers, 16% are divorced or separated, and 19% are never-married. Note, too, that two-thirds of all ever-married people are still married to their first spouse.

entire General Social Survey file from 1972 to 1989 (Davis and Smith 1972–1989). I will also cite data from the NORC/Kinsey study of 1970 (Klassen et al. 1989).

The two-part *Love and Marriage*/Gallup study is the first full-scale national probability sample study of sexuality and fidelity in marriage. It is a preliminary investigation which will doubtless be improved upon in further research. It also creates a tentative benchmark for measuring change in responses over time. It is based on two telephone surveys with random samples of 657 married couples, both partners age eighteen and over, living in the continental United States, for a total of 1,314 respondents, half men and half women. In surveys of this sort the sampling error which might occur (with 95% confidence) could be plus or minus four percentage points for items in one sample and less than plus or minus three percentage points for items in both samples.[14]

The present analysis is supported by data from the 1988 and 1989 General Social Surveys collected by NORC (788 and 847 married respondents, respectively) in personal interviews.

"Probability" sample—or "random" sample, as it is also called—have a technically precise meaning: each time a respondent is chosen, every other potential respondent in the population must have had an equal chance of being chosen (as if the population of married men and women over eighteen were on a giant roulette wheel that is spun for each choice). In the absence of such design, no valid generalizations can be made from the sample to the general population, no matter how large the sample may be, nor how closely it seems to match the population in its distribution on demographic characteristics.

Research based on other forms of sampling may make interesting reading, but it tells nothing about the behavior of the total population. When nonprobability samples such as the various Hite Reports (Hite 1977, 1981, 1987) are adduced to refute the findings of probability-based research, it is a process not dissimilar

---

[14]The original research carried out in the first survey was severely limited, both in sample size and questions asked, by the availability of funding. The findings were, however, so interesting that I decided to commission the second survey to provide both a larger sample base and more items. The two questionnaires are printed in the appendix. The major variables used in this report were in both surveys, with the exception of sexual satisfaction, working mothers, and divorce and reconciliation.

to forecasting the weather by reading the entrails of chickens in refutation of the techniques and findings of professional mete-orology.

An insistence on probability sampling is not a peculiarity of certain scholars. Nor does it represent only a "better" form of sampling in comparison with "good samples" taken by other researchers (such as Ms. Hite or the late Dr. Kinsey). It is the only sampling technique which enables a researcher to be precise about the odds that his/her sample will be different from the population sampled. No other method can exclude the possibility of mon-umental error because of a biased sample.

There is, alas, a version of Gresham's law in research: bad samples drive out good samples. Hence the researcher with the good sample must defend the honesty and representativeness of his/her respondents against those who have assembled the Con-ventional Wisdom by methods as scientific as wetting their fingers and holding them in the wind.

R E S E A R C H R E P O R T, N O T J O U R N A L I S M

The rhetoric of social research is different from the rhetoric of feature-article journalism. The former concentrates on the aver-age, the latter tends to concentrate on the unique case. The former is interested, for example, in the majority who do not engage in extramarital affairs, the latter is usually interested in the individual man or woman who does have such experiences. The former is more given to cautiously nuanced statements, the latter to sweep-ing generalizations. The former often seems, as a national news magazine once said of a report of mine on Catholic schools, to be mired in qualifications; the latter is concerned with broad and perhaps irresistible social changes. The world seen by the former is usually a world of multishaded gray, the world of the latter tends to be simple black and white.

The findings of social research are almost always less dramatic than the findings of popular journalism; the social research report almost always presents a more complicated and more intricate picture than does the popular article or TV special. The researcher almost always finds more stability and continuity than does the journalist. Finally, the research report is almost always content with more uncertainty, ambiguity, and mystery than the feature writer can tolerate.[15]

Both rhetorical games have their own rules and their own purpose and legitimacy—so long as the writer and reader agree on the nature of the game and the limitations imposed by the rules of each game and so long as both understand that the rules of one game cannot be imposed on the other game. The conflict occurs when the reader of feature articles discovers that the research scholar has called into question the mass media picture of reality which the reader has come to believe as unassailably true. Does not everyone know that there has been a dramatic increase in marital infidelity among women? In fact, is this not the reason why Senator Jesse Helms and his allies have tried to block government-funded research on human sexuality? Will not such research lead to even more adultery among women and the even greater deterioration of marriage and family life? How dare anyone jar this Conventional Wisdom about the real world with a report which suggests that generalizations about the so-called Sexual Revolution should be strongly qualified?

What can I tell you?

A reader often finds herself/himself caught in the crossfire between two needs—the need to admit that reality is complicated and intricate, and the need for simple and sure road maps with which to negotiate a path through the mazes that reality has created. The research scholar can only say that, in the reader's better moments, he/she knows that the world is a gray, messy, complex place and that any guide who suggests that it is not merits suspicion as either a fool or a charlatan.

This book is not a monograph on American marriage, because there are not enough data yet available to begin to think about such an effort. It is, rather, a report on two surveys designed as a benchmark which may eventually make such a monograph possible.

---

[15]I write "almost always" in this paragraph because there are some exceptions. In my own career as a sociologist the most notable case in which the survey findings were far more dramatic than those reported in the mass media was the response of American Catholics to the 1968 Papal Encyclical on birth control. Indeed, popular journalism has yet to catch up with the rejection of that teaching by both Catholic laity and Catholic clergy.

Finally, the book will be relentlessly factual, both because facts are what surveys are about and because there are so many myths about the condition of American marriage which need to be refuted.

Consider the following "facts":

1. Romantic love diminishes as the years of marriage increase.

2. For all the religious activity of Americans, religion is not an important part of American marital adjustment.

3. Sexual experimentation ceases to be important after a certain age in life.

4. Cohabitation facilitates adjustment to marriage.

5. Many Americans, if they had it to do over again, would marry someone other than their present spouse.

6. The pressures on a working mother reduce sexual satisfaction and marital adjustment.

7. Children diminish the happiness of marriage.

8. As the years go on, the spouse looks less attractive.

9. There are few ways to sustain sexual attraction in marriage over the long run.

10. Once a marriage has been in serious trouble, it is difficult to regain its former level of happiness.

All of the above "facts" seem reasonable enough. Indeed, most of us have read articles in newspapers or magazines which support them. They all have, however, one thing in common: none of them, as I shall demonstrate, are true.

E V E R Y O N E D O E S S U R V E Y S

All assertions about human behavior are based on surveys, either the formal surveys that the professionals take (with probability samples, quality control, and careful statistical analyses) or the informal collection of impressions from one's own experience that are often cited in dissent from formal survey findings.

Thus a reviewer in a national magazine said, in commenting

on the Kinsey/NORC book, "We also have to thank women, gays and lesbians, and young people, who demolished traditional myths, for the democratization of American sexuality. . . . These three groups demanded their share of the pleasure pie in a way that shook the patriarchy to its phallocentric core."

A more graphic statement of the Conventional Wisdom about the "Sexual Revolution" one could not imagine. The author of it implies that he has spoken with a sufficient number of Americans of the classes he describes to be able to generalize about their motivations and behavior.

The point here is not that he does not know what he's talking about. The point is, rather, that he has done his own survey, which he thinks is superior to that done by the professional scholars: he has spoken with people, he has noted their responses, he has analyzed these conversations, and he has generalized from his sample to the population.

The critic of the professional survey should realize that she/he has also made a survey to sustain his/her assertions, most likely of a biased and inadequate sample, with sloppy data collection, and imprecise statistical analysis. The frequent pretense of such critics to superior intelligence and sensitivity is a mask for the inadequacy of their data. If they assert that our respondents are deceiving us, we could just as gratuitously reply that perhaps their "respondents" are deceiving them.

METHODS

The professional researcher and the cocktail party amateur use the same basic analytic method: comparison. The former may assert that religiously exogamous marriages seem less harmonious and satisfying. The latter may assert that religiously mixed marriages work as well as other marriages. Both are comparing marriages about which they know something, the former from his/her data, the latter (presumably) from personal experience.

The professional researcher has a vast repertory of analytic techniques that he uses to make the comparisons which are essential to her/his analysis. Are younger women, for example, happier because they have had more sexual freedom (as the reviewer quoted above seems to imply), or does promiscuity lead to guilt in later life? A fair question, it would seem.

Or one might ask whether the apparent increase in romantic play among younger respondents appeals more to women than to men, or more to men than to women. One must ask not only whether these behaviors contribute more to marital satisfaction for one gender or the other, but also whether they contribute to a better image (or possibly a worse image) of the spouse for one gender or the other.

This often fairly intricate method of making comparisons is the analytic technique that I use in the present book. I also often combine various responses into clusters by a technique called "factor analysis." For the sake of concreteness, I most frequently use in my analysis only the item which correlates most strongly with the total factor.

I also use a technique called "multiple regression" (don't let the words bother you) to see how much of the variance between (let us say) the happily married and the unhappily married can be explained by a "model" combining a number of variables which correlate with reports of happy marriage. This technique also enables me to depict, for example, the relative importance of sex and religion in sustaining the "falling in love" phase of marriage. Once or twice I also make use of a technique called "log-linear model fitting" to explore the complexity of a set of relationships.[16]

In this book I have used figures to illustrate many points. Figures are nothing more than pictures and greatly facilitate, as do all pictures, understanding of what is being described. Consider Figures 11.5 to 11.11 (pages 129–33) which describe the impact of the "falling in love" phase of marriage on the sexual activities of men and women as they grow older. The straight lines across the figure for the sexual behavior of those who are in the romantic phase at whatever age tell the story powerfully: one is never too

---

[16]I will explain more about the multiple regression technique in Chapter 4. It is possible, I think, to understand that technique without knowing the mathematics involved, because it is inherently reasonable. I will not, however, try to explain log-linear model fitting because I have yet to find a way to make it inherently plausible to those who lack technical training. Sometimes I don't quite understand it myself and must call my colleague Michael Hout for guidance!

old to fall in love, never too old to be a romantic, never too old, if you wish, to be a romantic fool.

Indeed, if you will take a few minutes to become a skilled reader of figures, you can understand the themes of this book just from reading the introductions and conclusions of the chapters and studying the figures.

CONCLUSION

A final difference between the journalist and the professional researcher is that the latter must always be more restrained in his rhetoric. These first few thousand words of the present book are an exercise in restraint. I want to define as precisely as I can what I am about in this book, and what I'm not about. As the first (national sample) study ever attempted of fidelity and intimacy in American marriage, the book is necessarily a preliminary effort. It is neither a definitive nor a comprehensive study of marriage in our culture, although I hope it may be a contribution to an eventual study of such quality and quantity.

For all its preliminary nature and limitations and imperfections, I still feel that cautious analysis of the kind attempted here is a lot better than the equivalent of going into a self-induced trance and reciting visions about the present and future condition of American marriage out of the material which bubbles up from one's unconsciousness (about, for example, seizing a share of the pleasure pie and shaking the patriarchy to its phallocentric core).

Oracles may perform useful functions on some occasions, but survey research is more helpful for those who prefer facts to visions some of the time.

3. Americans Describe Their Marriages

In this chapter I present the basic findings of the Love and Marriage *research—how Americans portray their marriages in response to survey interview questions and address in detail the possibility that they are not telling the truth about their experience of marriage.*

MORE ON FIDELITY

The fidelity and chastity statistics in both *Love and Marriage* and GSS are virtually the same. In the former, 96% reported that they were faithful last year, and 38% of respondents in their first marriage say that they have had only one sexual partner in their life (30% of the men and 48% of the women). Ninety percent of the respondents (91% of the women and 89% of the men) say that they have had only one sexual partner for the duration of their present marriage. The last figures close the gap which existed in the GSS data—the number of partners between the beginning of marriage and last year.[17]

It would thus appear that the argument which attributes fidelity to AIDS will not stand up. The fidelity epidemic (pandemic, if you will) is not a recent development. To the extent that they take multiple sexual partners (and many do not do so at all), Americans do their explorations before or between marriages and not during them.[18]

There is surely more divorce in America than there used to be, but not much more infidelity.

Note that GSS and *Love and Marriage* are different studies conducted by different methods. The former is a personal interview survey on a wide range of variables. The latter was a telephone survey devoted entirely to marriage—with the sexual partner questions asked at the end of the interview. Yet the results are virtually the same. Both studies do prove that Americans are a most monogamous, a most faithful and a most—well, a *reasonably* chaste people.

Americans are also happily married and optimistic about their marriage. More than three-fifths say that their marriage is "very happy." Three-quarters say that their spouse is their best friend. More than four-fifths say they would marry the same person again if they had it to do over. Three-fifths reject the idea that children take the fun out of marriage. Almost half also reject the notion that as the years go on much of the fun goes out of marriage.[19]

[17] If those who refused to answer the questions are counted in with the assumption that *all* of them have been unfaithful or unchaste the proportions decline only a few percentage points. The refusals are also excluded from the articles done on the GSS data.

[18] Some divorced respondents may have experimented sexually before the previous marriage was ended. They would not be counted as having extramarital powers in a marriage unless they were unfaithful in their present marriage.

[19] The proportions in this paragraph are all the "strongly" agree (or disagree) percentages. If those who disagree somewhat are added, the proportion rejecting the decline of marriage with children and age increase to 82% and 70%. Older people are more likely to reject such statements than younger respondents.

P O R T R A I T   O F   T H E   S P O U S E

Americans like their spouses:[20] 82% (14%) say that their spouse is good with children; 77% (20%) say that the spouse is kind and gentle; 76% (21%) say the spouse is physically attractive; 66% (27%) think that the spouse respects the respondent's opinion; 66% (24%) say the spouse helps with household tasks; 64% (30%) agree that the spouse makes them feel important; 58% (34%) endorse a statement that the spouse is "exciting"; 51% (41%) contend that their spouse is romantic; 50% (37%) think the spouse is a skillful lover; 29% (40%) agree that the spouse is imaginative about sex; 18% (40%) think that their spouse is mysterious and intriguing; 10% (17%) say that the spouse is sometimes like a god.

Furthermore, criticisms of the spouse are usually rejected: 15% (37%) think that their mate does not understand their emotional needs; 11% (26%) agree that the spouse does not understand the respondent's work; 10% (24%) doubt that the spouse understands the respondent's physical needs. Only 7% (28%) admit that the spouse is overweight; 7% (17%) think the spouse cares more about work than about the respondent; 4% (3%) suspect that the spouse cannot be trusted; 3% (14%) think the spouse is dull; 2% (10%) say the spouse has bad manners; 1% (8%) say that the spouse has bad breath or body odor.

A woman colleague remarked to me that some people she knows who have divorced would have vigorously agreed with such a positive assessment of their marriage partner almost up to the bitter end, because they wanted to believe that the assessment was true and they wanted the marriage to work.

In fact, can spouses be the paragons that our respondents describe? Or are the respondents merely wishing and hoping that the spouses measure up to such criteria?

There's no way at present anyone could know the answer to that question. Longitudinal research that investigated the couples

[20] Most questionnaire items in the *Love and Marriage* study admit to three answers, a strong positive answer, a qualified positive answer and a negative answer. I will normally follow the convention of describing the strong response and putting the qualified response in parenthesis. The proportion giving a negative answer can be calculated by subtracting the first two proportions from 100.

years later could determine whether divorce is more likely to occur among those who give their spouses bad marks or among those who give them good marks. I am inclined to think that the enthusiasm of the unqualified response ought to be taken seriously as an indicator of how the spouse views the marriage in its good moments, and that the qualified response is one that hints at trouble. Minimally, the portraits of the spouse which can be drawn from *Love and Marriage* indicate a deep commitment to sustaining the marriage relationship.

In summary, perhaps a tenth of the marriages described in our survey seem to have serious problems and another quarter are not working as well as the respondent would like. The other three-fifths to two-thirds are at the moment perceived as doing all right.

A more refined picture of the quality of a marriage can be obtained from a question asking about which phase the respondent perceives the marriage to be in:[21] 17% describe themselves as "falling in love," 55% say that they are "settling down," 3% judge that they are "bottoming out," and 25% are "beginning again."

S P O U S E   A N D   R E S P O N D E N T   T O G E T H E R

The *Love and Marriage* respondents also report high levels of joint activity involving both husband and wife;[22] 71% (23%) contend that the couple works hard to make their marriage better; 64% (29%) discuss their marriage openly with each other; 63% (27%) report that they generally agree on how children should be raised; 57% (30%) discuss sex with each other openly; 52% (38%) talk privately and intimately together; 52% (30%) listen to music together; 49% (44%) tend to like and dislike the same things; 34% (27%) pray together; 30% (37%) go to parties together; 23%

---

[21] The survey question is stated thus: Many people think that marriages go through cycles— over and over again. If the cycles are falling in love, settling down, bottoming out and beginning again, where would you put your marriage at the present time?

[22] The first percentage is the proportion saying that the joint action happens "a lot." The second is the additional proportion saying that it happens "sometimes."

(32%) read the same books and magazines; 18% (27%) report that they work out or play sports together; 7% (24%) say that they go out dancing together.

In addition, 4% (12%) go to religious retreats together, and 2% (3%) go to marriage therapy together.

I S   S E X   I M P O R T A N T ?

Regarding sex and romance, 53% (34%) say that sex is very important in holding a marriage together; 51% (40%) say that they try to make their love life romantic; 48% (36%) say that they are very playful when alone together in private; 39% (39%) report efforts to try to improve their sex life together; 32% (43%) arouse each other sexually; 28% (40%) report mutual back rubs or massages; 27% (40%) help their spouse climax before or after they do; 10% (29%) take showers or baths together; 6% (26%) state that they abandon all their sexual inhibitions; 5% (29%) state that they go to a hotel or a motel to spend time with each other alone; 3% (16%) swim nude together; 2% (20%) make love outdoors; 2% (19%) watch x-rated videos together; 1% (19%) buy erotic underwear.

Furthermore, 45% (34%) of the survey respondents describe themselves as "moral about sex," 21% (54%) think they are skillful lovers, and 27% (45%) think of themselves as "sexual persons."

Not everything is perfect in the sex life of our respondents: 22% (39%) wish they were more confident lovers, and 3% (9%) (20%)[23] say that they avoid sex.

Are these proportions of joint activities high or low? Since such aspects of marital intimacy have never been studied before in a national survey, there is no way of ascertaining whether they represent increases or decreases from past levels of such activities. Did more or less than 22% of American married couples often or sometimes make love outdoors twenty years ago? Forty years

---

[23] The third percentage represents those who give the second qualified response (the statement applies to them "not too well") which is permitted on this question.

ago? Did more or less than 61% pray together thirty years ago? Fifty years ago?

For such questions there are no answers, though the items in the *Love and Marriage* survey provide benchmarks for the future. However, the picture of joint husband-and-wife activities described in the previous paragraphs surely do not indicate a total collapse of marital intimacy. In subsequent chapters we will see which activities seem best to account for fidelity, marital happiness, and romantic love.

ARE THEY TELLING THE TRUTH?

The statistics described in this chapter present a very different picture than that portrayed by mass media, which reports the "decline of the family" and the "Sexual Revolution." Indeed, some will be quick to dismiss our findings on the grounds that they are at odds with what everyone knows to be true. The respondents must be lying; they must be giving socially acceptable answers rather than telling the truth. The survey takers, it is said, have been deceived.

There are a number of responses to this objection, one which always arises, be it noted, when careful and objective research challenges the Conventional Wisdom.

First, consider the Conventional Wisdom. It is based on an occasional survey, such as the Hite Report, which is innocent of the techniques of probability sampling; on media feature articles or programs which generalize from the particular cases; on personal stories told by members of various social elites; on conservative lamentations; on liberal celebrations; and on problematic impressions. While no other national probability sample studies have focused on marital fidelity, the findings we report are consistent with *Sex and Morality in the United States* (the NORC/Kinsey Institute study in 1970—Klassen et al. 1989) and other analyses of survey data (such as the essay by Tom W. Smith in *Trends in Public Opinion*, 1989). When the findings of good research conflict with the findings of bad research or poorly documented and sloppily articulated impressions, the presumption ought to be in favor of the good research.

Second, given the fact that it is generally believed that most Americans engage in extramarital affairs and indeed that to have an affair is fashionable, the fidelity response is no longer the socially acceptable one. Our respondents are reporting behavior which they think is a minority behavior. Indeed, two-thirds of them think that fidelity is more important in their marriage than it is in most marriages ("your spouse and you are more concerned with being faithful than most people") and only a quarter "strongly agree" that most couples are faithful to one another.

If we should go back to our respondents and ask them if they agree with our findings—which they produced for us—they would very likely say that the findings couldn't possibly be accurate: all those other people aren't telling the truth!

We would have our work cut out for us to persuade them that *they* are the other people.

Third, the relationships among the variables in the study are internally consistent. Marital happiness, for example, correlates with a skillful lover as a spouse—a finding one would surely expect, but not if the respondents were trying to deceive the interviewers about their sexual lives. Moreover, cohabitation before marriage also correlates with skillful love, suggesting a period of practice without responsibility. On the other hand cohabitation correlates negatively with marital satisfaction. Thus the intricate relationship among the three variables—cohabitation, skillful love, and marital happiness—is not what one would expect from dishonest or careless respondents. Rather it represents a form of self-revelation which indicates an openness to the interview experience and not an intent to deceive. It is also the common experience of interviewers engaged in this kind of research that respondents are usually candid and helpful in answering questions about their intimate lives.

Thus it would seem that the difference between fact and impression about marital fidelity is an example of what sociologist Hubert O'Gorman (in Klassen et al., 1989) calls pluralistic ignorance: erroneous cognitive beliefs shared by some individuals about other individuals. The individual respondents in our surveys think their behavior is different from that of others, when in fact it is not. The vast majority accept the Conventional Wisdom as an accurate description of what others do, but as not applying to themselves. The majority, in other words, is firmly convinced that it is a minority—and may, if it is contentious enough, even attack research findings which condemn it to majority status!

Fourth, many of our respondents who portray pictures of faithful and happy marriages are quite honest about their own premarital experimentations. They do not attempt to present themselves as exemplars of virtue before their present marriage. Such self-disclosure is not compatible with intent to deceive and is congruent with a desire to answer questions truthfully.

Moreover, even if our respondents are merely giving socially acceptable answers it is significant that despite the prevalence of "Sexual Revolution" imagery, they still believe that responses of chastity and fidelity are socially acceptable. The "conservative" sexual morality displayed in our research is fundamentally continuous with that reported in the NORC/Kinsey study of 1970 (Klassen et al., 1989), just as that report is continuous with the conservative morality of the more distant American past.

Fifth, as I wrote in a previous chapter, all assertions about human behavior are based on surveys, either the formal surveys that the professionals take (with probability samples, quality control, and careful statistical analyses) or the informal collection of impressions from one's own experience that are often cited in dissent from formal survey findings.

If the critics of this research are not persuaded by these five arguments that there is solid probability that the respondents are in general responding truthfully, then the ultimate answer to them is that they should go collect their own data.

CONCLUSION

The majority of the respondents in the *Love and Marriage* survey seem happily married, content with their spouse and with the common life, and prepared to marry the same husband or wife again. While there are obviously discontents in some American marriages, the Conventional Wisdom about marriage in crisis cannot stand up to the description of marriage and spouse of a majority of Americans. Those who nonetheless believe that there is a crisis must claim that they know more about marriage in America than married people themselves do.

Is this a "conservative" or "optimistic" description of American marriage?

The two labels, it seems to me, are inappropriate. The description is merely factual. If it is "conservative" to report that traditional morality still seems to apply to extramarital sexual encounters, than the conservatism is in the married men and women and not in the report. If it is "optimistic" to report that most Americans feel they would marry the same spouse again, then the optimism is in the response and not in the report of that response.

Obviously there is pathology in some marriages. A quarter of Americans are not willing to exclude completely the possibility of a divorce in their marriage. More than a third have seriously considered divorce. A fifth say that both of them have considered ending the marriage. A quarter fight physically with one another. One out of every thirty married women has been forced by her husband to have sex. To these marital conflicts I turn in the chapters to come before trying to analyze the correlates of a happy marriage.

4. The Divorce Option

With divorce so easy and so frequent and with so many (alleged) pressures on married men and women, do those who are still married consider divorce a real possibility in their lives? Why is a divorce a possibility for some and not for others? What part do sex and religion play in impeding divorce? How many Americans have considered the possibility of divorce and rejected it? The answers to these questions establish that the respondents to the Love and Marriage *surveys are not looking at their marriages through rose-colored glasses and that they have purchased the (relative) happiness of their marriages at the cost of considerable effort.*

THE DIVORCE SITUATION

Some two-thirds of Americans are still married to their first spouse,[24] a little more than four-fifths of those who are married have or have had only one spouse—the difference being those who have divorced and not remarried (a third of the divorced men and half the divorced women). Within age categories, 71% of those over fifty are still married to their first spouse, as were 45% of those between thirty-five and fifty and 68% of those under

[24]The data in this paragraph are based on the General Social Survey, 1985–1989.

thirty-five. The projection that half of those ever married in America will eventually be divorced seems to be close to fulfillment for those in the intermediate age category.

The divorce rates, as was noted in an earlier chapter, have leveled off in the later 1980s, in great part, as Robert Michael has suggested, because the effect of the birth control pill and the availability of employment for women have worked their way through the population.

Andrew Cherlin (1981) has observed that the divorce rate has increased at a fairly steady rate for the past century. Nonetheless, it was only in the early 1970s that the number of marriages broken by divorce in the earlier stages of the life cycle exceeded the number broken by death at the beginning of the present century. Longer life—or perhaps the prospect of longer life—seems to have made its contribution to the increase of divorce.

While there are many theories to explain both divorce and the increase in divorce, there are no data sets which enable one to test the theories. Ideally, one would want to follow a probability sample of Americans from the beginning of their relationships and, at various points in the marriage cycle, study those relationships to determine why some end in separation or divorce and others do not. Studies of those who have reached the state where they are applying for divorce or have just divorced do not tell us how these couples differ from those who have not divorced or those who have thought about divorce but have decided against it.

The nature of the sample in the present study—presently married men and women—makes it impossible to say whether they will ever divorce or not. However, we can ask (1) how they estimate the possibilities of their marriage ending in divorce and (2) how those who considered divorce and rejected the possibility may have worked out their reconciliation (though the data do not allow us to ask why they decided against divorce, as opposed to those who decided for it).

Thus the questions which can be answered about marriage and divorce with the present data set are limited. However, they are questions which have not been answered before.

In the present chapter, then, I will consider the possibility of divorce and in the next chapter the dynamics of reconciliation.

NO SIMPLE EXPLANATIONS

In subsequent chapters I will consider the reasons, first of all, for the possibility of divorce and reconciliations after quarrels, then for sexual fulfillment and for happy marriages; next, the reasons for the falling-in-love phase of a marriage, then the reasons for the bottoming-out phase; and finally the reasons for marital fidelity. I will proceed in this fashion, since I think I can assume for the sake of the discussion that fidelity is the result in part of a happy marriage.

The reader must remember that the causality of human behavior is necessarily complicated (most of the time, anyway). Thus one might say trippingly on the tongue at a dinner party that drug abuse is the result of poverty. Someone else might say that, no, it isn't—many drug abusers are members of the white middle class who have been indulged by their parents. Then yet another someone might say that the problem with white middle-class drug users is not that they have been spoiled by their parents but that they have not been loved enough.

Such an exchange of assertions (perhaps fueled by the ingestion of a drug called alcohol beforehand) keeps the dinner table conversation from becoming dull and perhaps interferes with the digestive process. A mostly silent member of the dinner party might mutter occasionally that probably all the factors discussed were involved and many others too, all of them in complicated interaction with one another.

This mostly silent partner might be a sociologist (though some of them are not necessarily silent during such heated exchanges). She/he will likely be ignored because such observations spoil the fun of the debate. Yet unless the participants of the debate are fools (and the number of such is not small), they will acknowledge in their more sober and reflective moments that the mostly silent partner is probably right: not all poor people use drugs, not all indulged white middle-class young people use drugs, not all unloved white middle-class young people use drugs. The explanations, so passionately defended, are at best partial and limited, and they do not exclude one another.

The position taken by the quiet guest may be called multivariate analysis, a name which implies that explanations are complicated and at best limited, that there is no single explanation of human behavior and that all explanations and all combinations of explanations leave human behaviors only partially explained.

As I say, on sober reflection, most reasonable people would not deny the validity of such an approach. Yet one can nonetheless hear sober folk, even sober social scientists, indulge in such non-multivariate explanations as, "If they're faithful like you say, the reason is fear of AIDS."

One responds with something like, "Gimme a break!" Nonetheless one realizes that in similar circumstances, when faced with a phenomenon which occasions surprise, one is oneself very likely to respond with a similar single-variate explanation.

So in this and subsequent chapters I propose no simple and total explanation of, let us say, marital happiness. Moreover, the explanations I offer may, as they say in the popular media, leave many questions unanswered. They are also likely to raise new questions. Thus I report later in this chapter that the two strongest predictors of marital happiness are assertions that the spouse is kind and gentle and that the spouse makes the respondent feel important. Fair enough, one might say, and perhaps obvious enough, too. But how do you go about making a man (or a woman) feel important? And how do you go about being kind and gentle?

I might paraphrase the late Harold Macmillan and say that that's not a question for your sociologist but for your archbishop. Given the quality of archbishops these days I perhaps should change that to say that it is a question for your marriage counselor—although with sufficient time and resources sociologists could probably offer partial and complex explanations of what constitutes gentleness in the average marriage (and probably discover that even on the average there are very different components of gentleness for the two genders).

Finally, in the absence of data collected over time and from the same people, it is difficult to be confident that the causality flows from gentleness to marital happiness. For might happiness not lead to greater gentleness? And because the relationship is happy, might not a respondent be content with what passes for gentleness in a spouse? Thus one must be content with saying that the variables which correlate with happy marriage are at a minimum signs of happiness and not necessarily causes.

Why bother, then, with attempting explanations if they are to be so limited? The answer is that even imperfect light is better than darkness.

And why bother with complicated analysis of explanations that everyone knows to be true before you propound the explanation? The answer is that that which everyone knows to be true is often not true, and that which many would suspect not to be true often in fact turns out to be true. I doubt that many of my sociological colleagues would have agreed before the last chapter that frequent joint prayer is as important to marital happiness as it seems to be. Even if the light is there and you know it's there, it's still useful to learn how strong the light is.

The technique commonly used to explore multivariate explanations is called multiple regression analysis. It addresses the question of how much of the variance (in marital happiness, for example) can be accounted for by one or many other variables. When many variables are put into the regression equation, the analyst is also able to compare the relative importance of the different variables in explaining the dependent variable (marital happiness, in this case) net of one another. This "net" correlation is called a "beta," as opposed to the "r," which is the correlation between two variables (agreement on raising children and marital happiness, for example) without consideration of the impact of other variables (religious endogamy, for example).[25]

The correlation between the combination of explanatory variables and the variable to be explained is called "R." The square of R (i.e., R^2) is the amount of variance in the latter explained by the former. What are "decent" betas and Rs and R^2s in sociological analysis? They can be very modest indeed. The beta between school integration and achievement for black students is approximately .01—meaning that it accounts for 1% of the variance in academic achievement. An R of .15 (which would mean an R^2 of .023—two and a quarter percent of variance explained) is often not only accepted by a sociologist but warmly embraced.

Not much compared to what the physicists can do, you say?

Stars are simple compared to people, I respond. And, at the risk of mixing a metaphor, a little bit of light is better than no light at all. The amount of variance which will be explained by

---

[25] Endogamy is not an important direct influence on marital happiness because its influence is filtered through agreement on children.

the models of marital happiness to be developed in this chapter is extraordinary—which would lead the cautious analyst to suspect that the variables that do the explaining come close to being definitions of marital happiness.

The reader may be impatient with this methodological discussion. To such impatience I reply that you would not expect to learn much about how stars work without learning a little bit of geometry.

C H A N C E S   F O R   D I V O R C E

Three-quarters of the respondents in the sample said that divorce was "not at all likely" for them. One-fifth said that it was "not too likely," 3% said that it was "somewhat likely," and 2% said that it was "very likely." Thus 5% see divorce as more likely than not and another 20% are not willing to exclude it as a possibility. In these proportions, there were no differences between men and women, between Catholics and Protestants, and between those who went to college and those who did not. Nor was there any difference between those under thirty-five and those between thirty-five and fifty—about a third of each group did not rule out completely the possibility of a divorce—while among those over fifty, nine out of ten thought that a divorce was "not at all likely."[26]

There are five different classes of variables which correlate with the possibility of divorce—disagreement over values, communication, sexual satisfaction, the character of the spouse, and behavioral factors. Together, these factors account for about two-fifths of the variance on the possibility-of-divorce measure.[27]

[26] In this chapter the dependent variable, unless otherwise noted, will be a dichotomy between "not likely at all" and other responses.

[27] Neither education nor the presence or absence of children correlates with the propensity to divorce.

DISAGREEMENT ON VALUES

The respondents were asked to rate their marriages on a number of different important aspects: agreement on finances (60% say "very good"), ability to disagree (67%), agreement on basic values (74%), agreement on religion (68%), agreement on quality and quantity of lovemaking (56%). While all the variables related to confidence that there would be no divorce, only three remained statistically significant in their relationship after all were considered together: agreement on religious issues, agreement on financial issues, and agreement on basic values. The last named was the most important of all.

Of those who said their agreement on basic values was "very good," 17% saw divorce as a possibility, while 46% of those who did not think that basic value agreement was "very good" thought divorce was possible. Women were significantly more likely than men to display a correlation between value disagreement and divorce—54% versus 38%.

Lack of financial agreement was also a strong correlate of possible divorce—15% of those who said their agreement was very good thought that divorce might occur, as opposed to 40% of those who thought their agreement on finances was less than very good. On this matter there was no difference between women and men.

Disagreement on religion also had an impact on the possibility of divorce: 19% of those who said that their agreement on religious issues was very good thought that divorce was possible, as did 37% of those who said that their agreement on religion was less than very good. Similarly, those who said that they could disagree without threatening the relationship were only about half as likely to see divorce as possible (16% versus 40%). The strength of both correlations did not vary across gender lines.

When disagreement on basic values and inability to express disagreement are combined, 54% of those reporting both think divorce is possible as opposed to 13% of those who report neither—about a third of the intermediate groups report divorce as a possibility.

Three-quarters of married Americans report agreement on basic values, and 56% said that they had both agreement on basic values and the ability to disagree without threatening the relationship. Among this group, divorce seems most unlikely. Among the other 44% of the population the probability of divorce goes up to at least 35%, and is over half if there is neither agreement nor the freedom to disagree.

If, instead of considering all those who do not say divorce is not at all likely (25% of the population), one considers the much smaller proportion saying that divorce is very likely or somewhat likely (5% of the population), then one discovers that among those who say their agreement on values is very good, as is their ability to disagree, only 1% see a divorce as very likely or somewhat likely, while those who do not agree and are not able to disagree report a 20% very likely or somewhat likely chance of divorce. There are no gender differences in these numbers.

Clearly agreement on values and the ability to disagree constructively are important dimensions of the common life. Can we find any hint of the specific values about which there are disagreements?

Eight variables correlated significantly with value disagreement even when their joint influence is taken into account: religious disagreement, financial disagreement, the absence of "kindness" in the spouse, lack of mutual trust, the inability to compromise differences, the lack of excitement in the spouse, the inability of the spouse to talk about making the marriage better, and disagreement on the raising of children; together they explain more than a fifth of the disagreement in marriage.

Religious disagreement is the most powerful predictor of value disagreement (financial disagreement is also important). Those who agree with their spouse on religion are 27 percentage points more likely to report agreement on general values. This difference is particularly strong among those who go to church almost every week—36 percentage points. The religious effect on possible divorce is mediated through its impact on the whole value syndrome. There is no special religious effect on general value agreement in endogamous marriages as opposed to religiously mixed marriages.

Agreement on raising children is important, too; of those who said they agreed with the spouse on the raising of children, 80% also reported excellent value agreement; but of those who did not agree all the time on raising children, 60% said they had excellent value agreement.

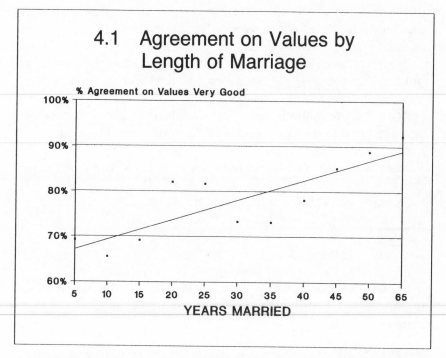

4.1 Agreement on Values by Length of Marriage

% Agreement on Values Very Good

YEARS MARRIED

Religious questions, financial issues, how to raise children, how to be kind, how to generate trust, how to compromise, how to be exciting, how to talk to one another—these are all challenges of value communality. The inability to process such problems is probably the sign and simultaneously the cause of a deeper and more complex difference of values between the spouses. Does this latent value stress increase or decrease in the course of the marriage?

The conflicts seem to diminish as the marriage goes on (see Figure 4.1).[28] But in fact the curve may be U-shaped: 31% of those with less than fifteen years of marriage report that they do not have "very good" agreement on values, 39% of those between sixteen and twenty-five years of marriage do not have such agreement, and likewise 18% of those who have passed their silver jubilee. It would seem then that there may be an ebb and flow in agreement about values and that the struggle to work them out goes on through the whole course of a marriage. However,

[28] In most of the line charts in this book, I will present the actual observations as symbols like "*" and "+" and the trend as a line "fitted" to the symbols; that is, the best straight line that can be drawn to fit the direction indicated by the symbols.

the "wave" in the figure is not statistically significant, and thus the trend line on it indicates a steady increase in value agreement as the years of marriage increase.

In either case it is not true that value conflict emerges only after husband and wife get to know each other well. It exists at the very beginning and diminishes as they get to know each other better (if they remain married—some of the improvement in value agreement might be the result of the dropping out of the married pool of those who disagree).

More study on the marital life cycle is required before one can speak with confidence about such ebb and flow.

Humans are value-oriented beings; hence it is not surprising that value conflict will have a powerful impact on human relationships. Quite the contrary: the opposite would have been' surprising. The question remains whether, in addition to being value-oriented creatures, put at risk by conflicting values, humans can be influenced by less intellectual dimensions of their organism which diminish to some extent the impact of value conflict.

C O M M U N I C A T I O N

Of American married men and women, 43% say that they talk to each other together without interruption often. The median number of hours a week they talk to one another is twenty. Both factors, along with the claim by 68% that they try very hard to make their marriage better, have an impact on the possibility of divorce. Of those who say they talk less than twenty hours a week, 28% think divorce is not impossible (opposed to 20%), as do 30% who do not try very hard to make their marriage work (22%) and 31% of those who say that they do not talk a lot without interruption (16%).

Talk and effort are not the same thing, as Figure 4.2 shows, but each makes an independent contribution of its own. Only 15% of those who do both (the bar on the far left) think divorce is not impossible, as opposed to 35% of those who do neither (the bar on the far right). Effort in the absence of talk (the second bar from the left) is more important in lowering the possibility

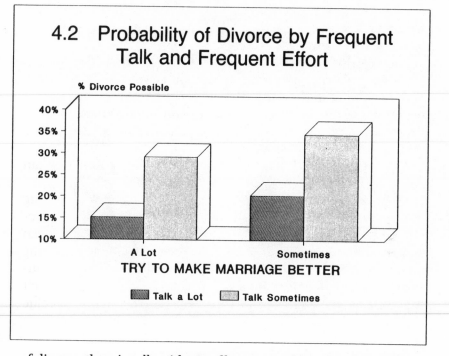

4.2 Probability of Divorce by Frequent Talk and Frequent Effort

% Divorce Possible

TRY TO MAKE MARRIAGE BETTER

Talk a Lot   Talk Sometimes

of divorce than is talk without effort (second bar from the right); 20% of those in the former category say divorce is possible and 30% in the latter category. Talk, it would seem, comes cheap when it is not matched with effort.

SEXUAL FULFILLMENT

Can sexual pleasure moderate some of the negative impact of value disagreement on marital stability? The realists might say no: if there is value disagreement, the sexual game may continue (with diminished pleasure, perhaps), but what happens in bed cannot compensate for disagreements in other realms of life. The romantics might say yes: sexual pleasure holds men and women together even when conflicts threaten to tear them apart.

The romantics seem to carry the day in this debate. A question was asked in the study about satisfaction with sex life, with a six-point response scale running from "a very great deal of satisfac-

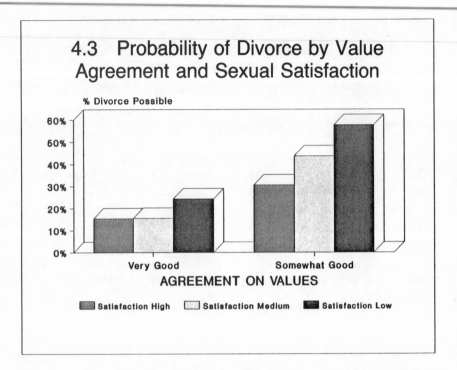

4.3 Probability of Divorce by Value Agreement and Sexual Satisfaction

% Divorce Possible

AGREEMENT ON VALUES

Very Good   Somewhat Good

Satisfaction High   Satisfaction Medium   Satisfaction Low

tion," through "a great deal," "quite a bit," "a fair amount," "some," "little," and "none." About a third of the respondents chose the top point, another third chose the second point, and the rest of the sample ranged through the remaining four points. Among those who reported value disagreement but a high level of satisfaction with their sexual life, the proportion who thought divorce might occur was 30%; among those whose satisfaction was in the middle range, the proportion thinking divorce possible rose to 44%, and among those with the lowest level of satisfaction the proportion reporting the possibility of divorce rose to 58%.

As Figure 4.3 demonstrates, sexual satisfaction depresses the relationship between value disagreement and divorce—sexual satisfaction cuts the proportion seeing divorce as a possibility in half among those who disagree (right-hand bars) on values ("somewhat good"). Among those with value agreement (left-hand bars), on the other hand, the negative relationship between sexual satisfaction and divorce possibility is not statistically significant. When value agreement is high, in other words, sexual satisfaction does nothing to lower of the possibility of divorce.

When value agreement is low, however, sexual satisfaction does reduce the possibility of divorce. Those with negative marks on value agreement and positive marks on sexual pleasure are only 5% higher than the average for the whole sample in reporting the possibility of divorce (30% versus 25%). The strength of this relationship is the same for men and for women.

Sexual pleasure among the human species is in itself a value-shaped reaction, so the sexual pleasure which reduces the impact of differences in basic values is also a value-drenched behavior. The nature of the values which influence sexual pleasure must be examined in more detail.

In a later chapter I consider the question of what makes for sexual satisfaction in marriage and the relationship between sexual fulfillment and marital happiness. For the present it suffices to say that it is very important in holding marriages together which are under pressure because of other matters.

The romantics do indeed win this one.

CHARACTER   OF   THE   **S**POUSE

Two variables which describe the character of the spouse also have an effect independent of values and sexual fulfillment: the spouse's kindness and whether the spouse treats the respondent as an equal. Of those who say that the spouse treats them as an equal, 17% see the possibility of divorce, as opposed to 48% of those who say the spouse does not treat them as an equal. There are no differences between men and women in this correlation.

The question arises as to whether these qualities of the spouse, thoroughly admirable as they may be, can explain why sexual satisfaction can depress the relationship between value disagreement and possibility of divorce. Even though there are value disagreements with the spouse, might the spouse have qualities of character that facilitate sexual love, and which together with sexual love mitigate the impact of value conflict?

It turns out that this is indeed the case. For those who have value conflict, the relationship between sexual satisfaction and the possibility of divorce is −.25. When the equality variable is taken into account the relationship diminishes to −.17 and when kindness is added to the equation it diminishes further to −.14. Thus a little less than half of the relationship between sexual satisfaction and the low possibility of divorce (for those where there is a value disagreement) can be accounted for by the kindness and respect for equality of the spouse. Kindness and equality also have direct effects on the possibility of divorce, but they also have this subtle indirect effect through their relationship with sexual love. Thus the propensity to divorce, as perceived by the respondent, is heavily affected by values, sexual pleasure and the character of the spouse.

I must note the fact that there is almost certainly a bidirectional relationship between character and sexual satisfaction. It is surely the case that the sexual pleasure in the relationship could and probably does make the spouse kinder and more egalitarian. Sexual pleasure, then, influences the possibility of divorce directly, indirectly through its impact on value disagreement (a subtle impact, as we have noticed), and also through kindness and egalitarianism, which influence it and which it also influences.

The four-variable model of kindness, equality, value agreement, and sexual satisfaction accounts for 23% of the variance on the possibility of divorce. The remaining eight variables to be discussed in this chapter add 13% more explanatory power.

B E H A V I O R A L   I N F L U E N C E S

Frequency of joint prayer, physical conflict between the spouses, a spouse who drinks, cohabitation before marriage, infidelity after marriage, two incomes in the family, flirting with other men and women, and separate bedrooms also affect the possibility of divorce.

Does prayer help marriages to stay together? Or is such a notion merely pious nonsense? How can prayer moderate the impact of serious value conflict or an unhappy sex life? Is one a pietist who believes prayer makes a difference, or, again, a realist who knows that it does not?

Joint prayer, in fact, is astonishingly important in checking fear of divorce, especially when combined with sexual satisfaction. Of

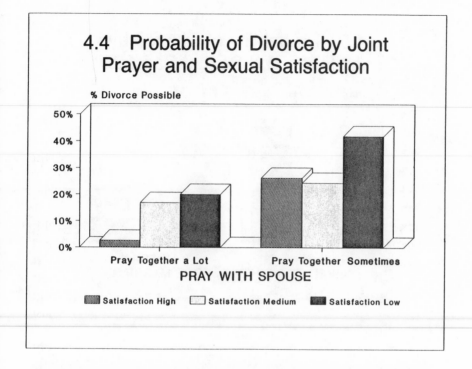

4.4 Probability of Divorce by Joint Prayer and Sexual Satisfaction

% Divorce Possible

PRAY WITH SPOUSE

Pray Together a Lot   Pray Together Sometimes

Satisfaction High   Satisfaction Medium   Satisfaction Low

those who don't pray together often, 30% think that divorce is possible, while only 11% of those who pray together a lot think that divorce is possible (29% do pray together often). Joint prayer has an interesting interaction effect with sexual satisfaction: only 1% of those who pray together often and report the highest quality of sex think divorce is possible. In fact, only those who do not pray together often and whose sexual satisfaction is low go above the average expectation (see Figure 4.4, the bar on the far right) of divorce, and they are twice as likely to expect divorce. Joint prayer and lovemaking, apparently reinforcing one another, seem virtually to eliminate fear of divorce.

On the other hand, 49% of those who sometimes occupy separate bedrooms (18% of the respondents) think that divorce is possible, as opposed to 21% of those who never use separate bedrooms. Of those who sometimes flirt with others (40% of Americans), 39% think a divorce may occur, while 16% of those who do not flirt consider divorce possible.

In addition, 40% of those who fight physically (11% of the population—a high level of physical violence) expect a possible divorce, against 23% of those who don't. Forty-five percent of

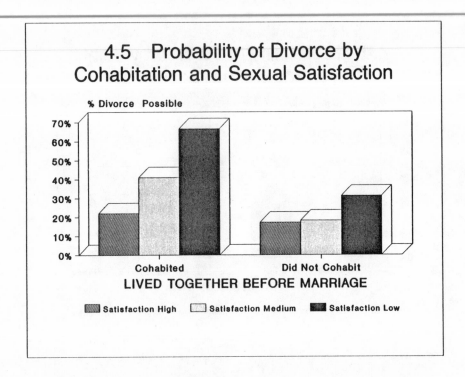

4.5   Probability of Divorce by Cohabitation and Sexual Satisfaction

% Divorce Possible

LIVED TOGETHER BEFORE MARRIAGE

Cohabited   Did Not Cohabit

▨ Satisfaction High   ▢ Satisfaction Medium   ■ Satisfaction Low

those whose spouses drink too much (9% of the population) think a divorce is possible. When the two variables of fighting and drinking are added together, the possibility of divorce goes up to 80%.

Of the members of two-income families, 31% consider divorce possible, as opposed to 20% of the one-income families.

Three-quarters of those who have been unfaithful (either in the last year or the course of the marriage) think divorce is possible, as against a fifth of those who have been faithful. Forty percent of those who cohabited with their present spouse before marriage (20% of the population) think a divorce might happen, while 21% of those who did not cohabit recognize the possibility of a divorce.

Cohabitation also interacts with sexual satisfaction (Figure 4.5). If the couple cohabited before marriage and the sexual satisfaction is low, the possibility of divorce rises to 60% (third bar from the left). Or to put it the other way around, if sexual satisfaction goes out of a marriage which was preceded by cohabitation, the marriage is in very grave jeopardy, while the same is not true if there was no cohabitation. Joint prayer on the other hand minimizes

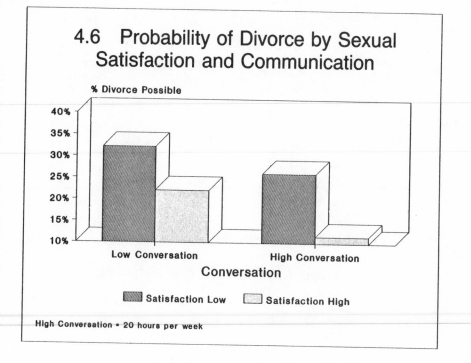

4.6   Probability of Divorce by Sexual Satisfaction and Communication

% Divorce Possible

Satisfaction Low   Satisfaction High

High Conversation • 20 hours per week

the risk to a marriage which had been preceded by cohabitation—only 19% of the cohabitors who pray often with their spouse think that divorce is possible, as opposed to 44% of those who don't pray often with their spouse.

Women are more likely to see the separate bedroom as opening the possibility of divorce than men. Men with wives who drink too much (5% of the population) are more likely to see divorce in the offing than women whose husbands drink too much. There are no gender differences in the other correlations.

Figures 4.6, 4.7, and 4.8 show the relationship between communication on the one hand and sexual satisfaction, premarital cohabitation and joint prayer on the other. When sexual satisfaction is high and there is frequent communication (bar on the far right of Figure 4.6), divorce is not very likely, as one might expect. Where both are low, the possibility of divorce is much more likely. But the interesting comparison is in the two middle bars. Just as conversation without effort is more likely to lead to divorce possibility than effort without conversation, so too is conversation without sexual satisfaction a more serious problem than sexual satisfaction without conversation. Communication, even

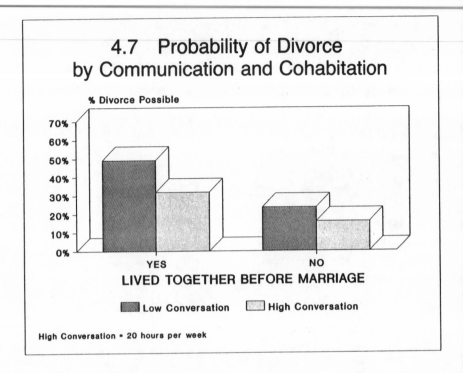

4.7   Probability of Divorce by Communication and Cohabitation

% Divorce Possible

LIVED TOGETHER BEFORE MARRIAGE

Low Conversation   High Conversation

High Conversation = 20 hours per week

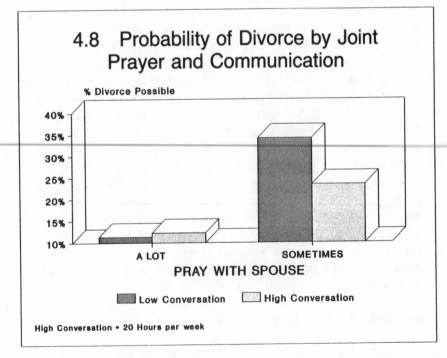

4.8   Probability of Divorce by Joint Prayer and Communication

% Divorce Possible

PRAY WITH SPOUSE

Low Conversation   High Conversation

High Conversation = 20 Hours per week

lots of it, without good sex, is not an effective antidote to fear of divorce.

The possibility of divorce is increased among those who have cohabited before marriage (Figure 4.7) if there is little communication between the two spouses, reaching nearly 50% (the bar on the far left). If you have cohabited before marriage, you perceive your chances of divorce as much lower if you and your spouse are communicating frequently with one another.

Finally joint prayer seems to be an effective substitute for conversation (Figure 4.8, two left-hand bars), but in the absence of prayer together, conversation does diminish the possibility of divorce. If spouses pray together, it would seem, they don't have to talk all that much to depress the likelihood of divorce—not, of course, that they are thereby dispensed from conversation with one another.

CONCLUSION

The family that prays together, it has been argued, stays together. To which might be added, *especially if they make satisfying love together*. The romantics and the pietists triumph over the realists on the importance of sex and prayer in preserving married love despite value conflicts. Prayer together is in itself a form of very intimate behavior, perhaps more embarrassing (and also more exciting) than other forms of intimacies between husbands and wives. As we shall see throughout this report, sexual intimacy and prayerful intimacy are a very powerful combination.

Value agreement, communication, the character of the spouse, sexual satisfaction, and various behaviors—past and present—create together a complex but powerful explanatory model that accounts for almost two-fifths of the variance in the possibility of divorce among married couples. A more simple model involving only values, character, and sexual satisfaction accounts for about a quarter of the variance.

There are, it hardly need be said, no simple explanations of why a couple leans in the direction of divorce. But there are some surprising aspects of the complex web of motivations and behaviors which constitute the matrix for divorce, especially the role of joint prayer and the combined role of joint prayer and satisfactory sex. If it be social policy to diminish the propensity to divorce, one must not forget the importance of sex and of prayer and especially the importance of the two of them working together.

God and pleasure are, quite literally, a hard combination to beat.

5. Reconciliation Within Marriage

Not all conflicts rupture marriages. Some dangers of separation have been overcome. While we cannot say anything in the present study about those who have ended their marriages, we can say something about those who considered ending their relationship and did not and examine the costs, if any, of reconciliation.

THE RECONCILED

Thirty-seven percent of married Americans admit that there was a time when they were prepared to leave their spouse or their spouse was prepared to leave them; in 22% of the cases both were prepared to leave each other. Of these, 40% say that divorce is still likely.[29] The other 60% say that divorce is not likely at all. This latter group would seem to represent a successful reconciliation after a marital crisis. The question in this chapter is whether we can discover a little bit more about the one-fifth of Americans

---

[29] In the sense of their not saying that divorce "is not at all likely."

who have successfully reconciled after a brush with divorce. How do they differ from those who stay together, but who still see divorce as a possibility, and from those for whom leaving or being left by the spouse was never a possibility? The five classes of variables discussed in the previous chapter on the prevention of divorce also affect the propensity to reconciliation as herein defined—values, communication, sexual pleasure, character of spouse, and behavior. However, the specific variables differ and have differential impact. Nonetheless, the explanatory model for reconciliation explains two-fifths of the variance.

Reconciliation is more likely to be observed among those who have been married more than twenty-five years and among those who have no children at home, the impact of the latter variable being mostly the result of the former. The higher rate of reconciliation among those who have been married longer may be the result both of the acquisition of skills at reconciliation through time and the dropping out of the married pool of those who were not able to reconcile.

Reconciliation does not correlate with gender or religion or education or the number of children a respondent has had. Nor does it correlate with the severity of the original conflict, save that those who did not seriously think about separation are more likely to be reconciled (78%).

V A L U E S

The pertinent "value" insofar as reconciliation is concerned is the ability to disagree without threatening the marriage.[30] Of those who affirm that such a joint value exists in their marriage, 73% are in the reconciled state, as opposed to 43% of those who do not see that value in their marriage. What constitutes the ability to disagree? Pretty clearly it is the ability to compromise (which 39% of all respondents say applies to their marriage), and indeed 78% of those who say their spouse is very good at compromise

[30] In most of this chapter, comparisons are between those who once were threatened with separation and now say there is no likelihood of divorce, and those who were once threatened with separation and now say that there is a likelihood of divorce. A comparison between the reconciled and the rest of the sample will be made at the end of the chapter.

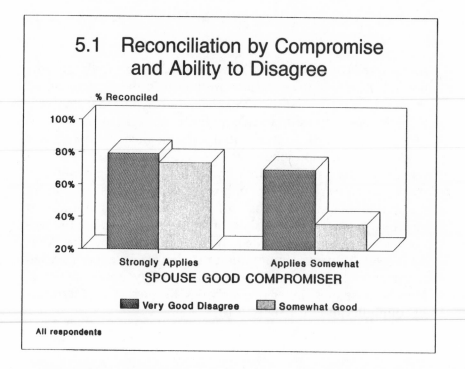

5.1 Reconciliation by Compromise and Ability to Disagree

% Reconciled

SPOUSE GOOD COMPROMISER

▨ Very Good Disagree   ▨ Somewhat Good

All respondents

are reconciled, as opposed to 52% who admit that their spouse is not quite so good at compromise.

How do the ability to disagree and the spouse's readiness to compromise affect one another? Obviously they are correlated. Among those married to a spouse who is good at compromise, the ability to disagree does not add appreciably to the propensity toward reconciliation. In Figure 5.1, the difference between the two bars on the right-hand side is greater than the difference on the left-hand side, which means that the ability to disagree leads to a notable improvement in the possibility of reconciliation only among those who do not find the spouse a good compromiser; about four-fifths of both groups have reconciled. But among those whose spouse is not rated as a good compromiser, the ability to disagree without threatening the marriage adds 26% to the probability of reconciliation. Your spouse may not be good at compromise, but if she/he is open to disagreement which does not threaten the marriage, the odds of reconciliation go up. In both cases the ability to process conflict seems to distinguish sharply between the reconciled and the unreconciled.

If you can't compromise, it still helps to be able to disagree.

C O M M U N I C A T I O N

Intensity of communication between spouses is even more important in achieving reconciliation than in avoiding divorce. Of those who are successfully reconciled, 78% report that they talk to their spouse more than twenty hours a week, as opposed to 50% of those who do not. The figures for those who say they talk a lot about improving their marriage are 69% and 54%; and for those who say they often try hard to make their marriage work, 65% are reconciled as opposed to 47% of those who don't make that claim. By themselves, these three "communication variables" explain about a sixth of the variance between the reconciled and the unreconciled. As we shall see, though, communication, however important it may be, is relevant only when frequent joint prayer or frequent sexual activity are absent—perhaps because these latter two activities are such powerful means of communication (or signs of it).

S E X U A L   P L E A S U R E

The romantics win the battle about the role of sex in fomenting reconciliation, but only among those who have been married less than twenty-five years: 61% of those who have sex once a week[31] or more are reconciled, as opposed to 34% of those who are not reconciled. Frequent sexual relations may be both the result of reconciliation and the cause of it—a sign and a reinforcement as well as a source of reunion. However, frequent sex does correct for the absence of the ability to disagree. In Figure 5.2, on both the left-hand and the right-hand sides of the figure, the light bars are higher than the dark ones, meaning that frequent sex contributes to the possibility of reconciliation—or is a sign of a reconciliation that has happened, or both—even when the ability to disagree is lower. Only 22% of those who have sex less than

---

[31] Note that in the question of reconciliation it is the quantity of sex and not the quality which makes the difference.

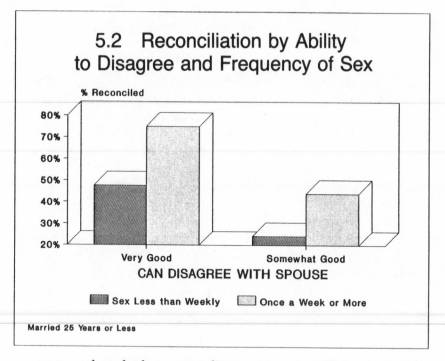

5.2   Reconciliation by Ability to Disagree and Frequency of Sex

% Reconciled

CAN DISAGREE WITH SPOUSE

Very Good   Somewhat Good

Sex Less than Weekly   Once a Week or More

Married 25 Years or Less

once a week and who cannot disagree are reconciled, as opposed to 72% of those who do both. In both cases, frequent sex adds to the propensity to reconciliation, suggesting that it does play something of a causative role itself, even in those circumstances where the value agreement (on the ability to disagree) is not so strong. Frequent sex also makes reconciliation ten percentage points more likely in each of the categories of compromise. Thus it seems to be an additional factor above and beyond the ability of the reconciled spouses to process conflict and something more than just a celebration of that ability.

This conclusion is confirmed by the fact that those married twenty-five years or less who say they are ashamed to be naked in the presence of their spouse are fifteen percentage points less likely to reconciled than those who are not so ashamed. Sexual energy seems to play a role of its own.

C H A R A C T E R   A N D
O V E R T   B E H A V I O R

The ability of a spouse to treat one as an equal is important both in avoiding the possibility of divorce and in reconciling after a brush with divorce (the "kindness" variable does not play a role in this later dynamic). Of those who report such a trait in the spouse, 74% are reconciled, as opposed to 36% of those who do not. A thirty-eight-percentage-point difference in reconciliation indicates just how crucial such a character trait is. It prevents an inclination to divorce and heals after divorce has been a threat.

Cohabitation before marriage seems to exercise a negative influence on the propensity to reconcile: 39% of those who cohabited have been reconciled with their spouses, as have 65% of those who did not cohabit. The proportions are roughly the same for those who have not been unfaithful and those who have been unfaithful. In the former case, it might be argued that since reconciliation correlates positively with the duration of marriage and since cohabiting is a custom which has increased among the young, the negative relationship between cohabitation and reconciliation may not be real.

In fact, when duration of marriage is entered into an equation along with cohabitation, the correlation diminishes (from .23 to .13), but does not become statistically insignificant.

Whatever the explanation of the cohabitation correlation, it hardly provides encouragement for those who think that living together before marriage and learning to cope with the problems of a joint life before making a permanent commitment is a good preparation for conflicts in marriage. It must be admitted, however, that without such preparation, those who elect to live together before marriage might have an even more difficult struggle to achieve reconciliation.

The highest level of reconciliation is to be found among those who engage often in joint prayer with their spouses: 85% of those who report such prayer have reconciled. Moreover, among those who pray every day, equal treatment, the ability to disagree, and even frequency of sex does not improve the probability of reconciliation, perhaps because an 85% reconciliation rate may well

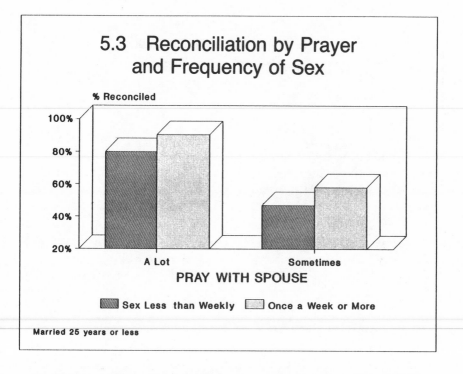

5.3 Reconciliation by Prayer and Frequency of Sex

% Reconciled

PRAY WITH SPOUSE

A Lot   Sometimes

▨ Sex Less than Weekly   ▢ Once a Week or More

Married 25 years or less

establish a ceiling. If a couple prays together often, nothing else seems needed to facilitate reconciliation. In the absence of frequent joint prayer, sexual pleasure, equal treatment, frequent conversation, and the ability to disagree do have an impact on improving the chances of reconciliation—with sexual frequency producing the highest level of reconciliation and equal treatment the strongest correlation. In Figures 5.3, 5.4, 5.5, and 5.6, there is virtually no difference between the light and dark bars on the left-hand side. The differences created by equal treatment, frequent conversation, the ability to disagree, and frequent sex are on the right-hand side of the figures—among those who do not pray often together with their spouse.

To oversimplify, if you don't pray together, frequent sex seems to be the best hope for reconciliation. If you don't pray together, at least play together.

Frequent communication (Figure 5.7) does not contribute to reconciliation in the absence of frequent sex. Only when there is sex at least two or three times a week does frequent conversation add to the proportion reconciled—and brings it to over 90%.

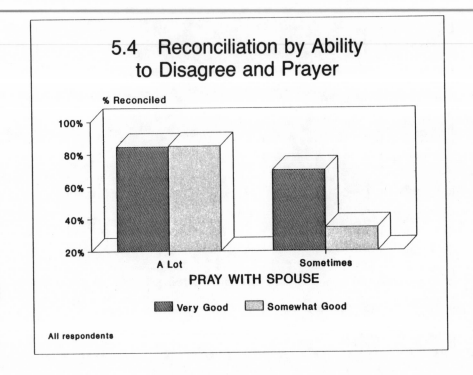

5.4   Reconciliation by Ability to Disagree and Prayer

% Reconciled

PRAY WITH SPOUSE

Very Good   Somewhat Good

All respondents

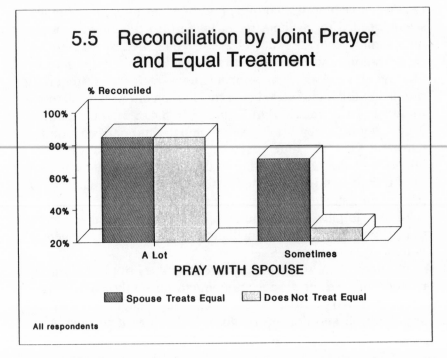

5.5   Reconciliation by Joint Prayer and Equal Treatment

% Reconciled

PRAY WITH SPOUSE

Spouse Treats Equal   Does Not Treat Equal

All respondents

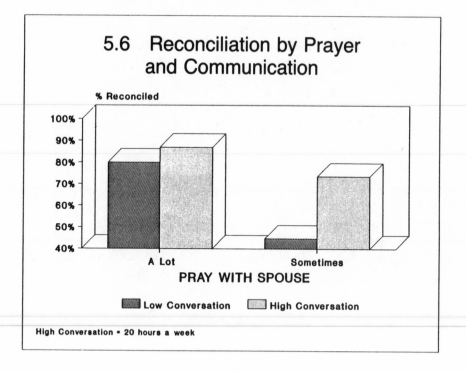

5.6   Reconciliation by Prayer and Communication

% Reconciled

PRAY WITH SPOUSE

Low Conversation   High Conversation

High Conversation = 20 hours a week

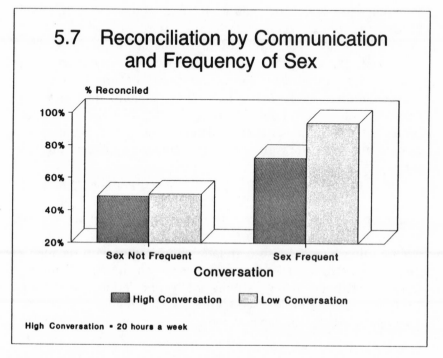

5.7   Reconciliation by Communication and Frequency of Sex

% Reconciled

Conversation

High Conversation   Low Conversation

High Conversation = 20 hours a week

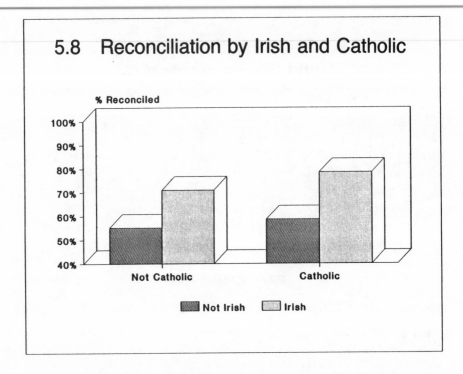

5.8   Reconciliation by Irish and Catholic

% Reconciled

100%
90%
80%
70%
60%
50%
40%

Not Catholic   Catholic

Not Irish   Irish

Frequent talk with your spouse and frequent sex with him/her virtually guarantee reconciliation.

When equality, communication, the ability to disagree, frequency of sex, joint prayer, and reluctance to be naked with the spouse are introduced into an equation, 30% of the variance in reconciliation is explained. When other variables such as years married, cohabiting, infidelity, and absence of children in the home are added, the variance explained rises to 43%. Thus more than two-fifths of the variance in reconciliation can be accounted for.

The standardized correlations for the seven-variable model are .21 for equality, .21 for prayer, .22 for conversation, .19 for frequency of sex, .17 for the ability to disagree, .15 for the ability to compromise, and −.11 for shame over nakedness.

One other variable also correlates significantly with reconciliation: Irish ethnic background. While there is no significant relationship between being Catholic and reconciliation, there is one for being Irish Catholic. (See Figure 5.8: the highest bar on the page is the one at the farthest right, representing those who are both Irish and Catholic). Thus, 73% of the Irish and 78% of the Irish Catholics are reconciled, as opposed to 56% of those who are not Irish. This relationship cannot be explained by frequency of joint prayer or frequency of sex among the Irish.

Moreover, when the variable is entered into the seven-variable explanatory model (prayer, conversation, disagreement, frequency of sex, equal treatment, ability to compromise, and shame), it remains durable and even contributes an extra 1% to the variance explained. Irish Catholics seem to have an advantage at reconciliation.

ARE THE RECONCILED DIFFERENT?

On none of the variables we have considered in this chapter are the reconciled significantly different from the rest of the sample. It would appear that those who have been through a brush with divorce, decided to continue in their marriage, and then concluded that divorce is unlikely are not different from the rest of married Americans. Those who are different are those who have been through the "near-divorce experience" and are not convinced that divorce is out of the question now. The unreconciled are those who need to be explained, not the reconciled. It is their difference from the rest of Americans that is partially accounted for by the six-variable model of equality, compromise, disagreement, prayer, frequency of sex, and shame over nakedness. Those who are unreconciled are more likely than all other married Americans (and not just the reconciled) to say that the spouse does not treat them as an equal, that they are not able to disagree without putting the relationship in danger, that the spouse is not good at compromise, that they do not pray together often with their spouse, that they have sex less than once a week, and that they are ashamed of nakedness.

The reconciled do not differ from other Americans in rating their spouse as their best friend, or in saying that they would marry the same person again. But there is one significant difference between the men in the two groups. Those men who are reconciled are significantly less likely to say that their marriage is very happy (67% versus 47%). The men who have been through the reconciliation experience therefore are not contemplating divorce, would marry the same person again, consider the spouse their best friend, but are not as likely to think of themselves as happily married.

Some of the men, it would seem, not so much have second thoughts as have accepted a situation which they feel is less than perfect.

With this single exception, it seems reasonable to assume that the exclusion of the possibility of divorce is simply another measure of marital happiness which ought to correlate highly with the other three that I have used—best friend, same spouse again, and very happy. This is indeed the case: the possibility of divorce correlates (negatively) with best friend and happy marriage at .5 and with same spouse at .35. Nonetheless, these correlations are sufficiently low that the possibility of divorce can be considered a measure of a somewhat different dimension of married life.

CONCLUSION

It is not surprising that the ability to work one's way out of a brush with divorce involves attaining the same skills as the rest of the population in compromise, coping with disagreement, and treating the spouse as an equal. It is the other half of the six-variable model which is the surprise: joint prayer, frequent sex, and the absence of shame, each of which make an independent contribution to reconciliation above and beyond the other two, and above and beyond the variables in the other half of the model. None of the orientations and behaviors in the model can be said to be essential for reconciliation. Yet all of them help (or are a sign of something that helps). To illustrate by a practical observation: marriage counselors routinely urge troubled couples to work on how they process conflict. They may also urge that the couple try to improve their sex life. But not very many counselors outside of rectories or parsonages (and not all in such places, either) would suggest that the husband and wife work on their joint religious life at the same time they work on their sexual relationship.

Yet the conclusion to be drawn from these last two chapters hardly seems disputable: the family that tends to pray together and tends to play together also tends to stay together.

6. Sexual Pleasure in Marriage

Just how important is sex in marriage? It is frequently said by self-appointed wise persons that it may not be all that important. Older married people will inform younger married people that its importance diminishes. Clergy, particularly celibate Catholic clergy (and especially hierarchy), will insist on the need for spiritual union between the spouses. Physical union, all seem to imply, is not so critical.

The hell it's not!

It is also said that the general sexual satisfaction of a sexual relationship doesn't depend on how frequently the spouses make love.

The hell it doesn't!

AN ARTISTIC MISTAKE?

The Catholic novelist Bruce Marshal once remarked that Jansenism (Catholic puritanism) was the quaint notion that God had made a mistake in ordering the mechanics and dynamics of the procreation and nurturing of human offspring.

Whoever is to be credited or blamed for human sexuality did indeed order that humans, like any other creature of which we have knowledge, be constantly preoccupied by sexual longing and need. For most people, in the ordinary course of events, those longings are fulfilled and those needs met with a more or less permanent sexual partner. In contemporary America that partner normally (in the statistical sense of that word) is the spouse. On a six-point scale of satisfaction ("How much satisfaction do you get out of your sexual relationship—a very great deal, a great deal, quite a bit, a fair amount, some, a little, none?"), a third of our husbands or wives reported "a very great deal" of satisfaction, another third "a great deal," and the final third positioned themselves on the remaining four points.

To those who challenge that evaluation and insist that the figure of one-third at the highest point on the scale is too high, I must reply that I am prepared to take the respondents' word for it. I know of no other way in which we can measure this satisfaction than by asking directly about it, save by interviewing God, who has thus far been unavailable to both NORC and Gallup. Those who are prepared to wet their finger and hold it up to the wind are entitled to do so. Survey research, however great its limitations, is somewhat better than hearing voices in the night, reading auguries, conversing with one's friends, or self-analysis.

But surely the survey taker cannot presume to explain sexual satisfaction in marriage, can he?

Perhaps not. But the survey taker can at least try to account for the variance on the six-point scale, which is better than writing off sexual pleasure as something understood only by the mystics, the psychoanalysts, and the editors of *Playboy*. In fact, the model around which this chapter is organized can account for half the variance on the six-point sexual-satisfaction scale, and does provide an outline of the ordinary course of sexual fulfillment in marriage by taking into account six sets of variables: the quantity of lovemaking, agreement with spouse, the experience of lovemaking, the behavior and character of the lover, religion, and preparations for lovemaking.

Gender, education, and religious denomination do not correlate with sexual satisfaction. Age does, as Figure 6.1 demonstrates: very great satisfaction declines from over 80% among those in their twenties to 25% among those seventy or over. Its decline is roughly parallel to the decline in the frequency of lovemaking, with more than 40% of those in their twenties making love more

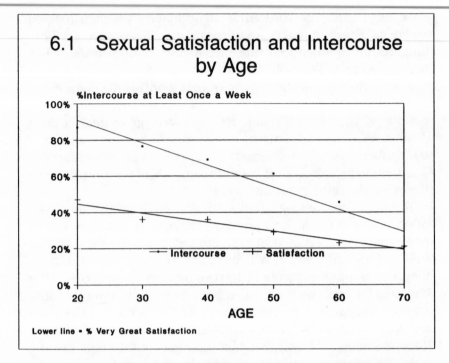

6.1 Sexual Satisfaction and Intercourse by Age

%Intercourse at Least Once a Week

Lower line • % Very Great Satisfaction

than once a week to less than half that of those in their seventies. In a subsequent chapter I turn to the question of sexual satisfaction in those over sixty.

A G R E E M E N T   W I T H   S P O U S E

Agreement with one's spouse on the quantity and quality of lovemaking and on sexual fulfillment are preconditions for sexual satisfaction. Half of those who say there is agreement on sexual fulfillment report a satisfying sexual life,[32] as opposed to 6% who report no such agreement. The numbers are virtually identical for those who say they agree on the quantity and the quality of lovemaking, though when the two are put into an equation together the former is twice as powerful a predictor of sexual plea-

---

[32] This phrase and others like it will be used for that third of the population which is at the top of the six-point scale.

sure. Together they account for half the variance on the scale. However, they will be left out of the model to be developed in this chapter because they run the risk of being too similar to the dependent variable—the six-point scale.

There are no differences between men and women in this correlation, nor are there any correlations with ethnicity and race—save for the Irish. Not only does being Irish correlate significantly (though barely—$r = .08$) with sexual satisfaction, the correlation for being Irish and Catholic and reported sexual satisfaction is even higher—.10. Moreover, when this variable is inserted into the model around which the present chapter is organized, it is remarkably durable, diminishing only to .08. Irish Catholics are 17 percentage points more likely than other Catholics who report very great sexual satisfaction, and also more likely than those who are not Catholic, to claim this highest level of sexual fulfillment. The difference between Irish who are not Catholic and others who are not Catholic is not statistically significant (Figure 6.5, page 76, the first two bars on the left). Thus the correlate of Irish and sexual satisfaction is a specifically Catholic phenomenon.

C O M M U N I C A T I O N

The communication variables I have been using in this report correlate with sexual satisfaction. Of those who say they are trying hard to make the marriage work, 41% report very great sexual satisfaction, as opposed to 21% who say they are not trying hard a lot of the time. Forty percent of those who say they talk often without interruption report that they are very greatly satisfied, versus 31% of their opposites. For those who talk more than twenty hours a week the rate is 40%, versus 31% for their counterparts. Conversation and sexual satisfaction then correlate, the former being perhaps as much as a sign as it is a cause of the latter.

Together they account for 6% of the variance in sexual satisfaction. However, they disappear in the final explanatory model as other and more powerful influences on marriage take over.

F R E Q U E N C Y

The frequency of lovemaking, as one might expect, is a powerful predictor of sexual satisfaction. Of those who report lovemaking at least once a week, 43% are at the top of the scale, as opposed to 17% of those who do not have weekly interludes of intercourse. Sexual relations at least every week are not essential for sexual satisfaction, but they clearly help. Again there are no differences between men and women on this item. Frequent lovemaking is as strong a predictor of sexual satisfaction for women as it is for men.

T H E   E X P E R I E N C E   O F   L O V E

The respondents were asked what their experience of lovemaking was like—what emotions they felt during and after lovemaking —83% reported physical satisfaction, 82% delight that they had pleased their spouse, 82% deep love, 59% pride, 58% ecstasy, 53% that they were sleepy, 51% desire for more, 50% healing of the strains and conflicts of marriage, 45% joy, 13% disappointment with themselves and 13% disappointment with spouse, 5% boredom, 4% embarrassment, and 2% shame.

Three of these experiences were especially powerful predictors of sexual satisfaction.

Of those who said that their sexual encounters with their spouse were ecstatic, 41% reported high sexual satisfaction, versus half that many of those who did not report ecstasy. Thirty-seven percent of those who do not experience disappointment with their spouse were extremely satisfied, as opposed to 17% of those who do experience disappointment with their spouse. Healing produced 39% high-level satisfaction and its opposite only 27% satisfaction.

The question naturally arises as to whether the quality of the sexual interlude can compensate for lack of quantity. Figure 6.2 shows that it is good to have both. Half of those who do experience ecstasy report very great satisfaction (the highest bar in the figure). But those who experience ecstasy (the far left bar) in less frequent

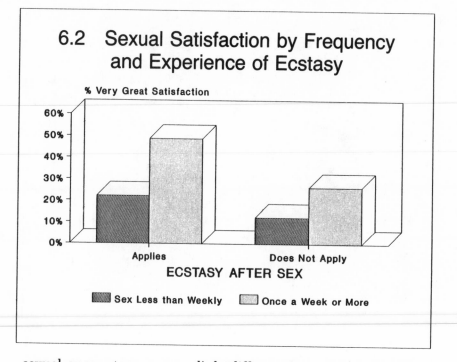

6.2 Sexual Satisfaction by Frequency and Experience of Ecstasy

sexual encounters are very little different from those who have frequent encounters without ecstasy (far right bar)—about a fifth in both cases. So quantity can indeed compensate for quality in marital sex, though the wise hedonist seeks both.

THE CORRELATES OF ECSTASY

The feeling of ecstasy during and after lovemaking is an important dimension of sexual satisfaction. Can we explain what factors contribute to this experience which three-fifths of American couples report as part of their sex lives?

Twenty-four variables correlated with ecstasy—characteristics of the spouse, sexual experimentation and playfulness of various types, and attitudes and behaviors which measured a willingness to let go of restraints and controls. Seven of these variables made a significant contribution to the experience of ecstasy when entered into an equation and explained a little more than a fifth of

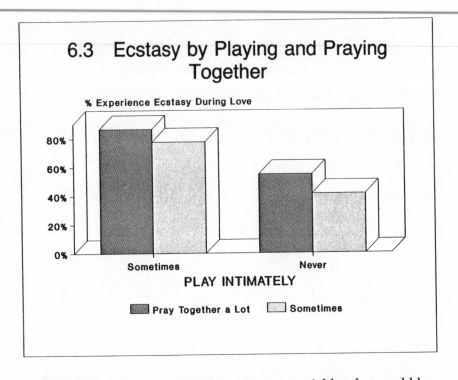

6.3   Ecstasy by Playing and Praying Together

% Experience Ecstasy During Love

PLAY INTIMATELY

Sometimes — Never

▨ Pray Together a Lot   ▢ Sometimes

the variance. They were for the most part variables that could be subsumed under the rubrics of "shamelessness" and the ability to yield control.

Not being embarrassed by sex (.17), a spouse who is imaginative about sex (.17), delight in undressing for the spouse (.11), sexual abandon (.10), making love outdoors (.08), not being ashamed of nakedness (.08), and being able to fight constructively with the spouse (.07) all help to provide a modest (pun only noticed after I typed it, so maybe it's a Freudian slip! Which might in its turn be another Freudian mistake!) explanation of sexual ecstasy. It comes especially to those who are willing to "let go" and give themselves over to their passionate feelings.

Prayer by the husband and wife together reinforces the ecstasy experience above and beyond the influence of, for example, long periods of sexual play (see Figure 6.3), though it has a greater effect on the ecstasy of those who rarely or never engage in such play than it does for those who engage in it sometimes (the two bars on the left of the figure).

Passion and prayer, playing together and praying together, con-

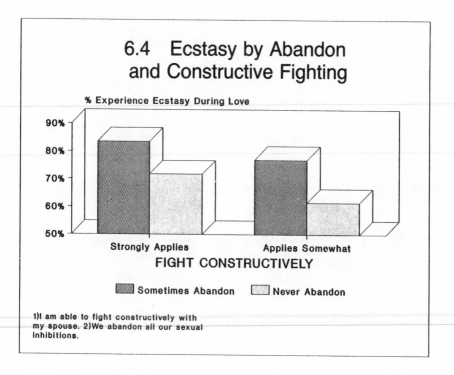

6.4   Ecstasy by Abandon and Constructive Fighting

% Experience Ecstasy During Love

90%

80%

70%

60%

50%

Strongly Applies   Applies Somewhat

FIGHT CONSTRUCTIVELY

▨ Sometimes Abandon   ▢ Never Abandon

1)I am able to fight constructively with my spouse. 2)We abandon all our sexual inhibitions.

tinue to interact with one another to produce both satisfying sex and happy marriages.

Those who are able both to abandon their sexual inhibitions at least sometimes and to fight constructively with their spouse (see Figure 6.4—the bar on the far left) are twenty-two percentage points more likely to experience ecstasy than those who do either less frequently or not at all. Ecstasy is not for the prudish or the prurient; it is for the playful and the prayerful.

It is also, it would seem, for those who are Irish and Catholic. As Figure 6.5 shows, 82% of the Irish Catholics (far right bar) experience ecstatic sex, as opposed to 70% on the average for both non-Irish Catholics and those who are not Catholic and not Irish. This correlation (− .09) does not diminish even when all the variables in the explanatory model for ecstasy are held constant. Just as they are more likely to reconcile and to report very great sexual satisfaction, Irish Catholics are also more likely to claim ecstatic sexual experiences. Their ecstasy accounts for their propensity to report very great sexual satisfaction: the latter correlation goes to zero when ecstasy is taken into account.

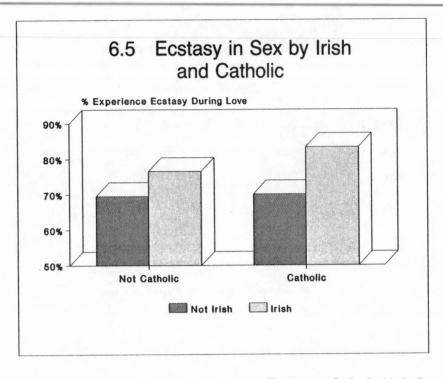

6.5   Ecstasy in Sex by Irish and Catholic

% Experience Ecstasy During Love

90%

80%

70%

60%

50%

Not Catholic   Catholic

▨ Not Irish   ▢ Irish

T H E   **S** P O U S E

As might be imagined, the person of the spouse also has a great impact on sexual fulfillment. If the spouse is a skilled lover, half of the respondents say that their satisfaction is very great. If the spouse is not rated as a skilled lover, the proportion declines to 16%. The same correlation is found with the description of the spouse as "romantic" and the respondent's judgment that the spouse rates the self as "romantic."

A fifth of those who say the spouse is interested only in work report very great sexual satisfaction, exactly half of those who report such satisfaction when they deny that the spouse cares only about work.

The love skills of the spouse also make up for infrequent lovemaking. In Figure 6.6 the two bars on the left represent the satisfaction of those who are married to a skillful lover. Note that the bar on the far left—those who do not have sex every week but who judge the spouse to be skillful—is higher than the bar on the far right, which stands for those who have frequent sex

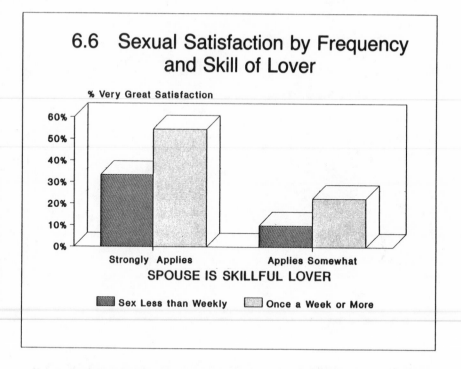

6.6   Sexual Satisfaction by Frequency and Skill of Lover

% Very Great Satisfaction

SPOUSE IS SKILLFUL LOVER

▨ Sex Less than Weekly   ▢ Once a Week or More

with a less skilled lover. Fifty-five percent of those who have both a skilled spouse and ecstatic sexual experiences report very great sexual satisfaction.

The quality of the lover makes up for the lack of quantity in the lovemaking, just as does the quality of the love experience.

A good-looking spouse also helps for good sex: those who say their spouse is good-looking are twice as likely to find very great sexual satisfaction as those who do not think so (39% versus 18%). However, it may also be that sexual satisfaction can *cause* a spouse to be perceived as good-looking. Surely the response does not mean youthful good looks, because it does not decline with the age of the respondent (and presumably the age of the spouse). A spouse who is good-looking and is a skilled lover produces a high level of sexual fulfillment (55%).

It also helps if you think your spouse judges you imaginative about sex (more than does your judgment about the spouse's imagination): 48% of those who feel they are being judged as imaginative report very great satisfaction, versus 29% who do not think their spouse judges them as imaginative.

None of these variables correlate with gender, and the dynamics

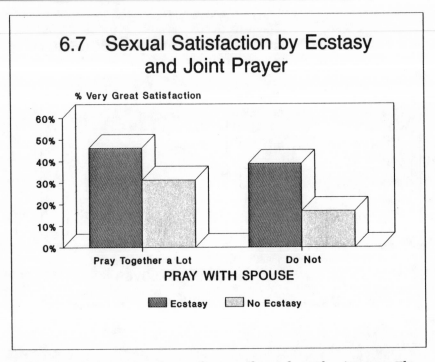

6.7   Sexual Satisfaction by Ecstasy and Joint Prayer

% Very Great Satisfaction

PRAY WITH SPOUSE

Pray Together a Lot   Do Not

Ecstasy   No Ecstasy

of interaction among them also are free of gender impact. The characteristics we are able to measure in this study which make for a good bed partner seem to be species- or at least culture-wide, and not gender linked.

R E L I G I O N

There is no correlation between denomination and sexual satisfaction, but two religious variables do influence that satisfaction: the feeling that the spouse is sometimes like a god, and joint prayer with the spouse. Two-fifths of those who think that the spouse is like a god report high sexual satisfaction, as opposed to a third who do not think of the spouse in this fashion. If the spouses pray together, the results are about the same. In both cases, religion increases the sexual satisfaction occasioned by other experiences, as Figures 6.7 and 6.8 demonstrate.

In Figure 6.7, the light bar on the left—those who pray with their spouse but report no ecstasy—is similar to the darker bar

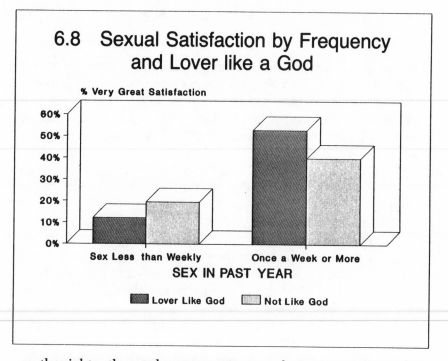

6.8 Sexual Satisfaction by Frequency and Lover like a God

% Very Great Satisfaction

SEX IN PAST YEAR

Lover Like God   Not Like God

on the right—those who report ecstasy and not prayer. Thus joint prayer makes up for the absence of ecstasy, though if you have both you are better off than if you only have one and much better off (twice as likely to report very great sexual satisfaction) than if you have neither.

Moreover, Figure 6.8 shows that if you judge your lover to be godlike and also have frequent sex (bars on the right), your satisfaction is more likely than if you have frequent sex with a less-than-divine lover. However, if you don't make love frequently with a divine lover, then your satisfaction is even lower than if you don't make love frequently with a less-than-divine lover (two bars on the left).

Religious images and devotion, then, continue to play an important role in marital happiness, even in the sexual relationship of the spouses. Religious imagery and devotion combine with sexual aspects of the common life to produce an even higher level of sexual satisfaction than purely sexual characteristics do. Perhaps one ought to conclude that religious imagery and devotion *are* sexual characteristics of the relationship.

S E X U A L **E** X P E R I M E N T A T I O N

Sexual experiments—various forms of love play, some of which might have seemed to an earlier age more than a little kinky—also contribute to sexual satisfaction, especially through a variable which is the response to a question "How often do you experiment with new ways of lovemaking?" A little more than half the sample said that they did experiment at least some of the time; that group is more than twice as likely to claim very great sexual satisfaction (44% versus 20%). Again there is no gender correlation.

This variable (along with "kind" and "exciting") is a conduit linking specific forms of love play to sexual satisfaction in the model around which this chapter is organized. However, apart from the model, the other forms of love do have a considerable impact on sexual satisfaction—which is doubtless the reason why men and women engage in them.

Thus, 49% of those who go to a hotel or motel for a weekend with the spouse,[33] 45% of those who bathe or shower with the spouse, 42% of those who swim in the nude with the spouse, 46% of those who undress one another, 44% of those who buy erotic underwear, 42% of those who make love outdoors, 41% of those who enjoy taking off their clothes for their spouse, and 37% of those who engage in prolonged intimate play report high levels of sexual satisfaction. Amusing oneself and the spouse with the spouse's body and one's own is hardly a new form of human behavior (and has not increased in the last five years, according to a retrospective question asked in the survey). It does, however, contribute substantially to sexual fulfillment, and going off for a romantic weekend contributes substantially, independent of all other variables.

It matters with which kind of body you are playing. If it is one

---

[33] In this section of the chapter, those who report engaging in these romantic behaviors "a lot" are linked with those who do them "sometimes." If only those who do them "a lot" are considered, the impact on high levels of sexual satisfaction is much larger, but based on a relatively small number of cases: 80% for making love outdoors, 61% for erotic underwear, 53% for playing together, 57% for undressing each other, 53% for the joint shower, and 46% for the nude swim.

These forms of sexual play are perhaps in part the result of a high level of sexual satisfaction as well as a cause. But they certainly correlate at very high levels with sexual pleasure, and they can't hurt.

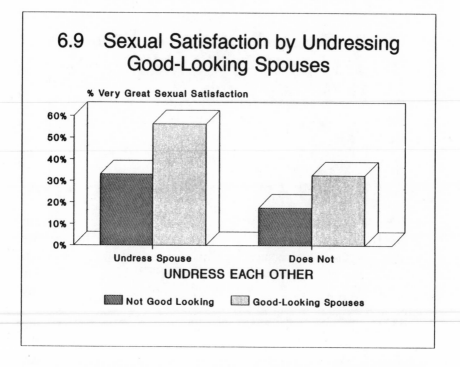

6.9 Sexual Satisfaction by Undressing Good-Looking Spouses

% Very Great Sexual Satisfaction

UNDRESS EACH OTHER

Undress Spouse   Does Not

Not Good Looking   Good-Looking Spouses

you judge good-looking (see Figure 6.9), your level of satisfaction goes up twenty percentage points (second left bar). Undressing a spouse whom you do not judge to be good-looking has no more payoff than not undressing a spouse you judge to be good-looking (first and fourth bars in the figure).

It must be noted that this is a subjective judgment of good-looking, one which does not correlate with either age or duration of marriage. Men are more likely than women to say that their spouse is good-looking (is this realism or romanticism? Don't expect me to answer)—82% versus 70%. Furthermore, 83% of the men over seventy and 62% of the women say that their spouse is good-looking.

What about undressing a god and being undressed by the same god? Might that be the ultimate sexual kick? As Figure 6.10 shows, if one undresses a lover who is like a god the chances of one reporting a very high level of satisfaction go to almost 60%. Sexual play and religious imagery working together have a very considerable payoff—indeed the sexual payoff in picturing your lover as like a god comes only if you undress him or her, and once more there is no gender correlation.

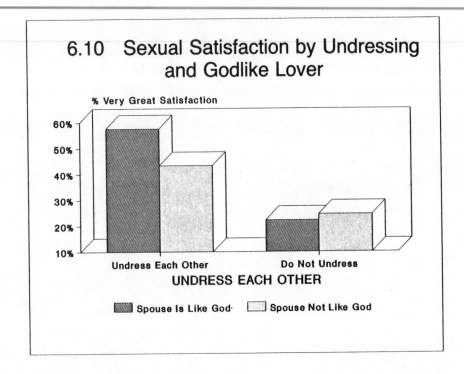

6.10   Sexual Satisfaction by Undressing and Godlike Lover

% Very Great Satisfaction

UNDRESS EACH OTHER

Spouse Is Like God·   Spouse Not Like God

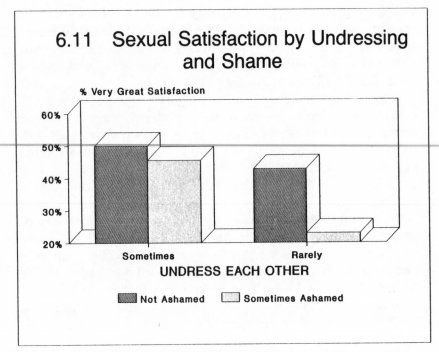

6.11   Sexual Satisfaction by Undressing and Shame

% Very Great Satisfaction

UNDRESS EACH OTHER

Not Ashamed   Sometimes Ashamed

Finally, if shame about nakedness (Figure 6.11—last bar) and the absence of mutual undressing are combined, only a fifth of those in that category report very great sexual satisfaction, as opposed to 50% of those who are not ashamed and do engage in mutual stripping. Those who are sometimes ashamed and yet engage in mutual undressing (second bar from the left) do not seem notably penalized for their embarrassment.

When the various play variables are submitted to the technique called factor analysis, two "factors" emerge. One includes mutual undressing, showers together, joy in taking off one's clothes for the spouse, and prolonged sexual play. The other includes nude swims, erotic underwear, love outdoors, and watching x-rated films. The former factor is the stronger predictor of sexual experimentation, frequency of lovemaking, and overall sexual satisfaction. Together the two factors explain half the variance in the sexual experimentation item, a third of the variance in the frequency of sex, and a fifth of the variance in sexual satisfaction. The first factor, involving various forms of naked play, alone accounts for 13% of the variance in sexual satisfaction. If the first factor could be considered traditional sexual play, and the second—x-rated videos, erotic underwear, nude swims—could be considered more modern or innovative amusements, then the former continues to be the more important type of sexual experimentation. But sexual play is an important part of sexual fulfillment in marriage and, as we shall see in the next chapter, becomes more important rather than less as life continues.

C O N C L U S I O N

Beginning with the mystery of sexual satisfaction, we have progressed through six sets of variables which might contribute to it—the quantity of lovemaking, agreement with spouse, the experience of lovemaking, the behavior and character of the lover, religion, and preparations for lovemaking. Each set of variables made a contribution. Since the order is logical and not chronological, it would be inappropriate to try to add them one by one to see how much is contributed by each new layer.

However, when twelve of the variables are entered into a multiple regression equation, the R is .72 and the R^2 is .52: half of the variance along the sexual satisfaction scale can be explained by these variables. The standardized correlations are skilled lover, .25; frequency, .33; spouse thinks respondent imaginative about sex, .15; romance, .15; sexual experimentation, .15; cares only about work, $-.14$; like a god, .11; exciting, .10; ecstasy, .09; naked sexual play, 08; spouse is good-looking, .07.

The model is gender-neutral: it works as well for women as for men. But doesn't everyone know that women react differently than men to sexual stimuli and responses?

Doubtless there are gender differences, but which gender would value ecstasy less? Or a skilled lover? Or an imaginative or romantic partner? Or a good-looking partner? Or sexual play? And which would value more a partner who cares only about work?

The gender differences are to be found, one suspects, in the variance not explained by the model—and in other characteristics of the spouse which are channeled into the relationship through romanticism and skilled love or imagination.

Obviously I have left out variables that might not be considered overtly sexual—save for the two religious measures about whose sexual impact there is both empirical evidence and theoretical expectation. I have done so intentionally because I want to try to explain (as far as one can with the fragile instruments of survey research—though these are no less fragile than other methodologies) sexual satisfaction in marriage in sexual terms. My assumption is that other variables, such as the quality of the whole relationship, are filtered into sexual satisfaction through intervening variables which are more or less explicitly sexual. Thus, when the two variables "kindness" and "equal treatment"—so important for the total relationship—are added to the model, they do not add to its explanatory power and indeed are not statistically significant.

That does not mean that they are not enormously important to the relations. Of course they are, but they exercise their impact through more explicitly sexual variables.

It might be said that the explanatory model in this chapter is drenched in romance—both as explicit variables and as surrogate variables like sexual experimentation, ecstasy, excitement, healing, and skill.

Romance is alive and well, if not in the species (though I suspect there, too), then in the culture.

Romance and religion. The impact of religion, both on sexual satisfaction directly and indirectly through its interaction with sexual stimuli, is consistently important.

7. Sex over Sixty

Sex among older people is often a snide joke among younger people, mostly because the latter forget that some day they too will be old. After a certain age in life, sex seems grotesque, the age depending on your own age—teens often seem to think sex between their parents is "gross." But human passion does not die, and neither does human sexual satisfaction. The proper question for this chapter is not whether there is passionate love over sixty, but who are the passionate lovers in the later years of life?

DOES PASSION DIE?

Figure 6.1 (page 70) in the last chapter showed the downward slide of both satisfaction and frequency of sexual intercourse as the years of life went on. The findings reported there will be a surprise to no one. Human passion seems to wane as the years go, in part for physiological reasons and in part too for psychological and cultural reasons. The mix of physiology (and especially endocrinology), psychology, and culture which contributes to this decline is extremely intricate.

The decline mapped out in Figure 6.1 is a decline of averages and tells us nothing about what happens to individuals. There are married men and women in their twenties whose sex life gives them something less than "very great" satisfaction and who en-

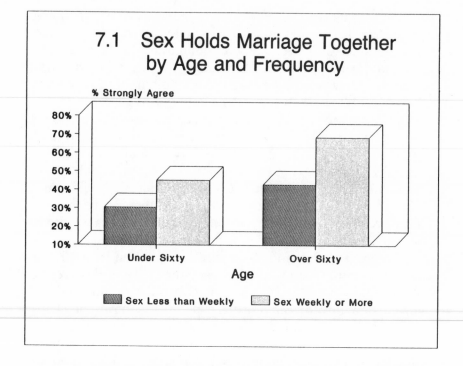

7.1 Sex Holds Marriage Together by Age and Frequency

gage in sexual intercourse less frequently than once a week. On the other hand, 42% of the married people in our study who are in their sixties report "very great satisfaction" from their sex lives, as do 20% of those in their seventies. Moreover, a fifth of those over sixty report intercourse at least once a week. It cannot be estimated from the data in this survey whether such proportions represent a decline in satisfaction and activity for the respondents, since we do not know what their activity and satisfaction were when they younger. However, they are able to maintain both the average activity and satisfaction level of married Americans despite their age. Thus age itself does not fate any given person to a low level of sexual activity and satisfaction.

There is certainly no inclination among the men and women over sixty to underestimate the importance of sex for holding a marriage together (see Figure 7.1). Of those over sixty 53% strongly agree that it is very important, against 42% of those under sixty. Moreover, agreement that sex is a strong bond for marriage rises to almost 70% (bar on the far right) for those over sixty who have intercourse at least once a week. Indeed, those over sixty who have sex less than once a week are as likely as those under sixty who have it once a week or more to see sex as binding force in marriage. It is simply not true that after a certain age in life the importance of the sexual bond diminishes. Those over sixty think it more important than do younger people, rather than less important. They may not engage in it as often, but it does not follow that they think it has lost its importance.

Why, given their agreement on the importance of sex, are some of those over sixty able to sustain a high level of activity and satisfaction and others are not? This survey cannot offer an explanation. One would have to know more about the health, physiology, life history, and culture of the respondents to undertake such an effort. However, one can ask whether there are behavioral indicators which account for the difference in sexual satisfactions and activities between the young and the not-so-young.

The more pertinent and more poignant question is whether a change in culture—a change in belief about sex in the lives of older people—would lead to a change in behavior among older people. The ability to sustain sexual experimentation, as this chapter shows, is a crucial indicator of activity and satisfaction after sixty. Is the decline in willingness to experiment a cultural phenomenon more than anything else? Can it be modified, if not in the present generation over sixty, at least in subsequent generations? Is there any good reason why sexual playfulness should ever stop in human life?

This report cannot answer those questions; it can, however, say that the ability of a substantial minority of men and women over sixty to be sexually playful suggests that these questions are worth asking.

S O M E   A R E   V E R Y   A C T I V E

Some of the older men and women are very active indeed: 15% of those over sixty and 10% of those over seventy report sex more than once a week; 40% of those in their sixties and 20% of those in their seventies say that they enjoy undressing for their spouse; 27% and 21% respectively say that they engage in mutual undressing with the spouse. A fifth of the former and a tenth of the latter report making love outdoors. Half the former and a fifth of the latter report prolonged sexual play. Furthermore, 16% and 12% report a shower or a bath together, and 38% of those in their sixties and 12% of those in their seventies say that they experience ecstasy during lovemaking.

Those over sixty are no less likely than those under sixty to say that their spouse is attractive and 55% say their spouse is a skilled lover (46% for those under sixty). Fifty-five percent say their spouse is romantic (52%). There is no significant difference between the two groups in those admitting they avoid sex or in those who say their spouse is attractive. Finally, 17% say that they swim nude with their spouse (34%), 41% report prolonged sexual play (38%), and 7% even report the purchase of erotic undergarments.

This is a picture of sexual activity among (some) older men and women which would seem to go against strong cultural expectations. Might they be exaggerating the quantity and quality of their sexual endeavors in order to give the impression that they have been able to retain their youthfulness? Or might they be so embarrassed at behavior which to others might appear ridiculous that if anything they would underestimate it?

The question about mutual undressing was asked before the age question and the question about undressing for one's spouse was asked after the age question. Both were asked after the question about the length of the marriage. The age question did not seem to make a difference in the responses. My guess—no more than that—is that an older person on the telephone would be more than a little embarrassed to admit pleasure in undressing for a spouse, however much she/he might actually enjoy the event, and that therefore the responses are not wild exaggerations. Hence I suspect that they are telling the truth: there is much more sexual activity and playfulness going on in the bedrooms of older men and women than the rest of the society seems to appreciate.

S A T I S F A C T I O N

If there is so much activity, why has the satisfaction level declined, as Figure 6.1 in the previous chapter demonstrates?

A general model which accounts for the variation in sexual

satisfaction by age also accounts for the different levels of satisfaction between those who are under sixty and those who are over sixty. Half the difference is the result of a lower level of frequency of sexual intercourse; 15% can be accounted for by the decline in the experience of ecstasy in lovemaking (74% to 54%); another 15% of the difference can be accounted for by the drastic falloff in experimentation with new ways of lovemaking (from 64% to 28%) and the accompanying decline in prolonged sexual play and undressing; and 7% can be attributed to the decline in the description of the spouse as godlike (net of the prior variables in the model).

Thus only 13% of the decline in sexual satisfaction remains unexplained, and that difference between those under sixty and those over sixty is statistically insignificant. There is less sexual satisfaction as humans age primarily because there is less frequent sex, less ecstasy in the sexual act, and less experimentation and playfulness before and during it. Or to put the matter differently, older men and women who are able to sustain frequency, ecstasy, experimentation, and playfulness (and some—about a quarter— are) are as satisfied sexually as younger men and women.

The importance of ecstasy in lovemaking is illustrated by Figure 7.2: those over sixty who experience ecstasy (second bar from the left) are more likely to report very great sexual satisfaction than those under sixty (second bar from the right) who do not experience the sexual act as ecstatic. The quality of the sexual experience itself easily compensates for age even if those under sixty who experience ecstasy (first bar from the left) are more likely to be very satisfied.

If one combines both the frequency of the sexual act and its quality (Figure 7.3), one sees, however, that for those over sixty who engage in intercourse at least once a week (two bars on the right), ecstasy has no impact on levels of satisfaction. If you have quantity over sixty quality doesn't make much difference. However, if you lack quantity, then quality makes up for the lack to some extent (two bars on the left).

When those under sixty are compared with those over sixty in their satisfaction by frequency and quality as represented in Figure 7.3, the levels of very great satisfaction do not vary significantly. Those who are high on quantity and quality over sixty are as likely to be satisfied with their sexual activities as those who are high on both under sixty.

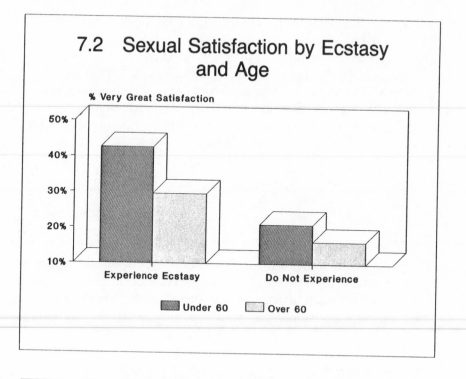

7.2   Sexual Satisfaction by Ecstasy and Age

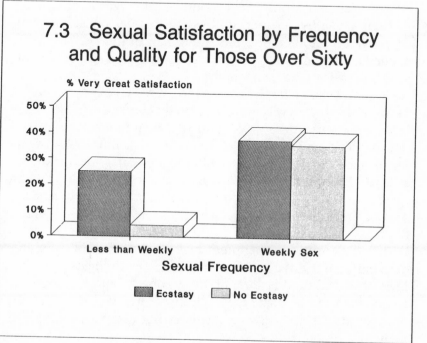

7.3   Sexual Satisfaction by Frequency and Quality for Those Over Sixty

Most of the decline, therefore, in sexual satisfaction among older men and women is the result of the decline in the frequency of sex and in the experience of sexual ecstasy.

Can these two be sustained after a certain age in life? Obviously they can, because some people do sustain them. Can more men and women sustain them over sixty than actually do?

The answer to that question is beyond the scope of this book. Just the same, the answer is "probably."

FREQUENCY

If half of the difference in sexual satisfaction between those over sixty and those under sixty (and half the correlation between age and sexual satisfaction) can be accounted for by the decline in the frequency of lovemaking, what in turn accounts for this latter decline? We find that 28% of the difference is accounted for by the decline in the proportion who say they experiment with new ways of lovemaking; 22% more can be accounted for by the decline of specific forms of lovemaking—prolonged intimate play, showers or baths together, undressing for the spouse, and undressing one another. The remaining half of the decline in frequency of lovemaking cannot be explained by any variable available in the data being analyzed.

Figure 7.4 illustrates the importance of sexual experimentation in sustaining high levels of sexual activity after sixty. In fact, there is no difference in the proportion reporting intercourse at least once a week between the two age groups for those who experiment at least sometimes—four-fifths of both categories make love at least once a week (the two bars at the left). It is only among those who rarely or never experiment (72% of those over sixty, 45% of those under sixty) that age has an effect on the frequency of intercourse (the two bars on the right).

The propensity to experiment may be the result of some underlying sexual drive (a combination of physiological, psychological, and cultural factors) and of feedback from frequent sex, so no claim can be made that it "causes" frequent sex. One can only say that in its presence, age does not make a difference in frequency of intercourse.

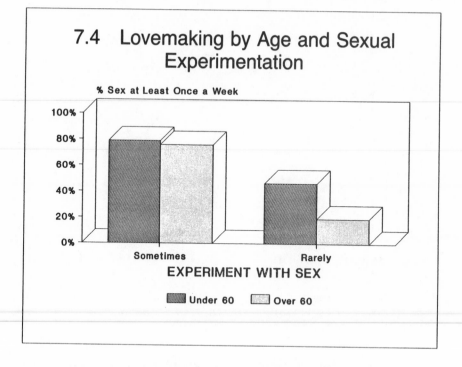

7.4 Lovemaking by Age and Sexual Experimentation

% Sex at Least Once a Week

EXPERIMENT WITH SEX

Under 60   Over 60

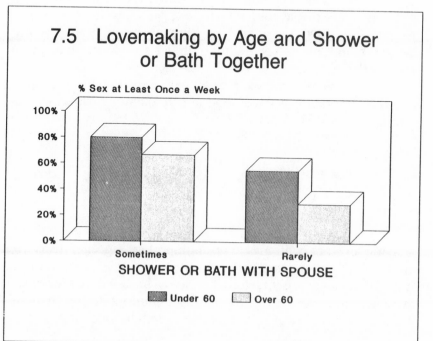

7.5 Lovemaking by Age and Shower or Bath Together

% Sex at Least Once a Week

SHOWER OR BATH WITH SPOUSE

Under 60   Over 60

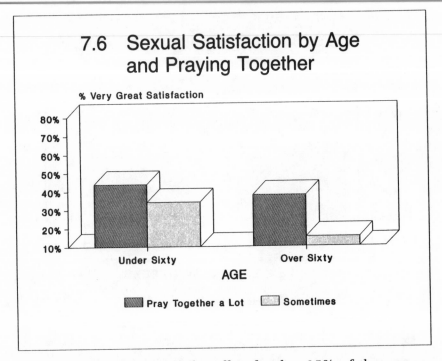

7.6 Sexual Satisfaction by Age and Praying Together

% Very Great Satisfaction

AGE

Pray Together a Lot   Sometimes

Figure 7.5 shows a similar effect for that 15% of those over sixty who report that they sometimes take showers or baths together. There is not a significant difference in frequency of sex between those over sixty and those under sixty if they engage in joint bathing.

In summary, for those who are sexually experimental and playful, the correlation between age and frequency of lovemaking vanishes.

P R A Y E R   A N D   S E X
F O R   T H O S E   O V E R   S I X T Y

Praying together continues to be an important aspect of the common life of husband and wife even after sixty, as Figures 7.6, 7.7, and 7.8 demonstrate. In figure 7.6, it is to be noted that for those who pray together "a lot," there is no significant decline at all in the level of *sexual satisfaction* after the sixtieth birthday (the darker

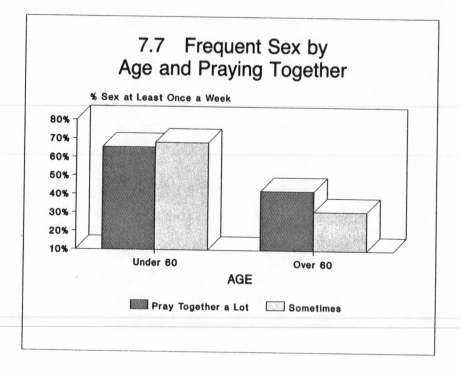

7.7 Frequent Sex by Age and Praying Together

7.8 Ecstasy by Age and Praying Together

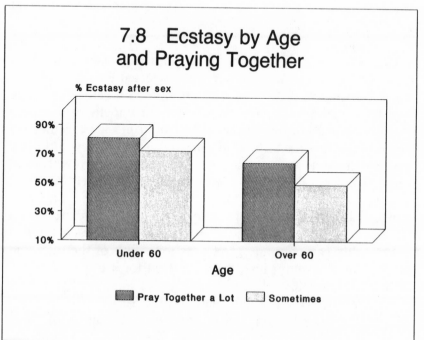

bars). Praying together cancels out the effect on sexual satisfaction of age—no small achievement, to put it mildly.

While the *frequency of sexual activity* declines after sixty even for those who pray together a lot (Figure 7.7), frequent prayer still correlates with more frequent sex for those who are over sixty (the two right bars). Moreover, the effect of prayer on sexual activity (or perhaps vice versa) is more pronounced after sixty than it is before sixty.

Finally, a similar phenomenon exists for *ecstasy in sex* (Figure 7.8): joint prayer correlates positively with ecstasy at both age levels, but more strongly for those over sixty. Moreover, there is only a small difference between the two middle bars in the figure: the proportion of ecstasy for those over sixty who pray a lot is only slightly lower than the proportion for those under sixty who do not pray together a lot.

In summary, if praying together (mixed with playing together) is an important correlate of sexual pleasure in marriage, its importance increases rather diminishes with age.

C O N C L U S I O N

Pretty clearly, and despite the hired-gun theologians of the Vatican, the human evolutionary process selected for forms of sexual mechanics and dynamics which bonded together the male and the female in an often passionate and sometimes intensely passionate relationship so that they would preside together (in some way) over the rearing of their offspring. The evolutionary process did not need to take into account the possibility that large numbers of humans would live long after their help was needed to protect neonates, infants, and children and long after the fertility of the female of the species ended. Therefore sexual attraction and frequent sexual activity in the already bonded relationship can continue (and does for a fifth of the men and women in our study) long after the need for it to continue the species has ended.

Rather little is known about this "senior" sexual activity, playfulness, and satisfaction. It has often been a matter for snide laughter among younger folk. Yet one suspects that the older lovers for whom passion and play have not stopped after a long life together of cherishing one another will have the last laugh.

They are entitled to that laugh, and they can afford to have it.

8. Forced Sex

This chapter looks at the hideous subject of rape. Using a question which almost surely leads to an underestimate of its incidence, the study discovered that 10% of married American women reported that sex had been forced upon them, usually by someone they knew and in about a quarter of the cases by their husbands.

Husband-rape is a disaster for a marriage. However, many women who have been raped by others are nonetheless able to have happy and satisfying marriages.

Ten percent of married women report that they have been forced to have sex against their wishes. Of these, 25% were raped by their husbands, 22% by a friend, 16% by a date or a relative, and 6% by a stranger. Sixteen percent would not or could not identify the one who forced sex upon them.

This proportion is substantially lower than reported by Diana Russell (1982) in her study of the same phenomenon (40% the target of attempted rape, 33% actually raped). However, Russell's questions were more elaborate and indirect—and better—than was possible in a single question at the end of a long interview. Nonetheless, it seemed useful to ask the blunt question bluntly to see whether it would produce an incidence of forced sex in marriage which was dismayingly high. The fact that 10% of married American women have been raped, almost 3% by their spouses, is profoundly disturbing evidence of the subjugation of some women by some men, especially since it is a conservative estimate.

The pertinent question for this chapter is whether rape as such has a negative impact on the marriage or whether the negative impact comes only from sex forced by the husband.

Those who have been forced into sex against their will are notably less likely to say that their marriage is very happy (47% versus 69%), and somewhat less likely to say that their spouse is their best friend (69% versus 79%) and that they would marry the same person again (74% versus 85%). Moreover, these figures were not affected by whether the attacker was their spouse or not.[34] If a woman has been forced to have sex, no matter who the assailant, she is less likely to be happy in her marriage.

She is also less likely to see her husband as kind (69% versus 81%), or to say that she is treated as an equal (59% versus 77%), and more likely to say that she is very ashamed to be naked (12% versus 2%). However, she is no less likely to have sex at least once a week and to report that her sexual satisfaction is "very great," or that she experiences ecstasy during lovemaking.

Figure 8.1 shows the effect of husband-rape and other-rape on various measures of marital fulfillment. The first bar in each group represents the proportion for those women who have not been sexually assaulted; the middle bar represents those who have been the victims of forced sex by someone other than their husband; and the third bar represents those who have been forced to engage in sex by their spouse. On each topic, sex forced by the spouse correlates with very low proportions of satisfaction—or both represent the effects of some antecedent problem. Only a quarter of such women say their marriage is very happy, and less than two-fifths say their spouse is their best friend. Perhaps astonishingly, 55% say that they would marry the same person again. Only half say the spouse is kind, and 25% that he is exciting. Half the women who have been raped by their husbands are considering divorce as at least a possibility.

Rape by someone other than the spouse has less effect on the six indicators than rape by the spouse. Notable differences exist between the first and second bars only in the group on the far

---

[34] It is possible that many of the unidentified attackers were also spouses.

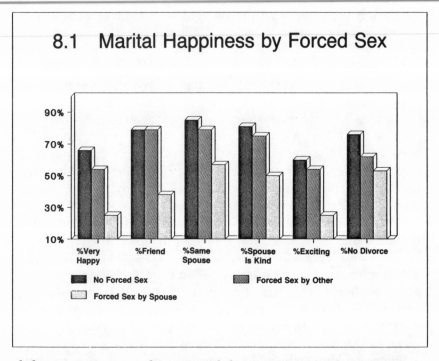

8.1 Marital Happiness by Forced Sex

left (proportion very happy) and the group on the far right (proportion considering divorce to be impossible). Husband-rape, then, depresses the satisfaction on all six measures, and rape by anyone effects both general marital happiness and the likelihood of divorce.

In answer to the question posed at the beginning of this chapter, the experience of rape by someone other than the spouse (perhaps long before the marriage) has some negative effect on marital satisfaction, though not on such key measures as judgment about the kindness of the spouse, the description of the spouse as best friend, and the conviction that one would marry the same man again.

However, husband-rape tends to be a disaster for a marriage, perhaps a marriage which is already a disaster area. The data available in this analysis enable us to say only that (a) rape must stop and (b) some women are able despite rape to put together happy marriages for themselves.

9. *Fear and Loathing in the Sexual Encounter*

The physical relationship between the sexes is not easy for many men and women. Almost a quarter of the married men and women in our sample admit that sometimes they avoid sex, and three out of ten say they are ashamed to be naked in the presence of their spouse. Whoever designed the species determined that sexual impulse and the impulse to sexual play would be difficult to resist but nonetheless resistible. Who are those who do resist and what impact does such resistance have on their marriages?

THE EXTENT OF FEAR AND LOATHING

Not all Americans, not even in this allegedly permissive era, enjoy sex. Some fear and loathe it:

- 47% of married men and women admit that they are shy at least some of the time with members of the opposite sex; 10%

concede that this shyness is frequent. There is no difference between men and women in the propensity to be shy.

• 20% respond that sex embarrasses them at least some of the
time—32% of the women and 15% of the men. Physical nakedness in the presence of the spouse upsets 30% of the respondents
at least some of the time—7% of the men and 32% of the women.

• 25% admit that they avoid sex at least some of the time—
40% of the women and 26% of the men; and 29% of the husbands
and wives say their spouse wants sex too often—46% of the
women and 22% of the men.

Whence comes this fear and loathing of sexuality which affects
substantial minorities of the population? Is it a holdover from
puritanism of one kind or another? Is it because the permissiveness of the Sexual Revolution has not affected older men and
women? Or is it a lack of sophistication among those who are
not so well educated?

When a factor analysis was performed to create clusters of these
variables, two factors emerged, the first emphasizing shame (nakedness, embarrassment, shyness) and the second a dislike of sex
(avoidance, spouse wants it too much). Neither of these two
factors correlated with religious denomination, biblical literalism,
or with income. There were, however, slight correlations with
age and college attendance and strong correlations with gender.

A G E ,   **S** E X ,   A N D   **F** E A R   A N D   **L** O A T H I N G

The age correlation with shame (measured by physical nakedness
in the presence of the spouse) in Figure 9.1 existed only for very
young wives, still in their early twenties. At all other ages physical
nakedness with the spouse is a problem for 30% of the women
and 8% of the men—no signs in either sex of a Sexual Revolution
on this measure.

Similarly (Figure 9.2), about two-fifths of the women in the
study admitted that they avoid sex at least some of time with no
variation by age. A little more than a quarter of the men also
admit that they avoid sex (a candid admission in a culture which

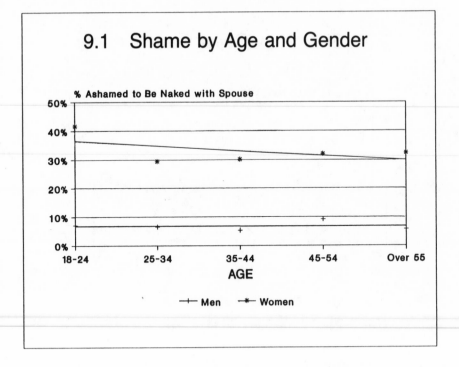

9.1   Shame by Age and Gender

% Ashamed to Be Naked with Spouse

AGE

— Men   —*— Women

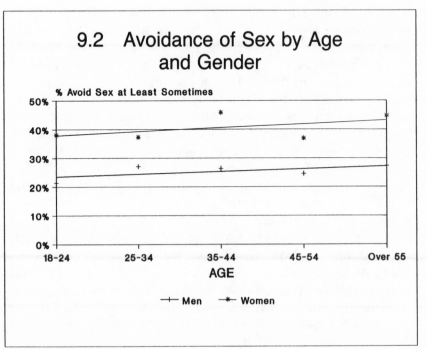

9.2   Avoidance of Sex by Age and Gender

% Avoid Sex at Least Sometimes

AGE

— Men   —*— Women

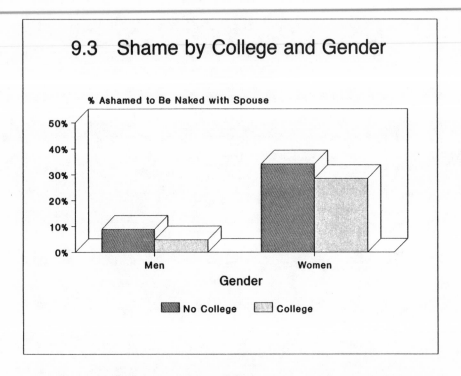

9.3   Shame by College and Gender

% Ashamed to Be Naked with Spouse

Gender

No College   College

prizes machismo) at least some of the time, with a slight increase in that proportion after they turn twenty-six. Shame and avoidance, then, are widespread in the society and correlate with gender, not age. Men are less bothered by shame (or less willing to admit it), but a surprisingly large proportion of them admit avoiding sex some of the time, and (as noted in a previous paragraph) nearly a quarter of the men think their spouse wants sex too often; this proportion does not vary with age (save among those over 55, where it declines). Thus a quarter of the men at the most virile periods of their life protest against a wife who is too lustful—a rather astonishing admission and so contrary to the stereotypes that it should put to rest the notion that the respondents in the survey were not being candid.

Does the sophistication added by college education diminish either shame or sexual avoidance? The answer (in Figures 9.3 and 9.4) is that higher education has no significant statistical impact on either phenomenon for either men or women. Whatever the reasons for sexual fear and loathing might be, they do not seem to be losing their impact in contemporary America.

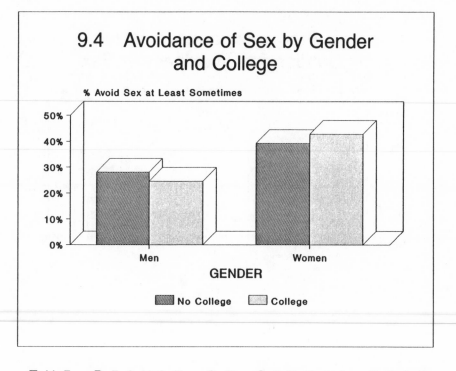

9.4   Avoidance of Sex by Gender and College

% Avoid Sex at Least Sometimes

GENDER

No College   College

THE RESULT OF SEXUAL FEAR AND LOATHING

Shame as such does not correlate significantly with judgments about agreement with the spouse on the quality and quantity of sexual life, or on the propensity for sexual experimentation, or general sexual satisfaction, or even, for women, the frequency of sex. For men, however, there is a significant correlation between shame and sexual frequency: those who do not feel shame are seven percentage points more likely to report sex at least several times a week (35% versus 28%).

With the exception of the small segment of the population which these men constitute, the energies of sexual demands break through the barriers of shame. Embarrassed, shy, uneasy about their naked bodies, husbands and wives nonetheless manage to make love and to enjoy it.

However, the propensity to dislike sex and avoid it has strong and equal impact on the sexual satisfaction of men and women

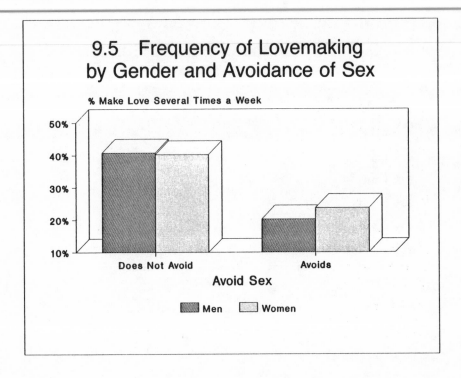

9.5   Frequency of Lovemaking by Gender and Avoidance of Sex

% Make Love Several Times a Week

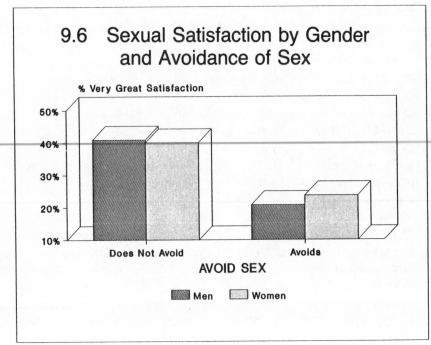

9.6   Sexual Satisfaction by Gender and Avoidance of Sex

% Very Great Satisfaction

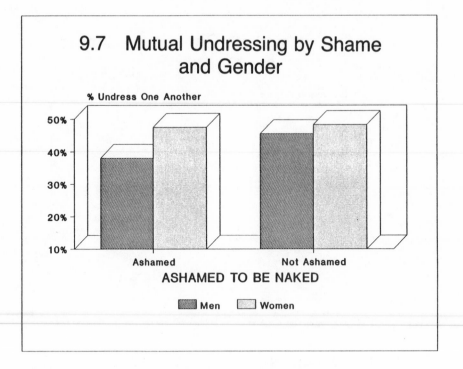

9.7   Mutual Undressing by Shame and Gender

% Undress One Another

Men   Women

ASHAMED TO BE NAKED

and their feeling that there is agreement between them and their spouses on the quantity and quality and fulfillment of their sexual lives (Figures 9.5 and 9.6). About two-fifths of those who do not avoid sex report frequent sex, as opposed to one-fifth of those who do avoid it. Similarly, approximately 40% of those who say they do not avoid sex judge their sexual fulfillment to be very great, as opposed to 20% of those who do concede that sometimes they avoid sex. One might have thought that the latter group was merely being more honest about their avoidance than the former, but it appears that avoidance also correlates with dissatisfaction, though the two phenomena doubtless influence each other.

Since 40% of American women report they avoid sex and 40% of that 40% are not fully satisfied with their sexual lives, there is a minimum of one out of every seven American wives who both avoids sex and is unhappy with her sexual life.

It is open to question whether the proportion ought to be and needs to be that high.

Women certainly cope with their feelings of shame better than the men who admit the same feelings. There is no difference between women who are ashamed of their nakedness and those

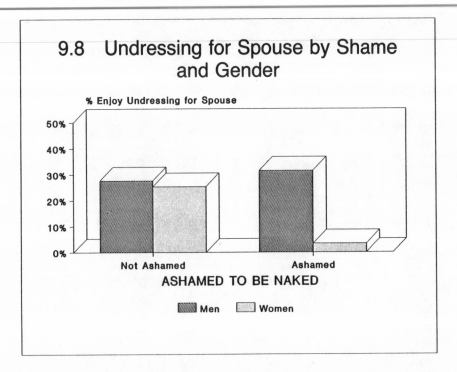

9.8   Undressing for Spouse by Shame and Gender

who are not (Figure 9.7, the two light bars) in their engaging in mutual stripping of clothes with their husband, while men who are ashamed of nakedness are only half as likely to report that they engage in such behavior.

But while women with a nakedness problem do engage in such behavior (perhaps *submit* to it), they are much less likely to enjoy taking off their own clothes to tease and arouse their spouse (Figure 9.8). Equal proportions of men, regardless of their shame, and women who are not ashamed report such exhibitions, but less than 5% of the women who feel shame report that they enjoy undressing for their spouse—as opposed to more than 30% of the women who are not bothered by shame.

The picture that emerges from these figures is of women who do not prevent their shame from interfering with the requirements of sex play but not particularly liking the violation of their modesty, a modesty which, be it noted, affects about 30% of American wives over twenty-five and 40% of those under twenty-five.

Yet the payoff in terms of sexual pleasure for women who are able to enjoy undressing for their spouse is considerable. Of those who are not ashamed of nakedness and do strip to tease their spouse (about one out of every three), 62% report sex at least several times a week as opposed to 29% of those in the opposite category. The 62% is the highest proportion on a table in which frequent sex is tabulated by gender shame and enjoying of removing one's clothes.

Moreover, that small proportion of women who are ashamed of their nakedness but nonetheless do enjoy removing their clothes for their spouse report exactly the same level of sexual activity. Pleasure at undressing for the spouse, in other words, has a considerable sexual payoff for a woman whether she is troubled by modesty or not.

C O N C L U S I O N

Shame is a much less serious problem for a married person than a dislike for sex. While both phenomena do not vary with age and both seem to be more prevalent among women than among men, shame limits the frequency of sex for men but does not impede their general satisfaction with their sexual life. However, dislike and avoidance of sex notably diminishes both the quantity and quality of sexual life for both men and women—and presumably for their partners too.

The tools available for this study do not permit further probing of the problem of fear and loathing, except to note that the absence of a major age correlation indicates that the problem is not an easy one to resolve—it goes away neither with age and experience nor with the advent of an allegedly permissive era. The results also suggest that it is a serious problem for somewhere between a quarter and a third of American married people—and that in some respects women are more likely to struggle successfully against this problem than are men.

As one might imagine, fear and loathing interferes with marital happiness, as we shall see in the next chapter.

10. Happy Marriages

Half the variance in marital happiness can be explained by rather simple models which include kindness, a feeling of importance, a sense that the spouse is exciting and trustworthy and a skilled lover. The spouse also must understand one's emotional needs, be good with children, help in household tasks, and agree on raising children. Finally, joint prayer and romantic eroticism also have a part to play in the construction of a happy marriage.

A MODEL FOR A HAPPY MARRIAGE

What, might one anticipate, would be the forces and the energies which combine in a happy marriage? A list would probably include—not necessarily in the order of their importance—mutual respect, interpersonal stimulation, cooperation in the family enterprise, agreement on the raising of children, mutual kindness, trust, responsiveness to physical and emotional needs, a satisfactory sexual relationship. One might want to add a satisfactory joint religious life and a willingness to engage in sexual experimentation.

Indeed, a model which incorporates measures for agreement on values, communication, sexual satisfaction, the character of

the spouse, and religion accounts for more than 60% of the
variance in a scale composed by combining (through factor
analysis) a marriage that is very happy, readiness to marry the
same person again, and conviction that the spouse is one's best
friend.

C H A R A C T E R   O F   T H E   S P O U S E

Since the marital relationship is between persons, and since the
character of the other person can be expected to have a notable
impact on one's response to that person, one would expect that
measure of the character of the spouse would be especially powerful in explaining the happy marriage. That expectation is certainly confirmed by the data. Five such variables account by
themselves for half of the variance in the marriage happiness scale:
the spouse makes one feel important, she/he is good with children,
she/he is exciting and kind, and she/he treats the respondent like
an equal. Since all the other variables that will be added subse-
quently to the model contribute only an additional ten percentage
points of explanatory power, it can be seen just how powerful
the influence of the character of the spouse really is. The other
variables are important too, however, because they are both the
results and the reinforcements of the respondents' judgments
about the spouse's character.

Figure 10.1 shows how important is the combination of a
spouse who combines both kindness and excitement: four out of
every five respondents in that category (far left bar) say that their
marriage is very happy, as do only one out of every five in the
opposite category (far right bar). If one must choose between
kindness and excitement (the two middle bars), not surprisingly,
given the fragility of the human personality, a kind and gentle
spouse is more important than an exciting one.

A similar phenomenon can be seen in Figure 10.2: a combination of a spouse who makes you feel important and treats you
as an equal produces an 80% response that the marriage is very
happy, while at the opposite (right-hand) side of the figure only
20% who can make neither claim for their spouse say that the
marriage is very happy. In a choice between equality and

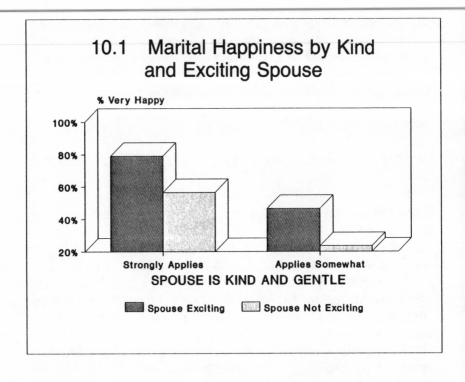

10.1   Marital Happiness by Kind and Exciting Spouse

10.2   Marital Happiness by Spouse's Behavior

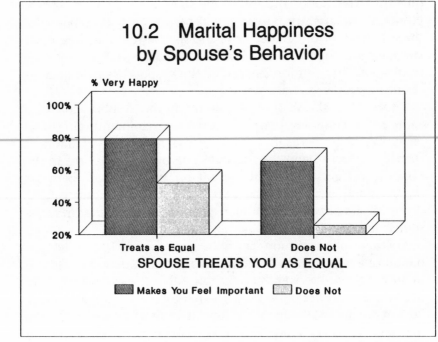

importance—the two middle bars—the feeling of importance turns out to be more powerful than a sense of equality.

That these variables (each one of which correlates strongly—.2—with marital happiness net of the others) are important is no great surprise. That they are as important as they turn out to be, especially since so little attention seems to be paid to them in what passes for marriage preparation in our society, is perhaps a surprise. To be both kind and exciting and to make another person feel both equal and important requires a high degree of skill which is, to put it mildly, not innate in the species.

VALUE AGREEMENT

Four "value" variables together explain 36% of the variance in marital happiness—general value agreement, the ability to disagree without threatening the relationship, and agreement on financial and religious values. The first two are the more important, relating to happiness, net of all the other value variables, at .3.

Thus three-quarters of those who agree on values and are able to disagree without threatening the relationship say that they are very happy, as opposed to one-quarter of those who disagree on values but cannot express that disagreement—the far left and the far right bars in figure 10.3. The two middle bars indicate that both variables are equally powerful in the absence of the other but that by themselves they produce only a 40% very happy score.

Almost exactly the same thing occurs when one compares the relative effect of financial and religious agreement (Figure 10.4). Those who have both are more than twice as likely as those who have neither to say that their marriage is very happy. In the choice between the two, each seems to be equally important—if you have to choose between religion and money.

It is impossible to sort out the influence of values and character on one another—if you admire the person, you are likely to admire the values, and vice versa. When the value measures are added to the explanatory model based on the character of the spouse, however, the predictive power is increased from 50% of the variance to 57%, so values add something to character as our

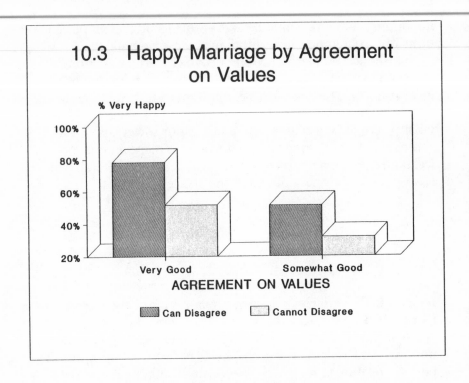

10.3 Happy Marriage by Agreement on Values

% Very Happy

AGREEMENT ON VALUES

Can Disagree   Cannot Disagree

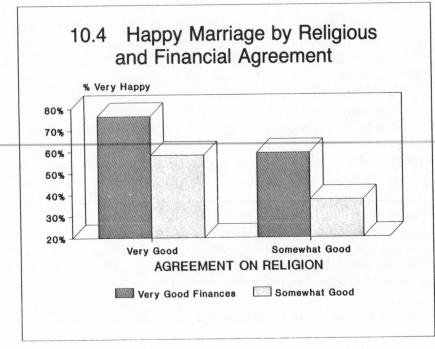

10.4 Happy Marriage by Religious and Financial Agreement

% Very Happy

AGREEMENT ON RELIGION

Very Good Finances   Somewhat Good

five measures specify character. Kindness and excitement do not necessarily guarantee value agreement.

C O M M U N I C A T I O N

The three communication variables considered in an earlier chapter add another 1% to the explanatory power of the model, which is not to say that they are unimportant. If I had begun the model with them—as I might have with the legitimate argument that communication is essential to both value agreement and character recognition—they would have explained 18% of the variance. Seventy-nine percent of those who say they try hard to make their marriage successful report a very happy marriage. Of those who say they talk often about their marriage, 75% also say that they are very happy; and 71% of those who say they talk more than twenty hours a week claim a very happy marriage. (The opposing numbers are 44%, 51%, and 59%.) When any two of these variables are combined, the proportion reporting a happy marriage goes up to nearly four out of five.

Without even considering sex, therefore, we can account for most of the variance that can be explained about marital happiness. However, sex cannot be that easily dismissed, because the sexual atmosphere of the relationship permeates all the other aspects of it.

S E X U A L I T Y

One could make an argument that if it were not for sexual differentiation there would not be marriage, and that one must begin with sex if one wants to explain marital happiness. If such an argument was accepted, the sexual measures available would account for a little more than one-fifth of the variance in marital happiness before anything else is considered. Indeed, almost 10% of the variance is accounted for by sexual satisfaction alone. Sexual avoidance and naked playfulness account by themselves for 7% of the variance, but when they are added to an equation

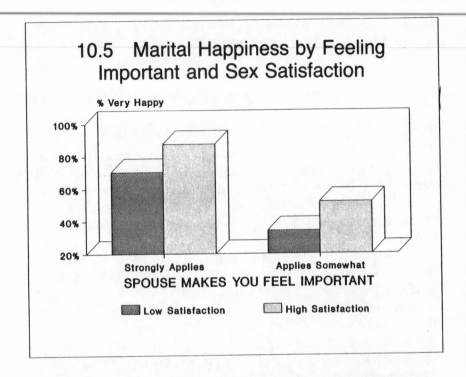

10.5   Marital Happiness by Feeling Important and Sex Satisfaction

% Very Happy

SPOUSE MAKES YOU FEEL IMPORTANT

Strongly Applies   Applies Somewhat

Low Satisfaction   High Satisfaction

which includes experimentation, sexual satisfaction, and ecstasy, avoidance continues to have a significant relationship with marital happiness, but shame does not. The *frequency* of lovemaking also has no significant relationship, when the other sexual variables are taken into account, with marital happiness.

How important, then, is sex to marital happiness? Clearly it cannot be excluded, but just as clearly it is not as important as the character of the spouse—though both judgment on the latter subject and sexual satisfaction clearly influence one another.

When character and sexual satisfaction are combined, as they are in Figure 10.5, it can be seen that the feeling of importance is more powerful a predictor of marital happiness than sexual satisfaction (the two bars on the left), but sexual satisfaction does make a contribution of its own above and beyond that made by the spouse's ability to make the respondent feel important.

Of those who report both very great sexual satisfaction and the feeling of importance, 84% are very happily married, but even those who report importance without such a high level of sexual satisfaction, 65% say they are very happy. This is as good an

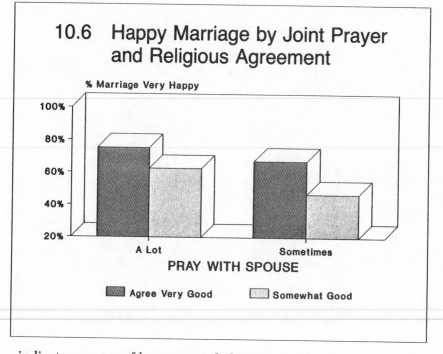

10.6 Happy Marriage by Joint Prayer and Religious Agreement

% Marriage Very Happy

PRAY WITH SPOUSE

■ Agree Very Good   ▨ Somewhat Good

indicator as any of how sex and character of the spouse interact to produce high levels of marital happiness—and of the relative importance of the two.

R E L I G I O N

When all the religious variables available—prayer, joint prayer, church attendance, endogamy, spouse's church attendance, and agreement on religious values—are put into an equation with the marital happiness scale, only joint prayer and agreement on religious values have statistically significant relationships with marital happiness. Together they account for 10% of the variance, religious agreement being twice as important as joint prayer.

Joint prayer, however, makes a contribution of its own to happiness above and beyond agreement on religious values (Figure 10.6). Those who have both to a high degree are thirty percentage points more likely than those whose religious agreement is some-

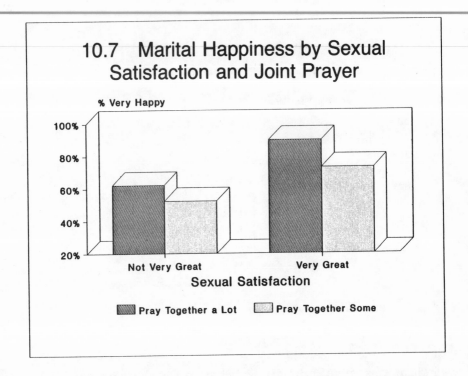

10.7 Marital Happiness by Sexual Satisfaction and Joint Prayer

% Very Happy

Sexual Satisfaction

Not Very Great   Very Great

Pray Together a Lot   Pray Together Some

what good and who pray together sometimes to say that their marriage is very happy. A high degree of one without a high degree of the other produces a 65% proportion, so that frequent joint prayer without a high level of religious agreement cancels out the effect of religious agreement without prayer.

Joint prayer for its part when combined with a high level of sexual satisfaction pushes the proportion who are very happy up to 90% (Figure 10.7), and even 60% of those who pray together often without a high level of satisfaction say that their marriage is very happy.

What is the relationship between prayer and character?

Character as measured by the spouse being exciting is obviously more important than prayer (Figure 10.8), though prayer does add its own layer of marital happiness both for those whose spouses are exciting and those whose spouses are not exciting, moving the level of satisfaction up ten percentage points for those whose spouses are exciting and twenty percentage points for those whose spouses are less than exciting. It helps to pray together even if your spouse is exciting, but especially if she/he is not exciting.

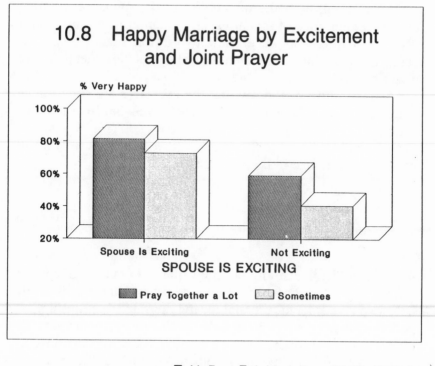

10.8   Happy Marriage by Excitement and Joint Prayer

% Very Happy

SPOUSE IS EXCITING

Pray Together a Lot   Sometimes

THE FINAL MODEL

When all the variables discussed in this chapter are put together in a general model, the most important direct influences on a happy marriage are a spouse who makes you feel important (.19), the ability to disagree (.15), an exciting spouse (.15), a kind and gentle spouse (.15), sexual satisfaction, value agreement (.12), a spouse who is good with children (.10), financial agreement (.09), and sexual experimentation (.09). Sex and character combine to be the most powerful influences on marital happiness. Moreover, it is not the frequency of sex that shapes marital happiness, but its quality and its openness to new ways of lovemaking.

I was almost tempted to write that the picture of a happy American marriage presented by this model is a comfortable one. The values have been straightened out, the sex is satisfactory, the communication functions well, the husband and wife have learned how to be good to one another. They have reason to be satisfied and perhaps not a little complacent.

While there would be an element of truth in that summary, it would overlook both the description of the spouse as exciting and the importance of sexual experimentation (more important than the frequency of sex). These two factors suggest more adventure in the relationship than the stability of the general picture might suggest.

A fairer picture would say that the marriages are comfortable with a touch of excitement and a lot of love—hard-earned love perhaps.

As for wild adventure in marriage, that will have to wait till we turn to romance in the next chapter.

CONCLUSION

A very considerable amount of the variance in marital happiness can be accounted for by those characteristics which traditionally have been considered essential for the marriage relationship, especially kindness, trust, excitement, skilled love, and being made to feel important by the spouse. The reason that so many Americans perceive themselves as happily married is that they perceive these needs being met in their marriage relationship.

Are the needs met better or worse than they were ten, twenty, a hundred years ago? In the absence of longitudinal data there is no way to answer that question. The levels of satisfaction in our benchmark observations seem reasonably high.

I remarked earlier that I felt somewhat uneasy at the large amount of variance that these models explain. Never in my three decades as a sociologist have I seen such successful models. My mentor Peter Rossi once remarked, "When it goes above .2, recompute." Yet I don't think that the powerful relationships presented in the figures in this chapter are merely definitional. If the models are so successful at explaining the variance[35] in marital happiness (and if the differences between men and women and younger and older are relatively minor), the reason in part might be that there is so much traditional and folk wisdom about the factors that correlate with or are signs of a happy marriage. This

---

[35] The explanatory power of models in subsequent chapters is not nearly so powerful. In a sense I may have "spoiled" the "general reader" with this chapter explaining more than half the variance. Such results happen once in a lifetime.

wisdom must have been in the back of our heads when George Harris and I designed the questionnaire for the *Love and Marriage* study. It turns out, not unsurprisingly perhaps, that the folk wisdom is largely correct. It is useful, however, to know that it is correct, and to be able to say which components of the traditional explanations are the most important.

Are the models developed in this chapter clichés?

Maybe, and to some extent. Nonetheless, there is nothing wrong with clichés so long as they turn out to be true. And there's nothing wrong with validating clichés as long as they are in doubt and especially when "revolutionary" developments call them into question or when worn-out and presumably discarded clichés, like the one about the importance of intimacy in prayer, turn out to be unexpectedly true.

11. Romance!

Romantic love persists in part because of a combination of erotic playfulness and religious devotion. This intricate pattern is not a function of fundamentalist literalism about religion.

CAN LOVE BE ETERNAL?

Love, says the Brazilian proverb, is eternal, but it does not last.

This wisdom, both traditional and conventional, seems at first obvious enough. Romantic love may be necessary for marriage to occur, but it surely is not necessary to sustain the marriage relationship, which is based on more durable, less ephemeral qualities. Occasional bursts of romantic love may be useful, but they are not really required.

Falling in love is a delicious experience, obsessing, delightful, fatiguing, exhilarating, frustrating, wonderful, terrifying. Perhaps it is understandable that most men and women are relieved, if somewhat disillusioned, when it fades away. When one is in love,

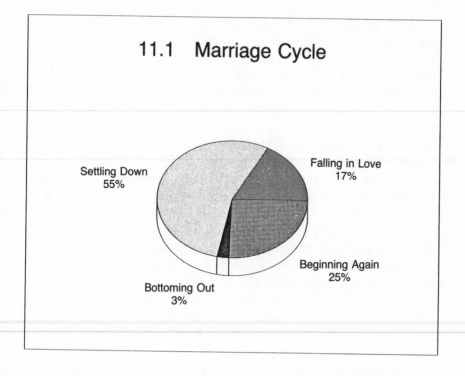

11.1 Marriage Cycle

Settling Down
55%

Falling in Love
17%

Beginning Again
25%

Bottoming Out
3%

one is absorbed, preoccupied, tense and intense, and filled with a sexual longing which permeates the rest of existence, making it both glorious and exhausting.

Wonderful as the interlude is, it is not clear that a whole life in love would be tolerable.

And it certainly seems to fade away quickly. In the *Love and Marriage* survey, 47% of those in the first year of marriage said they were in the falling-in-love phase, 35% in the second year, and 13% in the third year. Two years of romance seems to be the ration for most marriages.

Nonetheless, 17% of the respondents in the *Love and Marriage* survey said that they were in the falling-in-love phase (Figure 11.1), while 55% said they were settling down, 3% bottoming out, and 25% beginning again. Moreover, this response does not correlate either with age or duration of marriage. Those in the falling-in-love phase are remarkably satisfied with their marriages: 90% of them say that the spouse is their best friend (as opposed to 72% of the rest of the population), 96% would marry the same person again (versus 79%), 81% say that they are very happy in their marriage (as against 57%). All these are unqualified responses—"strongly agree" or a similar answer.[36] Falling in love certainly seems to bind a couple together. It surely does no harm. Not, as the Irish would say, at all, at all.

There is some cyclic movement in the falling-in-love phase, but 60% of those who are in love now said they were five years ago, 70% said they were in love two years ago, and 83% expect to be in love five years from now. It is not, then, a completely permanent condition, but it does have a continuity, and four out of five of those who are presently in the condition expect to be in it five years into the future (most of the rest think they will be "settling down").

They are certainly absorbed with one another—in fact 60% say that they are absorbed, as opposed to 30% of the rest of the population. Furthermore, 74% report sex more than once a week and 54% say that there is a very great deal of satisfaction in their sexual life (31%). Thirty-two percent make love outdoors (22%); 28% swim in the nude (19%); 18% engage in prolonged sexual play a lot (11%); 28% engage in mutual undressing (9%); 40% enjoy stripping for their spouse (20%); 57% take showers or baths together (38%).

Feeling that you're in love with your spouse correlates with (and probably is both a cause of and an effect of) a very different kind of sexual and interpersonal life than that reported by other Americans. Those who are falling in love seem truly to be by love possessed.

The eyes of romantic love see the spouse in a very different light than do the eyes of those not in that phase of the cycle: 88% say the spouse is exciting (versus 53%); 91% (versus 74%) say the spouse is kind; 74% say the spouse is playful (versus 44%); 78% report that the spouse is romantic (versus 47%); 31% say the spouse is mysterious and intriguing (as opposed to 16%); 47% report that the spouse is godlike (versus 24%).

They surely sound like people in love.

An issue for novelists, poets, and philosophers surely, but also

---

[36]The question about the four phases of the marriage cycle was based on work by Anzia and Durkin (1980), which assumed that the phases were regular events through which most marriages passed. It may be, however, that in addition to some married couples passing from phase to phase, others remain in one phase for most of their marriage. There is no correlation between falling in love and either age or duration of marriage, suggesting that for some respondents it may be a constant state.

for sociologists and psychologists, is whether so defining a spouse actually enhances the spouse's ability on these qualities.

Don't bet against it.

M O D E L S   F O R   R O M A N C E

"Romance"—the "falling-in-love" phase—seems to result from a combination of religious and erotic behaviors which do not substitute for one another. The elaborate model used to explain marital happiness fails rather notably when applied to falling in love.[37]

The best model explains 16% of the variance and is composed of spouses talking together, spouses praying together, frequent sex, a high level of sexual satisfaction, mutual absorption, the spouse being like a god, the spouse making you feel important, and the spouse being mysterious. The strongest predictors in the model are the feeling of importance (.17), sexual satisfaction (.16), and the spouse like a god (.14).

Not only does a sense that the spouse is mysterious affect the romance experience, but the romance experience is sufficiently mysterious to be opaque to a comprehensive explanation—although an explanation of 16% of the variance is no small achievement in much social research.

S E X   A N D   G O D

Frequent sex is a critically important part of falling in love, both, one supposes, as a cause and as an effect. More than a quarter of those who say that the spouse makes them feel important and who have frequent sex (Figure 11.2) say they are falling in love, and so do 15% of those who do not report a spouse who makes them feel important but who still engage in frequent sex, the same

---

[37]This is true both when "love" is dichotomized against the rest of the population and when the marriage cycle is considered a continuum with bottoming out low and falling in love high.

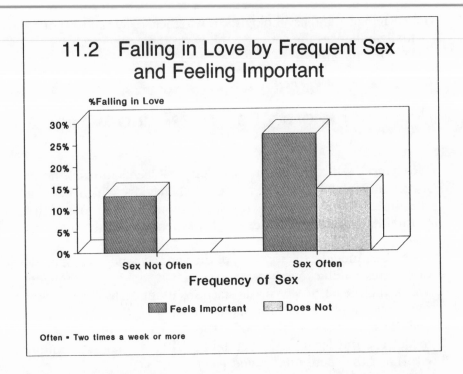

11.2   Falling in Love by Frequent Sex and Feeling Important

%Falling in Love

Frequency of Sex

Feels Important   Does Not

Often = Two times a week or more

proportion reported by those with a sensitive spouse and less frequent sex. None of those respondents who lack both frequent sex and a sensitive spouse say they are falling in love.

The two religious variables, joint prayer and feeling the spouse is like a god, have a powerful impact on (or result from) romance. Half of those who pray together with their spouse often and who think that the spouse is godlike say that they are falling in love (Figure 11.3), as do a third of those who feel the lover is godlike who do not pray together with the lover. A lover who is godlike is more important than prayer together, but when prayer is added to such a love, then the chances of being in the romantic stage of the married cycle are even—one out of two. Religious imagery, symbolism, and behavior are intimately connected to romance: the presence of God seems to make it a *ménage à trois*.

And if She/He is present, She/He is seeing a lot of lovemaking: half of those who think the spouse is godlike and who make love frequently—see Figure 11.4—say that they are falling in love, as do only a fifth of those who make love frequently and do not see the spouse as godlike (the two light bars). Thirty percent of those who see the spouse as a god and do not make love so frequently

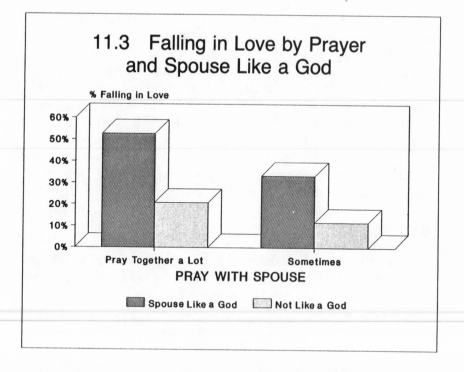

11.3   Falling in Love by Prayer and Spouse Like a God

% Falling in Love

PRAY WITH SPOUSE

Spouse Like a God   Not Like a God

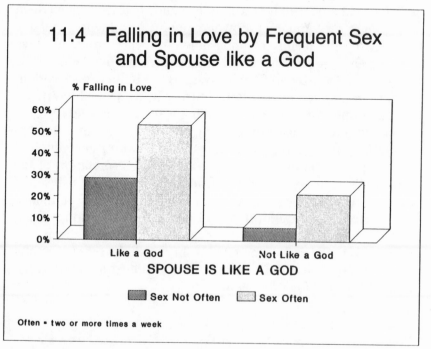

11.4   Falling in Love by Frequent Sex and Spouse like a God

% Falling in Love

SPOUSE IS LIKE A GOD

Sex Not Often   Sex Often

Often = two or more times a week

also report that they are in the romance phase. The greatest payoff in romance, in other words, comes from (or relates to) a mix of religion or religious images and frequent sex.

The interaction between the religious and the erotic is intricate: both add independent explanatory power. Thus, for example, when one cross-tabulates romance by joint showers and joint prayer, one finds that 9% of those who do neither, 20% of those who do one or the other, and 30% of those who do both are in the romantic phase. When the effect of religious retreats and skilled lover are combined, the proportions are 6%, 24%, and 35%. One-third of those who attend retreats at least sometimes and who say the spouse is a skilled lover are in the romantic stage, almost six times as many as those who do neither. In a combination of time alone in a hotel and being made to feel important by the other, the rates are 5%, 15%, and 25%—those who engage in romantic interludes in a hotel and feel important are five times as likely to say they are falling in love as those who do neither.

Using a technique called log-linear model fitting (you don't want an explanation of this if you don't already know what it is), it is possible to test the notion that the interaction between religion and eroticism is crucial to romantic love. A model which says that retreats and joint showers combine to influence romantic love, while the feeling of importance influences romantic love separately from these two working together, fits the data.[38] Thus there are at least two different "systems" of influence at work in shaping romantic love (and presumably being shaped by it).

The connection, indeed the intimate (you should excuse the expression) relationship of sex, religion, and love is not a function of the fact that the rigidly religious insist both on devotion and an image of a happy marriage. When the interpretation of the Bible question (see *Love and Marriage II*, question 31) is inserted into the regression equation which is represented by the model, it does not relate at a level of statistical significance to romantic love and adds only slightly to the explanatory power of the model; moreover, it diminishes the relationship of all the other variables in the model by only .01 at the most. ("Skilled lover" declines from .12 to .11, for example.)

---

[38] For the technicians it cannot be rejected. $\chi^2 = .489$ with 4 degrees of freedom $P = .975$.

Which comes first? Are these spouses in love because they have been able to mix religion and eroticism in their lives, or does the mix come because they are in love?

Obviously the relationships cannot be sorted out with any confidence in the absence of longitudinal or retrospective data. It is at least arguable that religion provides the courage for romantic experimentation.

R O M A N C E   A N D   A G E

Thus far the behavior I have described in this chapter may seem to the reader characteristic of sixteen-year-olds in love for the first time, young adults on the rebound from disturbing relationships, crushes between men and women who ought to know better. Surely an experienced person ought to be able to grow out of such passing fantasies and settle down to the mature responsibilities of life.

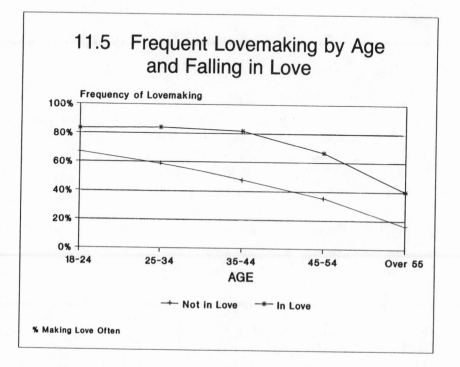

11.5 Frequent Lovemaking by Age and Falling in Love

However, as I noted earlier, romantic love does not correlate with either age or duration of marriage. Those who are in love do not "grow up." They continue to be romantics, even perhaps romantic fools.

As the remaining figures in this chapter demonstrate, age may diminish somewhat the lovemaking rates among the romantics, but the romantics continue to be sexually playful and their advantages over those in other phases of the marriage cycle is enhanced, not diminished, by age. Romantic fools they may be, but they still seem to be enjoying life.

First of all, the frequency of lovemaking, as seen in Figure 11.5, is greater for those in love even at the beginning of marriage and remains unchanged even into the late forties, while it diminishes sharply for the rest of the population. Even when it begins to decline for those in love, they still maintain a lead over those who are not in love which is larger (and much larger proportionately) than it was in the early years of marriage. Of those in love, 40% report frequent lovemaking, even when they are older than fifty-five!

Sexual experimentation also declines with age but much more

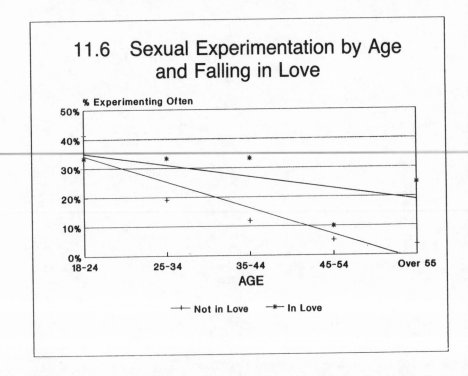

11.6   Sexual Experimentation by Age and Falling in Love

% Experimenting Often

Not in Love   In Love

AGE

sharply for those who are not "in love" (Figure 11.6): 20% of the romantics are still experimenting after fifty-five, while experimentation has ceased completely at that age for those who are not in romantic love.

Intimate play actually increases with age for those who are in love (Figure 11.7). They start out, in the early years of marriage, less likely than those not in love to engage in prolonged intimate play. But the lines cross in the early thirties: play diminishes for those who are not in love and increases for those who are, so that after fifty-five, those who are in love are four times as likely to report frequent and prolonged intimate play (20% versus 5%).

Nor does mutual undressing or the view that the spouse is attractive diminish with age for those who are in love (Figures 11.8 and 11.9). In fact, while the proportion who think the spouse is attractive diminishes with age for those who are not in love, it increases with age for those who are—so that nine out of ten of those who are in love over fifty-five insist that their spouse is attractive.

All the more reason, it would seem, to undress him or her. The rate of this behavior remains constant at 40% through the whole

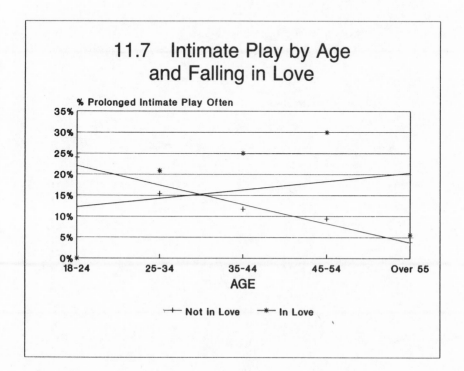

11.7   Intimate Play by Age and Falling in Love

% Prolonged Intimate Play Often

AGE

—+— Not in Love   —*— In Love

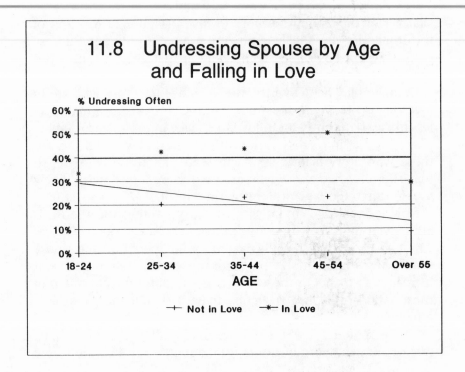

11.8   Undressing Spouse by Age and Falling in Love

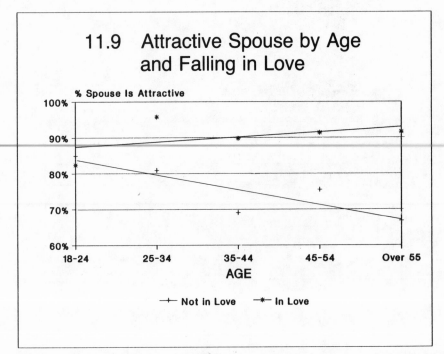

11.9   Attractive Spouse by Age and Falling in Love

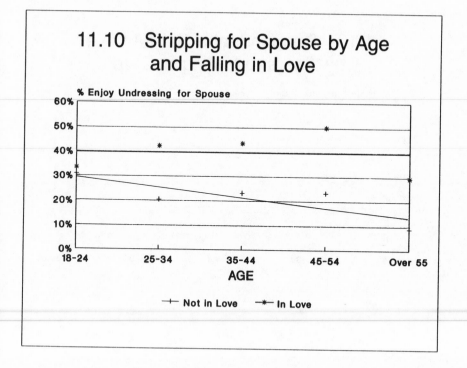

11.10   Stripping for Spouse by Age and Falling in Love

% Enjoy Undressing for Spouse

AGE

—+— Not in Love   —*— In Love

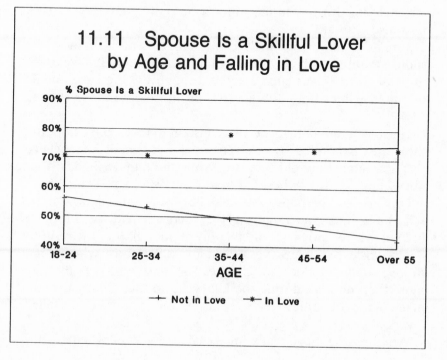

11.11   Spouse Is a Skillful Lover by Age and Falling in Love

% Spouse Is a Skillful Lover

AGE

—+— Not in Love   —*— In Love

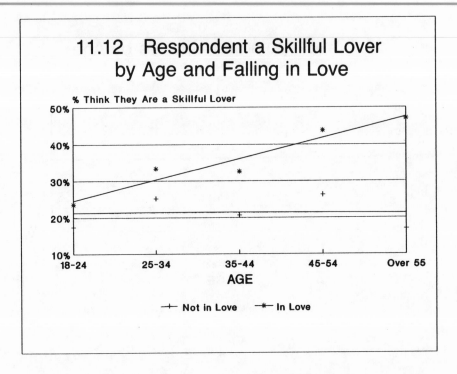

11.12   Respondent a Skillful Lover by Age and Falling in Love

% Think They Are a Skillful Lover

Not in Love   In Love

AGE

---

life cycle for those who are in love, but falls from 30% to 10% for those who are not.

Similarly, removing one's clothes to tease and delight the spouse is not a pastime which declines among those in love: two-fifths of them report such activity through the life cycle, while the rate declines from 30% to 10% for those not in love (Figure 11.10).

Those who are in love are also constant in their conviction that the spouse is a skilled lover: seven out of every ten of them believe this no matter how old they are, while the rate declines to four out of ten for those who are not in love (Figure 11.11).

Finally—and perhaps most incredibly of all—the image of the self as a skillful lover (Figure 11.12) increases with age for those in love. At the early ages of life, only about a fifth of the respondents considered themselves skilled lovers. For those who are not in love, that rate does not change. For those who are, the rate more than doubles during the life cycle, so that almost five out of ten of the romantic lovers over fifty-five say that they are skilled lovers.

Whether they have really improved as lovers or whether they

only think they have because of the response of their spouse is a question that cannot be answered with the present data, and perhaps need not be answered. It may be enough that you think you are a good lover to make you one.

The thick black lines in Figures 11.5 to 11.12 tell an astonishing story of the continuation and enhancement of romance through the life cycle for those who have somehow found the magic to sustain their love affairs.

Whenever I report the data in this chapter to an academic seminar, the group, no matter how solemn and reputable it may be, turns giggly. Some scholars take me aside after and assure me that while they have an excellent relationship with their spouse, they don't really think it would be proper or accurate to say that they were falling in love.

To which protestation I routinely reply that I'm merely analyzing response patterns and have no intention of offering either recommendations or moral prescriptions. It's not an answer that seems to be satisfactory.

Do the figures present a picture of how man and woman ought to relate to one another throughout the course of their marriage? Is it for this kind of intimacy that the species was designed by whatever or Whoever was responsible for the design?

It surely does not behoove a celibate to answer that question, but I'll answer it anyhow: all the data show is that, for some people at any rate, such a life is possible. Data do not impose obligations. However, data may open up possibilities. Further than this, said celibate sayeth not.

QUESTIONS ABOUT ROMANCE

Romantic love does not correlate with either age or education, so it is something that money apparently cannot buy, and if it increases, the reason will not be the upgrading of the educational attainment of Americans.

Yet another issue is whether romantic love is an option which can be exercised, a choice which can be made, a goal which can be pursued. While prayer and showers, hotels and retreats will not automatically cause an enhancement in romantic love, they will certainly not hurt it. Are there more complicated strategies which can be pursued in the quest of romance?

The poet in me is displeased with the question. Love happens. The storyteller in me is more tolerant: love can be developed and renewed by generosity and courage. The sociologist is fascinated by the research possibilities. And the priest who believes that God is not only love but young love is delighted.

The impact of romantic love on one's impression of the spouse is virtually the same for men and women, save for the relationship between romance and seeing the spouse as divine. Husbands are more likely to make that judgment than wives. However, because of the stronger correlations on this variable for women, there is no difference between men and women who are in love with their spouse in the proportion who say the spouse is godlike—a little less than half for both genders.

Oh, yes, they're in love all right!

A romance situation, as perceived by the wife, also increases the proportion who say the husband helps with household tasks, pushing the rate up above half—57%, as opposed to 46% for those who do not perceive themselves in the romantic-love phase.

Every little bit, presumably, helps.

CONCLUSION

Romantic love persists among some married men and women because of (or in relationship to) a complicated interaction of chemistry, history, psychology, sensitivity, and religion. The romantic marriage is not a typical marriage. In fact it probably represents a form of marital intimacy that most married people do not think possible or reject if they think it remotely possible. Life is too busy, too serious, too filled with responsibilities to pursue hearts and flowers and lace except on Saint Valentine's Day.[39]

Yet romance as a sustained pattern of marital intimacy not only happens, it happens with about a sixth of the married population.

---

[39] I'm not sure that the patron saint of romantic love is pleased at romantic love which surfaces one day a year and then creeps back into the dark basement of the preconscious.

Moreover it produces an extraordinary life of sexual activity and playfulness.

It is difficult if not impossible to sort out the natural history of such a sustained love affair without detailed information following such couples through a long period of their relationship. How the various dynamics at work interact as mutual cause and effect is something about which we can at present only speculate. We do not know how such love affairs are launched, how they are sustained, or how they survive. We can only give a few hints about such relationships as they are observed in a snapshot photo of a survey.

Romantic lovers are deliriously content with their spouses, whose admirable characteristics they praise in overwhelming numbers. Do these admirable characteristics produce the romantic love and the signs of it we are able to observe in their religious and sexual behaviors? Are they so grateful to God for the paragon they have found that they feel constrained to be devout? Are they so hopelessly in love with the wonder spouse that they spontaneously engage in the kind of erotic behavior which either pleases the spouse or does not displease him/her? Or do they consciously pursue both the religious and sexual aspects of their romance?

If I were forced to answer, I'd guess that the wonder in the spouse is at least in part the result of the spouse having been perceived and defined all through the relationship as being wonderful.

To put it another way, you can't beat for a turn-on the experience of being judged wonderful!

Nonetheless, developing a unified field theory in physics which combines explanations of electromagnetism and gravity will be a cinch compared to developing a theory which will provide a comprehensive explanation of romantic love.

Is all the data analysis worth the effort to come to such an agnostic conclusion? Don't we already know, or couldn't we have guessed, most of the hints about romantic love which I have discussed in this chapter?

Gimme a break!

The romantic lovers doubtless know about the importance of religion in their ongoing love affair, but did you, gentle reader? Were you not at first inclined to be skeptical and to write it off as a kind of Marabel Morgan Protestant Fundamentalism? If you are part of the media or academic elites, particularly living in or having passed through New York, Boston, Washington, the Bay Area, or Los Angeles, are you not still skeptical? Are you not convinced in your heart of hearts that religion cannot be all that important to ecstatic love, save for the uneducated and unsophisticated, especially if they live between the Hudson River (or the Appalachians) and the Berkeley Hills?

As a sociologist suggested to me, these romantics with their enthusiasm for their marriage must be a bit tiresome. Are they?

What feature article or TV special or academic study has considered the relationship between prayer and the persistence of romantic love?[40]

The entire study was worth doing if only to nail down the relationship between romantic love and religious devotion.

---

[40] There was one such (Greeley 1980). You never heard of it, and neither did the leadership of the Church, about whose people it was written.

12. Marriages in Trouble

Those respondents who describe their marriage as "bottoming out" are somewhat more likely to be older. They have a very low opinion of their spouse, whom they are more likely to describe as dull and ill-mannered, unkind and untrustworthy. Their spouse seems to be indifferent and insensitive. It may be possible, however, to revitalize such marriages and move them into the next phase of the cycle—beginning again. For those in that phase there is a closer relationship between erotic playfulness and marital happiness than for those at other phases of the cycle. It may be that, as Anzia and Durkin have argued, sexual love can carry a couple through the phase of beginning again to the phase of falling in love.

THE BOTTOM OF THE HEAP

Some 4% of the sample report that their marriage is at the opposite end of the cycle from that described in the previous chapter: it has "bottomed out." Their marriages are clearly in trouble, though it does not follow that they are either more likely to be unfaithful (they're not, by the way) or that they are headed for the divorce court (though many of them don't rule out that possibility). Only longitudinal research could tell us what proportion of American marriages that are in this phase are able to escape it.

Only a quarter who are at the bottom of the cycle say they were in the same place five years ago, though two-fifths say they were at the bottom two years ago. So for many of those in a troubled marriage, the problems are relatively recent. Moreover, they also seem to see the light at the end of the tunnel, because four out of five predict that they will be out of this phase five years into the future, three out of ten saying that they will be beginning again.

Nonetheless, they do not rule out the possibility of divorce. A quarter of them consider it very likely, and three out of five think that divorce is at least somewhat likely. Only two out of five of those at the bottom of the cycle exclude the possibility of divorce completely.

These are distinctly unhappy marriages. Only a fifth of the respondents in this phase say that they are very happy, and only two-fifths report that their spouse is their best friend and that they would marry the same person again if they had it to do over.

Just as the person in love sees the spouse as a paragon of virtue, so the person at the bottom of the marriage cycle sees the spouse as dull and unattractive. Only 40% think of the spouse as kind and gentle, 25% as exciting, 16% as mysterious and intriguing; 24% regard their mate as a skilled lover, less than half as many as the other respondents; 12% regard the spouse as playful, and only 28% say the spouse helps with chores; 39% think the spouse cannot be trusted (as opposed to 6%); 53% think the spouse is dull (as opposed to 14%); 45% regard the spouse as bad mannered (as opposed to 10%); 19% think the spouse has bad breath or body odor (versus 9%).[41]

A mere 12% of the women who are in the bottom of the cycle say their spouse helps with household tasks! And only 35% of the men!

Grounds for fury!

Whether this view of the spouse is the result or the cause of the condition of the marriage is our by now familiar unanswerable question. Are the bad manners more obvious because one does not like the spouse? If one was in love, would one simply not see the bad manners and not report them? Or do the bad manners actually lead to the deterioration of the marriage and then perhaps

---

[41]The proportions in this sentence represent a combination of the unqualified and the qualified responses.

become even more obvious? Is the spouse so detested that his/her efforts around the house are not seen? Or is she/he in fact indifferent to household responsibilities?

There are three possibilities, it would seem, for such marriages: divorce, renewal, or James Thurber's "lives of noisy desperation," a continuation of the present insensitive routine.

In either case, most such marriages are in deep, deep disarray.

Those over fifty are more likely to report that they are at the bottom of the marriage cycle (11% versus 3%), though there is no relationship with gender or income or college education.

The natural history of a marriage which bottoms out and stays there is as complicated a story as the natural history of a marriage which remains romantic. The former is a tragedy, the latter a comedy. A comprehensive account of either story is beyond the capabilities of a "snapshot" study and probably beyond the capabilities of even the most elaborate social science at the present. So I will be content with a description of the "signs"—the correlates—of a marriage in this kind of trouble.

MODELS OF TRAGEDY

Because of the small proportion of respondents in this phase of the cycle, regression analysis cannot be used. Instead I turn to what the pros call a "non-parametric" statistic called "gamma" to describe the correlates of bottoming out.[42]

The most important gamma relationships for bottoming out are as follows: spouse not trustworthy, .77; does not make me feel important, .73; unable to disagree without threatening the relationship, .72; spouse is not kind and gentle, .66; disagreement

---

[42] The statistic was developed by my friends Leo Goodman and William Kruskal. Its explanation has always delighted me. Assume that you are told that in the course of a day you will meet a hundred people, exactly half of whom are in the bottom phase. By merely flipping a coin to make your prediction of who was who, you would be right about half the time. The gamma is the measure of the increase in accuracy of your prediction over chance if you know some characteristic of the person. So if you know (to choose deliberately a ludicrous example) that the person you encounter either has or has not purchased and used erotic lingerie, your probability of making an accurate prediction is improved over chance by a gamma of .73 if you always predict that the non-purchaser is at the bottom of the marriage cycle. You multiply .5 by .73 and add the result to .5 and discover that your prediction will be accurate more than 80% of the time.

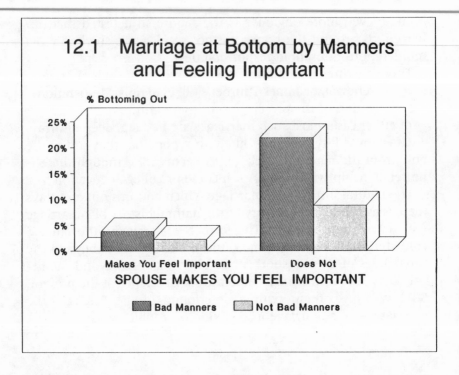

12.1   Marriage at Bottom by Manners and Feeling Important

% Bottoming Out

SPOUSE MAKES YOU FEEL IMPORTANT

Makes You Feel Important   Does Not

Bad Manners   Not Bad Manners

on basic values, .66; spouse is dull, .63; spouse is bad mannered, .60; sexual satisfaction, .58; physical violence, .58; spouse drinks too much, .57; frequency of sex, .43; and sexual experimentation, .33.

The picture is a portrait of the horrors which can occur in a marriage. The horrors become worse when they are combined, as they often are. Thus in Figure 12.1, when bad manners and insensitivity are combined, one out of five who fall in that combined category say that their marriage has bottomed out—the spouse appearing very much like a rude brute. The combination of insensitivity and infrequent sex also notably increases the probability of the respondent being at the bottom of the cycle (Figure 12.2). On the other hand (far left bar in Figure 12.2) when the spouse makes one feel important, the absence of frequent sex increases only slightly the possibility of being in the bottom phase.

The same effect occurs (Figure 12.3) when the spouse is both insensitive and dull, not bad mannered but perhaps, as young people say, *boring!* One out of five respondents in that category say that they are at the bottom of the heap.

When a dull spouse is combined with infrequent lovemaking

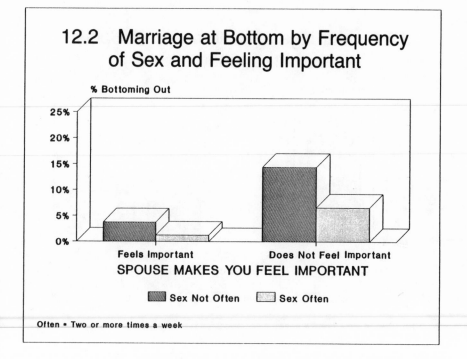

12.2 Marriage at Bottom by Frequency of Sex and Feeling Important

% Bottoming Out

SPOUSE MAKES YOU FEEL IMPORTANT

Sex Not Often   Sex Often

Often • Two or more times a week

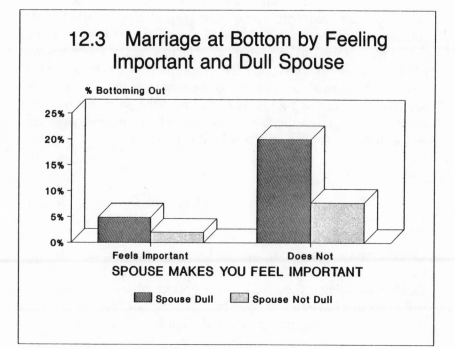

12.3 Marriage at Bottom by Feeling Important and Dull Spouse

% Bottoming Out

SPOUSE MAKES YOU FEEL IMPORTANT

Spouse Dull   Spouse Not Dull

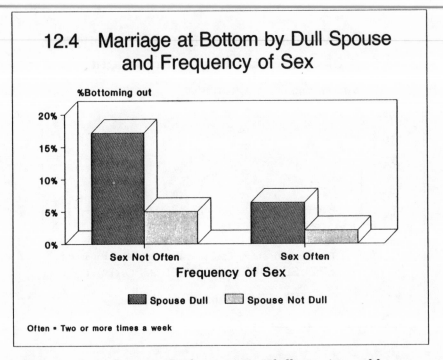

12.4   Marriage at Bottom by Dull Spouse and Frequency of Sex

%Bottoming out

Frequency of Sex

▨ Spouse Dull   ▢ Spouse Not Dull

Often • Two or more times a week

(Figure 12.4), the rate climbs to 15%—dullness, it would seem, must be combined with some other aggravation to produce a substantial propensity to feel that your marriage is in trouble.

The most powerful combination of factors occurs when insensitivity (failure to make one feel important) is combined with drinking (Figure 12.5): half of the respondents in that category say that they are at rock bottom. Almost the same proportion admit that their marriage is in trouble when physical violence and a drinking spouse are combined (Figure 12.6).

B E G I N N I N G   **A** G A I N

Can the vitality of a marriage be recaptured? No doubt the revitalization task is difficult. However, more than four-fifths of those who say that they were at the bottom phase both two and five years ago have now moved out of that phase, more than half to the "beginning again" phase and most of the rest to the "set-

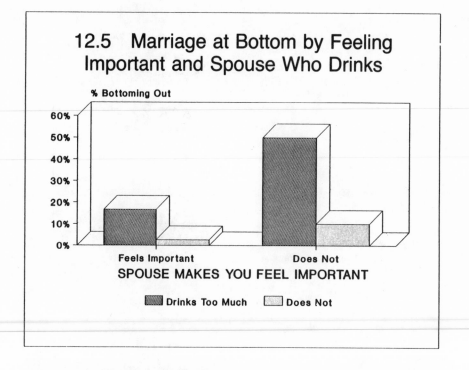

12.5 Marriage at Bottom by Feeling Important and Spouse Who Drinks

% Bottoming Out

SPOUSE MAKES YOU FEEL IMPORTANT

Feels Important   Does Not

▧ Drinks Too Much   ▭ Does Not

tling down" phase. Thus, if a marriage survives at all, it tends not to remain at the bottom.

Sexual activity is especially affected by the phase of the marriage cycle (Figure 12.7). While marital happiness deviates significantly from the average only for those who are bottoming out, there is a change in frequency of sex for each phase of the marriage cycle. The decline in sex begins in the second phase (settling down) and the decline of marital happiness becomes sharp only at the third phase (bottoming out) and then rebounds. Thus the marriage cycle is a more sensitive indicator of sexual activity than the happiness reported in the marriage.

Those in the beginning-again phase are, compared to those in the bottom phase, more likely to say that the spouse is sensitive, is not bad mannered, and is kind and gentle, and also more likely to report sexual experimentation and indulgence in erotic play and amusements.

Thus, there might well be an improvement in manners in creating the feeling of importance, in kindness, and in erotic activities. The last phenomenon is in keeping with the suggestion of

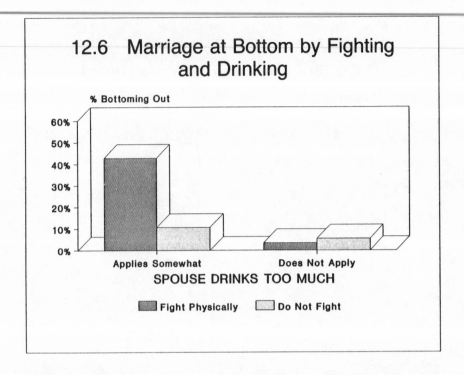

12.6   Marriage at Bottom by Fighting and Drinking

% Bottoming Out

SPOUSE DRINKS TOO MUCH

Applies Somewhat   Does Not Apply

Fight Physically   Do Not Fight

Anzia and Durkin, that erotic love is most important at the "renewal" phase—not the most frequent, perhaps, but the most important in getting up off the bottom.

The data from the *Love and Marriage* study provide some confirmation of this hunch. As Figure 12.8 indicates, the correlations between sexual activity and the marital happiness scale are higher in the bottoming-out and beginning-again phases than they are in the other two stages. While the two dark lines representing the last two phases of the marriage cycle are the lowest on the figure because married happiness is the lowest in those two phases, both lines move up more sharply as the amount of sex increases, while no such change occurs in the top two phases. The quantity of sex is more important when you are trying to piece your marriage back together again, and the quantity is most important of all in sustaining marriage when it is at its nadir.

The number of cases is very small, but 20% of those who do not have frequent intercourse in the bottom of the cycle expect to be in the beginning-again phase five years from now, as opposed to 60% who do report frequent intercourse (at least two

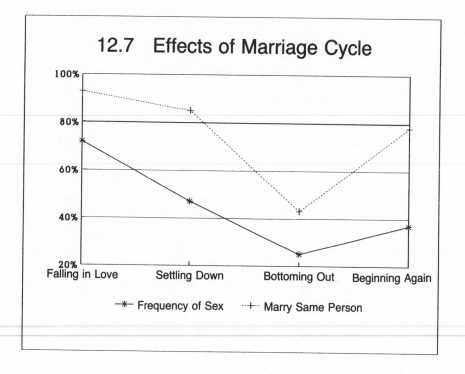

12.7   Effects of Marriage Cycle

times a week). Sex gives them some hope, it would seem, for their future.

Similarly, among those in the beginning-again phase, 36% of those who have frequent sex expect to be in the falling-in-love phase in five years, as opposed to 21% of those who do not have frequent intercourse. Lovemaking may spur the hope or it may reflect it or, more likely, they may influence each other. But sexual activity is certainly an indicator of how much hope there is for a marriage in serious trouble.

CONCLUSION

That less than one out of every twenty married Americans puts the marital relationship in this lowest stage of the marriage cycle is evidence that most married Americans do not see their marriages as troubled. We remain faced with the inevitable question

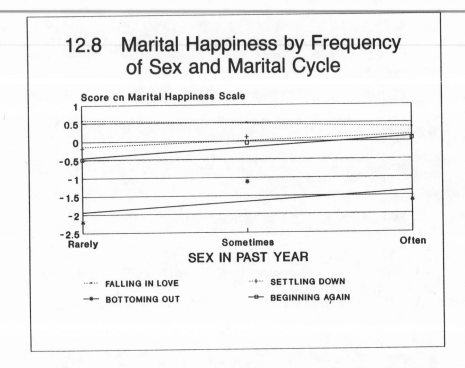

12.8   Marital Happiness by Frequency of Sex and Marital Cycle

Score on Marital Happiness Scale

SEX IN PAST YEAR

Rarely — Sometimes — Often

···▲··· FALLING IN LOVE   ···+··· SETTLING DOWN
─*─ BOTTOMING OUT   ─□─ BEGINNING AGAIN

of whether some of our more optimistic respondents are kidding themselves and perhaps us. Are they engaging in monumental deception and/or self-deception? Should more of them put themselves in the "bottom" phase of marriage?

If they are deceiving themselves, God alone knows it—unless a journalist or social scientist or a cleric or some other expert has the gift of *scrutatio cordium,* the ability to read minds and hearts. The best we can say in response to such a question is that most Americans think that their marriages are not in grave trouble.

If they are deceiving us, then they have shown remarkable ingenuity in making their deception systematic and effective. They would have had to understand the different relationships between erotic playfulness and marital happiness at the different phases of the cycle, a difference predicted by the Anzia and Durkin theory, and then adjust their responses to fit that theory, which is by no means self-evident and, alas, is not well-known.

If such brilliantly executed deception is indeed taking place in our sample, then it seems unlikely that any other method of examining American marriage would break through the deception. Those who are convinced that the picture of American marriage is notably different than that reported by the *Love and Marriage* sample will have to content themselves with arguing either from what they know to be true without any data, or what they know to be true from their own experience, or what they know to be true from talking to their families and their friends (who are, by definition, telling the truth).

Such a form of argumentation, heaven knows, is not unknown in American society (or the human condition); it is not indeed unknown even among those who claim, often with reason, to be scholars. It is not, however, scholarship.

13. Working Mothers and Marital Satisfaction

The proportion of working mothers has increased dramatically in America in the last quarter century. Dire predictions were made about what this increase would do to marriage. It certainly seems to have given women economic independence, which makes divorce easier. But has it also led to a deterioration in the quality of the relationships in many marriages as many recent stories have suggested?

Women are surely under more pressure in working-mother families, but the results for family relationships do not seem as dire as predicted.

TWO-INCOME FAMILIES

Popular fiction and Sunday feature articles warn of the dangers to marital happiness of the two-income family. The argument rages back and forth as to whether women "can have it all"— careers (though most working mothers have *jobs* rather than careers) and family. Marriage is under severe strain, some say, because women are determined to have it all, often without much help from their men. Others assert that men are beginning to enjoy their role as helpmates at home.

On the other hand, the data analyzed already in this report suggest that working mothers and their husbands are as happy with their marriages and their families as anyone else in the country and that, while younger working mothers suffer cross pressures, they still tend to be happy with both their families and their jobs, if not also with the pressures (to which pressures I return in Chapter 20).

What impact, then, on marital happiness does the working mother have? Does the relatively benign picture of marriage presented here thus far persist also in families with two incomes and children?

Twenty-nine percent of American families have a full-time working mother (with a child present in the home). In 22% there are no children and the wife is not working full time. In 7% of the families the wife works but there are no children present, and in the remaining 43% children are present but the mother does not work.

KIDS AND JOBS

Children correlate positively with most measures of marital happiness. While the correlations are modest, it is nonetheless the case that the more children respondents have, the more likely they are to be satisfied with their family life, to say their spouse is their best friend, and to assert that they would marry the same person again. For example, 44% of those with children say that they are very satisfied with their family life, as opposed to 34% of those without children.

However, the combination of a two-income family and the presence of children in the house (a different measure than whether the respondent has ever had children, since many older respondents have children who are not living with them) produces more complicated results.

First of all, if children are present in the home, marital happiness declines, especially for women (see Figure 13.1): 64% of non-working mothers say their marriage is "very happy" as opposed

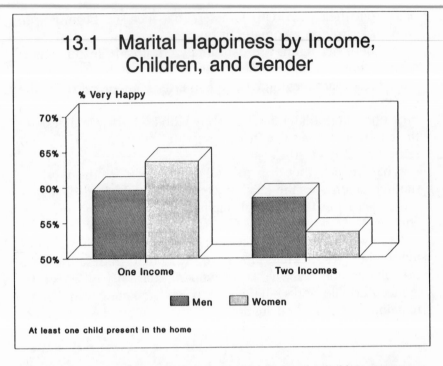

13.1   Marital Happiness by Income, Children, and Gender

% Very Happy

At least one child present in the home

to 54% of the working mothers (the two light-shaded bars). Moreover, 34% of the respondents who have a working mother in the family say that divorce is possible, as opposed to 21% of all other families—with no gender differences. The facts that working mothers with children at home are younger and that younger people are more inclined to believe that divorce is possible account for four percentage points of this difference, and five more percentage points are accounted for by the decline in marital happiness among families with working mothers. The remaining four-percentage-point difference is not statistically significant.

Thus the two-income, child-present[43] marriage is at greater risk of divorce because its level of marital happiness has diminished.

One would expect such a result from the work of Michael (1988), in which he argued (and demonstrated) that the possibility of financial independence for a woman because she had a job of her own would make divorce more likely.

However, the Figures 13.2 to 13.5 indicate that on other measures of marriage and family satisfaction, the working-mother

---

[43] How many children present does not affect the relationship.

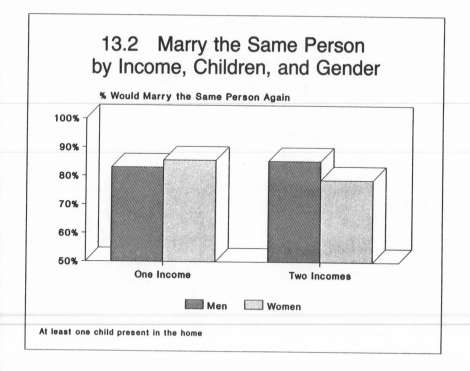

13.2   Marry the Same Person by Income, Children, and Gender

% Would Marry the Same Person Again

At least one child present in the home

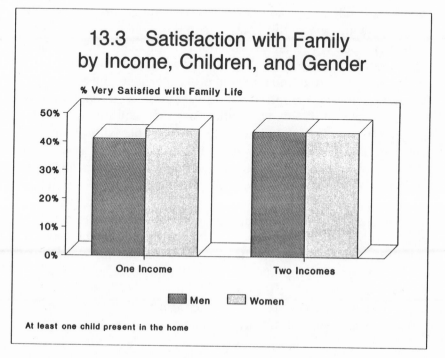

13.3   Satisfaction with Family by Income, Children, and Gender

% Very Satisfied with Family Life

At least one child present in the home

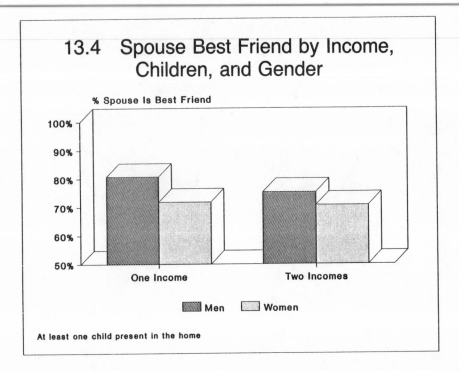

13.4 Spouse Best Friend by Income, Children, and Gender

% Spouse Is Best Friend

At least one child present in the home

marriage is not at a disadvantage. Its participants are as likely to say they would marry the same person if they had to do it again, that their spouse is their best friend, that they are very satisfied with their family life, and that they have no more trouble with their children than do members of other marriage units—though mothers, working or not, are about ten percentage points more likely to say that they have trouble with their children. (Possibly they are more likely than fathers to have trouble with them precisely because they are assumed to be responsible for them.)

The picture is therefore mixed, although not inconsistent. The proportion who say that divorce is "very likely" or "somewhat likely" increases by five percentage points in the marriages with working mothers. But the proportion saying that it is "very likely" is 2% in both family types. The change, then, for families with working mothers (and it is the same for men and for women) is an increase in the proportion who say that divorce is "somewhat likely" or "not too likely"—a shift, but not a shift which could be expected to affect notably the other four measures. You might very well say without any inconsistency that you would marry

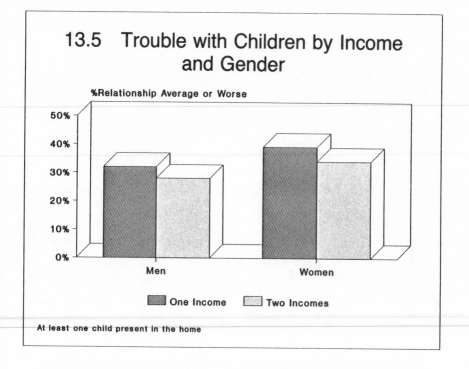

13.5 Trouble with Children by Income and Gender

%Relationship Average or Worse

One Income   Two Incomes

At least one child present in the home

the same person again, despite the strains, and still see the possibility of separation inch up because of the strains.

So the working-mother family has some problems, but among those who are still married, the problems do not seem to be catastrophic. Indeed, they are not nearly as great as the popular imagination suspects.

What about the alleged decline in sexual satisfaction and activity in working-mother marriages? In fact, respondents from working-mother families are *more* likely to report frequent sex and high levels of sexual satisfaction: 69% of members of working-mother families report intercourse at least once a week, as opposed to 59% of those in other marriages. However, the strains of being mother and worker do not account for the higher levels of lovemaking. Members of families with working mothers are younger; once age is taken into account, there is no correlation at all between sexual satisfaction and frequency of intercourse. Members of such families do not make love any more often, but not any less often either. Nor do they enjoy sex any more, but neither do they enjoy it any less.

H O U S E   H U S B A N D S ?

The ability of some women to more or less successfully "have it all" is not the result of more help from their husbands, though younger men are more likely to think that they help. Four-fifths of the men surveyed and half the women report that their spouse helps with household chores. This response does not correlate with age or with whether the wife works, save among working-wife families in which the respondent is over fifty: in these households, three-quarters of the men help with the chores (which are not likely to include the raising of children).

Since there is a question about how you think your spouse views you as helping with the chores, we can establish a tentative picture from both sides of the marriage. Three fifths of men in their twenties think that their wives see them as helpful. But only half the women in their twenties—no more than older women—see their husbands as helpful.

If there is a group where there is especially likely to be a house husband, it is men over fifty with a working wife.

While younger men are no more likely to help with chores than older men, even if the wife is working, nonetheless half of them do (according to their wives), which may be an improvement over the past. But the fact that only half the husbands of full-time working wives are described as helping with chores surely proves that, while women may have come a long way, they still have a long way to go.

The relationship between working mothers and a propensity to divorce disappears when frequency of sex is taken into account (see Figure 13.6). The inclination to divorce rises to 50% among those working-mother marriages in which intercourse occurs less than weekly (the light bar on the left) and remains at about 20% for all the other groups.

Frequent joint prayer has an impact similar to that of frequent sex (see Figure 13.7): 40% of those in working-mother marriages (far right bar) where there is less than frequent mutual prayer do not rule out the possibility of divorce. Finally, prayer together diminishes considerably the likelihood of divorce in families with working mothers. In fact, working mothers who pray often with their spouse (Figure 13.7, second bar from right) are lower in their propensity to divorce than nonworking moth-

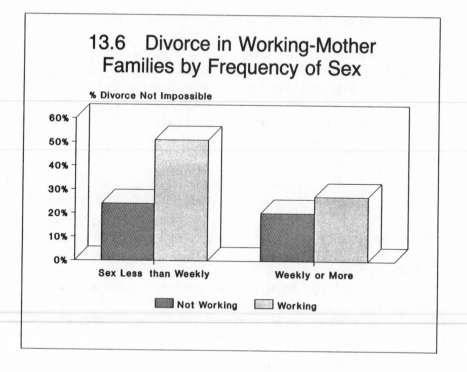

13.6   Divorce in Working-Mother Families by Frequency of Sex

% Divorce Not Impossible

Sex Less than Weekly · Weekly or More

Not Working · Working

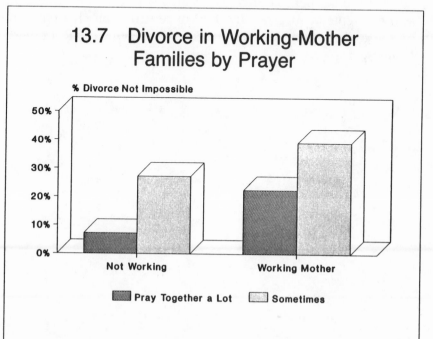

13.7   Divorce in Working-Mother Families by Prayer

% Divorce Not Impossible

Not Working · Working Mother

Pray Together a Lot · Sometimes

ers who do not pray often with their spouse (second bar from left).

When joint prayer and frequent sex are combined, only 18% of working-mother families say that divorce is not impossible, while in working-mother families where neither is present the possibility of divorce rises to 57%. Praying together and playing sexually together is especially important in working-mother marriages.

C O N C L U S I O N

There are stresses and strains in working-mother marriages, but among those who are still married, these stresses and strains increase only the proportion of those who say that divorce is somewhat likely, and diminish only a few percentage points the proportion who say their marriage is "very happy." As for other variables, the working-mother family either has no effect on marital satisfaction (as we can measure it in this survey) or the effect (as in more frequent intercourse) is an age phenomenon. As far as the parents in such families are concerned, their children are no more likely to be seen as presenting problems than in other families.

14. The Fidelity Syndrome

Fidelity is invariant with most social and demographic influences. Age, education, income, gender, and region, for example, do not influence it. Rather, an intricate model involving sexuality and morality accounts for about 13% of the difference between the faithful and the unfaithful. There is no evidence that attitudes toward fidelity have changed, or that the practice of infidelity has increased or is increasing.

FIDELITY AND MARITAL CONTENTMENT

It may seem reasonable to believe that there is a connection between marital happiness and marital fidelity—those who are happily married are more likely to be faithful, are they not? Should there not be a relationship between the portrait of marital happiness that I have presented and the high level of fidelity reported by our respondents?

At first glance this seems to be the case: 64% of the faithful[44]

---

[44] "Faithful" here means marriage-long fidelity. The same models work for fidelity over the last year.

say their marriage is very happy, as opposed to 42% of the unfaithful; 83% of the faithful and 74% of the unfaithful would marry the same spouse again; 78% of the faithful and 61% of the unfaithful say that their spouse is their best friend.

Yet if one considers those numbers, there is still a bit of a surprise. Three-quarters of the unfaithful nonetheless would marry the same person, and three-fifths say that the spouse is the best friend. Infidelity is compatible with a high degree of satisfaction with the spouse.

In the models I constructed to explain the difference between the faithful and the unfaithful, marital satisfaction does not have a direct influence on fidelity. Other attitudes and experiences intervene: a lack of erotic playfulness, a lower value on fidelity itself, a conviction that one is a highly sexed person, premarital sexual experience, marriage therapy, and especially a willingness to cheat on one's spouse if one thinks one can get away with it.

Men and women become unfaithful, it seems, for many other reasons besides an unsatisfactory marriage (hence there is no correlation between "bottoming out" and infidelity) or a delightfully happy marriage (hence there is no correlation between "falling in love" and fidelity). Moreover, it must be remembered that there is no age or gender correlation with fidelity. The unfaithful are just as likely to be over fifty as under thirty-five and to be women as well as men (whether this latter has always been true we are unable to say).

Despite these demographic similarities, the unfaithful person is a little different from almost everyone else in her/his attitudes toward marriage and sexuality.

A MODEL FOR FIDELITY

Sociology works with averages. It has nothing to say about individual cases. It does not purport to offer an explanation of why a given person might be faithful or unfaithful. It makes no judgments on the motives or the dynamics of individual behavior, and makes no attempt to describe what happened in any single instance of infidelity (or any other behavior). It does not therefore depict why someone you know might have been unfaithful.

Moreover, while explaining 13% of the variance (20% for women) for the average infidelity is a presentable achievement, it leaves much of the average behavior unexplained.

It is much easier to make sweeping, single-variable explanations (from the pulpit, for example). Such pronouncements purport to explain all the variance in, let us say, marital behavior with one or two abstract variables, like the "contraceptive mentality." Such rhetoric may be fun and it may even be appropriate for some occasions, especially if you are a bishop or a pope (though *I* don't think so), but it is not scholarship and it isn't even a precise or responsible description of reality. Those most likely to be unfaithful are those who do not believe that fidelity is important in a marriage, those who have cohabited, those who would be willing to have an affair if they were sure their spouse would not find out about it, those who consider themselves erotic persons, and those who have been in therapy with their spouse.

The faithful person is more likely to think that fidelity is important in marriage than does the unfaithful, and more likely to think it is more important in her/his own marriage than it is in other marriages. Moreover, the faithful person is more likely to want to know if the spouse had an affair. The unfaithful person is more likely to claim to be a "sexual person," and more likely to have experienced marital therapy.

One way to summarize the findings about infidelity is that the unfaithful person does not regard marriage as such too highly. Thus in Figure 14.1, the lowest fidelity rate (under 60%) is to be found among those who have cohabited before marriage and would have an affair if they could get away with it—the bar on the far left. Similarly, in Figure 14.2 the lowest fidelity rate is also the bar on the far left, a little more than 60% for those who would have an affair and do not think that fidelity is important. In both cases the addition of the cohabitation variable does not increase the fidelity rates greatly, suggesting that the moral attitude revealed by the willingness to have an affair if one could get away with it is crucial to the decision to be unfaithful. Such an underlying moral perspective disposes men and women both to cohabitation and to infidelity.

Marital therapy correlates positively with marital happiness, so it cannot be "blamed" for infidelity. Indeed, for those who are happily married, therapy does not correlate with infidelity. However, among those who are not "very happy" in marriage, 28%

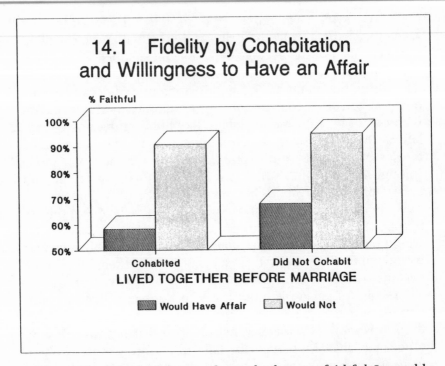

14.1   Fidelity by Cohabitation and Willingness to Have an Affair

of those who have had therapy have also been unfaithful. It would appear that this group represents those among whom unhappiness and serious emotional problems combine to correlate with unfaithfulness, either before or after the fact.

"MORALITY" AND FIDELITY

Marital fidelity is both important to men and women and a critical moral norm. The advocates of free love, such as there may be at the present time, would have us believe that fidelity is important only because oppressive leaders have made it a moral issue. However, it seems more likely that fidelity has become a moral norm precisely because the bond between man and woman is so important. Those who have displayed some lack of concern about the importance of the bond either through cohabitation before marriage or premarital sex are more likely to be unfaithful in marriage. But the question remains: Does the previous behavior

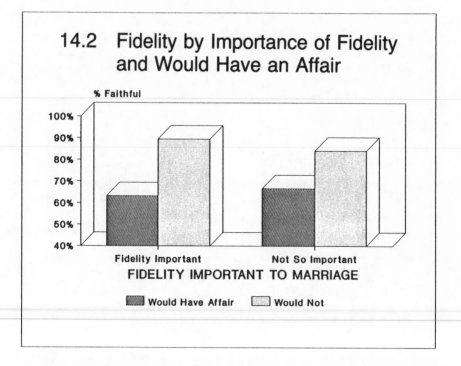

14.2   Fidelity by Importance of Fidelity and Would Have an Affair

actually cause the more recent behavior, or do both reveal an underlying lack of concern for integrity in human relationships?

Thus those who have cohabited before marriage but would not cheat on their spouse if they had the chance to do it without getting caught are as likely to be faithful as those who have not cohabited (Figure 14.1). Cohabitation makes a difference only among those who are disposed to cheat if they can get away with it (the darker bars).

Moreover, neither an emphasis on the importance of fidelity nor a happy marriage adds anything to the rejection of cheating as a predictor of fidelity (Figures 14.2 and 14.3). Only among those who would cheat if they could does a conviction about the importance of fidelity or a happy marriage increase the fidelity rate. When another factor is added to a willingness to cheat, then the fidelity rate plunges to between 50% and 60%—and the infidelity rate increases to between 40% and 50%.

There is no difference between the genders (Figure 14.4) in the fidelity rate when there is no propensity to cheat if one can get away with it. However, among those who are predisposed to

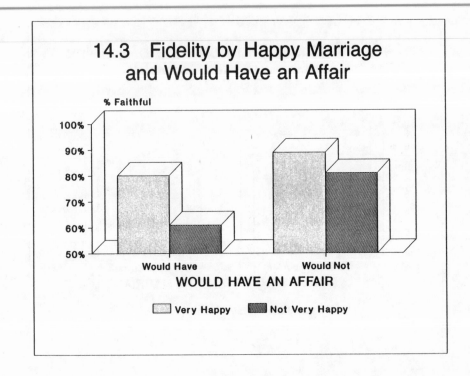

14.3 Fidelity by Happy Marriage and Would Have an Affair

% Faithful

WOULD HAVE AN AFFAIR

Would Have   Would Not

Very Happy   Not Very Happy

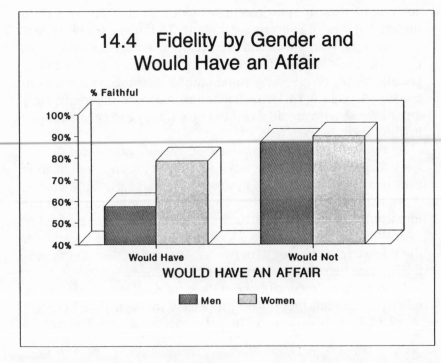

14.4 Fidelity by Gender and Would Have an Affair

% Faithful

WOULD HAVE AN AFFAIR

Would Have   Would Not

Men   Women

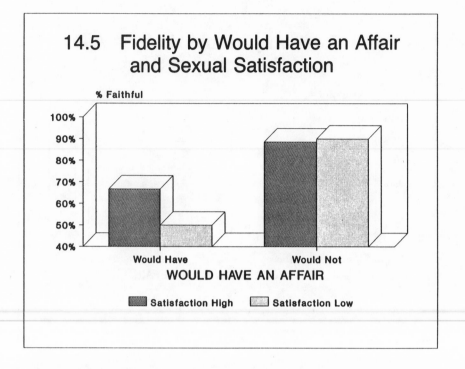

14.5 Fidelity by Would Have an Affair and Sexual Satisfaction

% Faithful

WOULD HAVE AN AFFAIR

Would Have   Would Not

■ Satisfaction High   □ Satisfaction Low

cheat, more than one out of five women and two out of five men have been unfaithful.

These patterns are repeated when the other variable is sexual satisfaction (Figure 14.5), frequency of sex (Figure 14.6), pre-marital sexual experiences (Figure 14.7), or even a feeling that one is less than completely moral about sex (Figure 14.8). Each of them has an impact only when the respondent is already disposed to cheating. Then the other variables increase the likelihood of infidelity.

Is the refusal to consider cheating a moral constraint or is it something more basic and primordial? In fact, a sense of morality about sex adds only marginally (Figure 14.8) to the fidelity of those who say they would not cheat if given a chance without fear of being caught. Morality is involved indeed, but the bond of fidelity seems to be something deeper and stronger than mere moral rules.

I'll repeat a previous argument: it may be that our respondents are exaggerating their own virtue. But even such exaggeration, should it exist, is evidence of how important, even in an alleged age of permissiveness, the bond between a man and a woman is

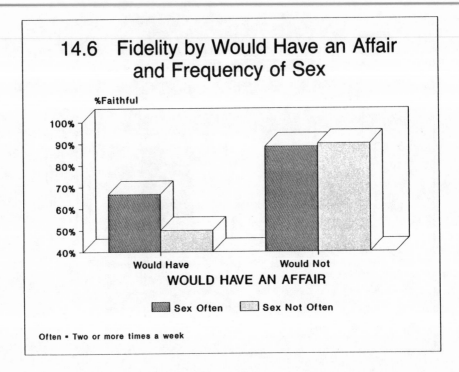

14.6   Fidelity by Would Have an Affair and Frequency of Sex

Often • Two or more times a week

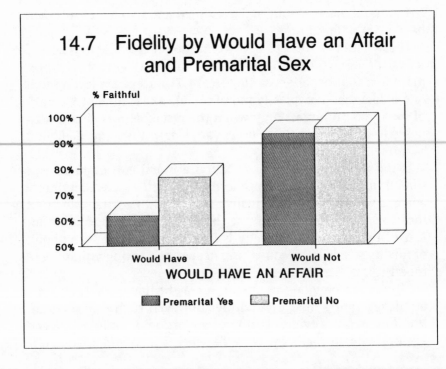

14.7   Fidelity by Would Have an Affair and Premarital Sex

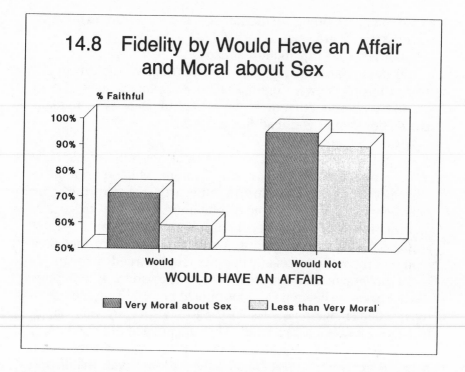

14.8   Fidelity by Would Have an Affair and Moral about Sex

% Faithful

Very Moral about Sex   Less than Very Moral

WOULD HAVE AN AFFAIR

supposed to be. That one would want to present oneself as faithful would be proof that fidelity is still believed to be enormously important, if not in one's own mind, at least in the minds of others.

Will romantic play tend to keep such a person in the marital bed? It's not needed in the absence of premarital experimentation and a spouse who imagines the self as sexual. With such a spouse, especially if there are problems which have driven the couple to therapy and the person doesn't value fidelity as much as others do, a high level of erotic activity might tend to help a little.

The words "might," "tend," and "little" are especially relevant here.

Human behavior is never simple, and explanations for it are never simple. A chemist would be ashamed of a model which explains only 13% of the variance. A sociologist is pleased with it. A chemist would say, "That little?" A sociologist would say, "That much?" Infidelity is a poignant, potentially disastrous form of behavior. To be able to say that it results in part from moral attitudes about infidelity, in part from emotional problems, and in part from an intricate combination of sexual orientations and experiences, including premarital sex and sexual excitement in the marriage, is no small achievement.

You knew that explanation already?

You knew that romantic play in a marriage would cancel out the relationship between premarital sex and extramarital sex? You would have written that down on a piece of paper as a confident expectation before you read this chapter?

Again, gimme a break!

As hardly need be said, the unfaithful are not typical. They seem to be driven by energies and demons which do not affect other people, at least not in the same way, not with the same intensity, and not in the same combination. They are statistically deviant, although judgments about their moral deviance are not appropriate for the sociologist. There is no evidence that they represent the vanguard of any important social trend or any major social movement as magazine articles or the various Hite Reports might suggest. They tend to be troubled and unhappy people— twenty percentage points less likely to say they are very happy in the *Love and Marriage II* study. They are not part of a revolution; nor, it would seem, victims of it. If they become heroes and heroines of certain kinds of fiction, the reason may be that fiction on occasion is indeed stranger than truth.

C O N C L U S I O N

Two sets of dynamisms determine marital fidelity, as best we can account for it at all—moral convictions about the importance of fidelity in marriage and complex sexual and emotional needs that are not being met in marriage and perhaps cannot be met in marriage. Since moral attitudes on extramarital sex have not changed in recent years (save for an increase in opposition to it), and since it is unlikely that the sexual needs of human beings have altered much, if at all, there continues to be a high level of marital fidelity. One could not dismiss on the basis of the data in this book the possibility that there has been a very slight increase in infidelity for women, despite the fact that it does not correlate with age for either women or men. Younger women are in fact no more likely than older women to have had extramarital affairs, and the rates of infidelity for men and women in the last year are the same. Perhaps at some time in the past women were even more faithful than they are today. It would have been difficult for the rates to be much higher, however, than they are now.

Whence comes the popular impression of a notable increase in infidelity for women?

It may be that in certain small segments of the society, too small to be caught in a modest probability sample, extramarital affairs for women have been increasing. Perhaps in the worlds of the academy and the national media fidelity rates among women are plummeting, as did the premarital chastity rates during the last twenty years—though perhaps fidelity was always less honored in these realms than it is on Main Street and State Street. Perhaps those who write about the extramarital affairs of women are merely writing about their families, their friends, the women they know.

Or perhaps they are writing about fantasy and not about reality—their own fantasies and the fantasies of their readers. There are no data on infidelity fantasy rates, though I would be surprised if they were much less than 100%, not that there's anything wrong with that. But might not much of the writing, fiction and nonfiction alike, be an appeal to active fantasies instead of an accurate representation of reality?

Is humankind a monogamous species? Surely not like Gambel's quail or even timber wolves. Patently humankind can and does engage in a wide variety of sexual practices, most notably polygamy and including on occasion infidelity. It would appear, the sex ratio being what it is, that most humans have had no choice but to be monogamous. As for fidelity, surely it is not locked into the human genes to be faithful. Whatever programming may exist is not irresistible: some humans have had considerable success in resisting it.

Yet there surely seems to be in America today (and in England, according to the study done there) a strong propensity to fidelity, one that is unshaken by other changes in sexual mores.

From free love, for weal or woe, we seem to be a long way.

15. The Gender and Generation Gaps

Women and men have rather similar views about the condition of their marriages. However, women in general are more critical of their spouses than are men. Men and women agree that women work harder at the marriage than do men. Men either are more romantic or have more illusions about their spouses than do women. Despite these differences, the portraits of marriage constructed by the two genders are not greatly different, perhaps not as different as one might have expected.

Positive evaluations of the marriage relationship generally do not diminish with either age or duration of marriage. However, some of the amusements of romantic eroticism are less prevalent among the older than they are among the younger, though by no means do they vanish among the older. While older women become more likely to complain about their husbands' weight problems, older men are even more likely to adore their wives. Are the younger cohorts different from the way their predecessors were when the latter were the same age as the younger are now? It is difficult to be certain. There is no evidence that the younger generation is more committed to romantic eroticism than the older generation was at the same age.

HOW GREAT A GAP BETWEEN THE GENDERS?

In the earlier chapters, I have reported on the happiness and the anguish in contemporary American marriage with only brief reference to the social and demographic characteristics which might produce different responses to marriage. In this and the next chapter I tie together the references and investigate the possibility that there might be radically different approaches to marriage between genders and generations and among various social, regional, and religious groups.

While there are such differences and they are surely important, it is nonetheless basically true that the different population groups agree much more than they disagree about their marriages.

Men and women generally agree about the condition of their marriages, although women are somewhat more critical of their spouses than are men (whether deservedly so I will not judge). None of the differences of opinion are particularly surprising, but they do suggest that the respondents have done their best to answer truthfully.

There are no differences[45] between men and women either in the proportion that say their marriage is very happy or that assert that they would marry the same spouse again if they had it to do over. Men are more likely[46] than women (80% versus 73%) to say that their spouse is also their best friend, perhaps a reflection of the fact that men are reputed to find it more difficult to make same-sex friends as women. Men are twice as likely as women (22% versus 10%) to say that they are in the falling-in-love phase of marriage, but there is no difference between the genders in the proportion who report that they are "bottoming out." Most of the difference in the falling-in-love response is made up by the fact that women are more likely than men to say that they are "beginning again" in marriage.

---

[45] In this book I am reporting only differences that are statistically significant at the .05 level or higher. That means that in ninety-five cases out of a hundred, when one accepts such a difference as reflecting one that exists in the sampled population, one will not be in error. Many of the differences *are* significant at the .01 or even the .001 level, but I decided not to burden the "general reader" with these matters.

[46] In this chapter I cite proportions giving the unqualified answer, unless I note otherwise.

Women are more likely than men (19% versus 13%) to agree or at least agree somewhat that with the coming of children the fun goes out of marriage. However, the overwhelming majority of both sexes disagrees. Women are more likely than men (84% as opposed to 75%) to say that fidelity is important in marriage, although there is no difference in their conviction that most other people are not faithful to one another. Men are more likely than women (57% to 48%) to feel that sex is important in binding a marriage together. Sixty percent of the men and 78% of the women agree (either strongly or somewhat) that women work harder than men at making a marriage last. Three out of five respondents, regardless of sex, agree that sex is more important to men than to women.

There is no difference between men and women in the reports of sexual satisfaction and sexual frequency.

MARRIAGE, SPOUSE, AND SELF

There are no statistically significant differences in the way men and women describe the state of the marriage relationship or the erotic and romantic activities in which husband and wife engage. However, they do differ in the way they describe the spouse and themselves. Women in general are more critical than men.

Seven-eighths of the men and three-quarters of the women agree that the spouse is good with children. Four-fifths of the men and half the women say that the spouse helps with the household chores. A quarter of the women and a fifth of the men say that their spouse cares more about work than about them. These differences may be the result of different perceptions, though more likely the perceptions also reflect different realities. Women traditionally have had charge of the children and responsibility for the household chores, while men were supposed to be more concerned about work. In the absence of longitudinal data, we cannot say whether there is more male involvement in household chores and less obsession with work than there was in the past.

Women are more ready to contend that their spouses are good

at sex than are men. However, women are also less likely to depict their spouses as sexually alluring than men.

Of the women, 59% say the spouse is a skilled lover, and 34% say that he is imaginative in sex, as opposed to 48% and 27% of the men, respectively. On the other hand, 81% of the men and 73% of the women say that the spouse is good-looking; 56% of the men and 49% of the women say that the spouse is romantic; and 21% of the men and 16% of the women consider the spouse "mysterious and intriguing."

Moreover, a fifth of the women as opposed to a tenth of the men find their spouse at least somewhat dull, 18% of the women and 7% of the men agree at least somewhat that the mate is ill-mannered, and 56% of the women and 46% of the men agree at least somewhat that the spouse does not understand the respondent's emotional needs.[47]

It may be that women have higher standards in these matters than their husbands—that they demand higher levels of performance before they admit that a man is romantic and mysterious and sensitive to emotional needs. They may also have higher standards of physical attractiveness. Or it may be that in fact men are more likely to be dull and ill-mannered and unromantic and uninteresting—despite their apparently superior skills (as women see them) in lovemaking. Women may, in other words, have fewer romantic illusions, or they may experience in men less that justifies illusions.

In one respect, however, men seem to be more likely to be romantic than women: 36% of the men as opposed to 19% of the women say that sometimes their spouse is like a god to them. Men, it would seem, are more likely to put their wives on a pedestal than vice versa—though the reason may be that the wives are more likely to merit adoration.

Women are less likely to be sexually confident than men. We find that 32% of the men as opposed to 24% of the women are ready to describe themselves as a "sexual" person, 27% of the men and 19% of the women think of themselves as a "good lover," and 74% of the men and 61% of the women deny that they ever avoid sex (52% of the women and 47% of the men considers themselves to very moral in sexual matters). It does not

---

[47]There is no difference on the subject of recognition of physical needs.

follow that women are indeed less confident than men, but only that they are less likely to think they are confident than men are.

The differences between men and women in their view of the spouse are almost stereotypical: men more involved in work and less involved with children and household responsibilities; men more skillful at sex but less sensitive, less romantic, less mysterious. Men are more likely to adore; women more likely to think men dull, uninteresting, and boorish. Women are more convinced, in sum, that men are just a little childish.

These stereotypical differences are not unimportant. In the absence of data from the past, one can only speculate as to whether the statistics represent a change from the past—though analysis of age differences in the next chapter might give a hint of change.

Nonetheless, on most of the judgments about the spouse the differences are not as great as they might be. Nor do they cancel out the single most important finding in this chapter: whatever the differences in the evaluation of the spouse, there is little disagreement between men and women on the condition of the marriage. That men and women describe the marriage similarly in virtually the same proportions despite different ratings of the spouse suggests that they are in fact validating the report on the marriage relationship that the opposite gender has given.

Men and women agree that marriage in America is not about to go out of fashion because of dissatisfaction with the marriage relationship.

A G I N G   A N D   M A R I T A L H A P P I N E S S

The advance of the years does not seem to affect the marital satisfactions of Americans. There is no significant relationship between either age or duration of the marriage on the one hand and the proportion who say their marriage is very happy, the proportion who say the spouse is their best friend, the proportion who declare that they would marry the same person again, and the proportion saying that they are in the falling-in-love phase. Moreover, there is no significant relationship between age and the suspicion that the fun goes out of marriage as one grows older. Finally, fidelity is not affected by age or duration of marriage, neither the fidelity during the last year nor the fidelity during the entire marriage.

AGE, GENDER, AND MARRIAGE

Most of the marital happiness indicators do not vary with age. Differences between men and women in the descriptions of the spouse do not change among younger cohorts. Whatever the age, for example, women are less likely than men to say that the spouse helps with the chores and that the spouse is good with children. Moreover, there is no evidence that, in the eyes of the spouse, men have improved at either helping with chores or caring for children.[48]

THE DECLINE OF PASSION?

Some things do change with age, however, most of them relating to erotic passion. Of the three cohorts (under thirty-five, between thirty-five and forty-nine and over fifty) the youngest is more likely to say that spouses discuss their marriage and their sexual relationship (69% and 50%), the middle somewhat less likely (65% and 42%), and the older less likely still (61% and 31%).

Most such indicators vary with age but without any significant change in the relationship between the variable and gender. For example, the proportion of those who say that they discuss their marriage with their spouse declines with age. But the differences between men and women at each age remain trivial.

Older men and women are also more likely to say that their marriage has bottomed out—9% of the men and 13% of the women. The older and middle cohorts are more likely to say that their spouse is overweight (39% agree at least somewhat), as opposed to 29% for the younger. The older cohorts are less likely

---

[48] It does not follow that younger men do not do more around the house than older men, only that their wives are no more likely to judge that they are helpful.

to say the spouses go out dancing together (23% versus 36%) and more likely to agree at least somewhat that the spouse is like a god (30% versus 25%).

Most of these differences suggest a certain weary slowing down with age. However, these changes in what one might call the physical stamina of the relationship do not affect its basic happiness. There is nothing in the data to suggest to younger married Americans that they will grow weary of one another, even though they may grow somewhat weary with age.

Confidence in one's abilities as a lover diminishes with age: 18% of the younger say that they are not confident, as do 25% of the older; 64% of the older say they never avoid sex, whereas 69% of the middle group and 71% of the younger cohorts say likewise; 45% of the older, and 55% of the younger, say that their spouse is a skilled lover.

These differences may or may not be a function of aging. It is possible that the younger age cohort are better lovers than their predecessors were at the same age and that they will continue with this advantage through life. There is no way to determine this from the data available to us at present. However, in a 1965 fertility study done by Westoff and Westoff (1967), the per-month rate of sexual intercourse for married women under forty-five (the population that was studied) was 6.7. For a comparable group in the General Social Survey of 1989—a quarter century later—the rate was exactly the same 6.7. It simply remains to be seen whether on the average the present cohort of younger married couples is more sexually sophisticated than its predecessors. The comparison is merely about the quantity of sex, not the quality, yet if there is no difference in quantity, it certainly remains open to question whether quality has improved all that much, especially since the rates of shame and avoidance do not vary with age.

EROTIC AMUSEMENTS

The younger are surely more likely to engage in erotic amusements than the middle and older generations do at the present: 28% of the younger, 24% of the middle, and 9% of the older swim in the nude at least sometimes; 64% of the younger, 41% of the middle, and 16% of the older take showers or baths together; 39% of the younger, 21% of the middle, and 7% of the older buy erotic underwear; 34% of the younger, 26% of the middle, and 11% of the older make love outdoors; 34% of the younger, 24% of the middle, and 10% of the older watch X-rated videos together.

For men and women alike, the erotic playfulness measure described in Chapter 11 correlated powerfully with the judgments that the spouse is exciting, mysterious, and playful. For women it also correlated significantly with the judgments that the marriage is happy and that they would marry the same person again.[49] Though there is an impression that men may push some of these exercises in sexual playfulness more than do women, the evidence seems to indicate that the amusements are more important to women in their evaluation of the marriage—perhaps because the play gives attention to her as a person and as a woman.[50]

There is a powerful correlation between age and romantic play (Figure 15.1). Younger respondents are far more likely than older respondents to score high on the playfulness measure, but though there is only a few percentage points difference between men and women at all ages, the men are more likely to report romantic play than women. One can therefore conclude that, as with most other explicitly sexual activities, the memories of husbands and wives are virtually the same and hence validate the testimony of each other.

Those under thirty-five obviously did not invent any of the pastimes. Whether the younger groups will continue these practices in their senior years, and to what extent, remains to be seen. However, retrospective questions did not indicate any higher level of romantic play than five years ago.

---

[49] The r, or simple correlation, is a measure of how much the variance on one item can be explained by variance on another. The amount explained is the square of the r. Thus when I report that the correlation between the erotic amusement scale and the judgment that the marriage is "playful" in private is .40, I am saying that 16% of the variance on one variable can be explained by the variance on the other. Does the respondent mean by "playful" erotically playful? On the basis of the correlation it would seem so. The correlation with "exciting" is .25 and that with "mysterious" .20. In most social research these correlations would be considered quite high. The correlation for women between erotic amusement and marital happiness is .14, and for "the same marriage again" is .23.
[50] The only women I know really well, the fictional women in my novels, surely need play, as T. George Harris has pointed out.

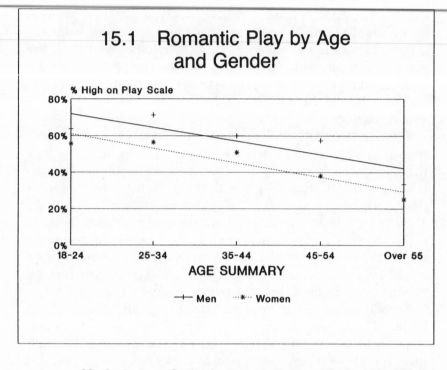

15.1   Romantic Play by Age and Gender

% High on Play Scale

AGE SUMMARY

—+— Men   ...*... Women

M O R E   A D O R A B L E   W O M E N ?

There are some interesting twists in the relationship among age, gender, and marriage. Younger men are slightly more likely than younger women to say that the spouse is overweight. In the middle level, however, while both men and women are more likely than younger ones to say that the spouse is overweight, women are more likely than men to complain about an overweight spouse. Among the older group there is no significant difference, because there is less complaint from women about overweight husbands.

Do men put on weight more than women between thirty-five and fifty or are women merely more likely to complain? Do men lose weight after they're fifty, or are women now less likely to complain? Perhaps the answer to the first question is that men do put on weight during those years and to the second that women no longer bother to complain.

Women's evaluation of their husband as godlike declines with age and more sharply than the evaluation declines among men

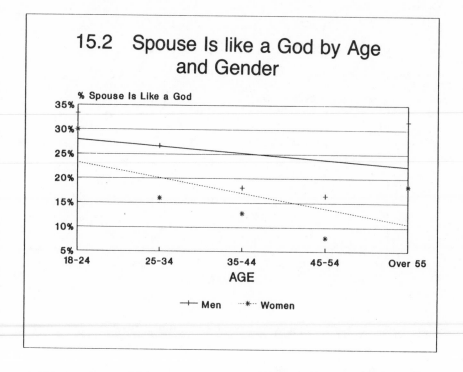

15.2   Spouse Is like a God by Age and Gender

(Figure 15.2). Thus at older ages there is a greater difference between women and men in such adoration than there is at younger ages. Whether the wives become relatively more adorable or the men love them even more is a question which need not be answered. The phenomenon itself should be encouraging enough to women—though perhaps it is not a substitute for help with the chores!

The judgment that the spouse is a good lover also declines more sharply for women than for men, though the differences at any age level are not statistically significant (Figure 15.3).

Men are more likely to increase their rating of the self as a lover with age, while women are more likely to lower theirs. Thus the difference in self evaluation which is not significant in the younger years becomes so in the older years (Figure 15.4).

There are no simple answers to the question of whether the attitudes and behavior of a young cohort represents a social change or merely a life cycle phenomenon. Does the youthful cohort really experience a more erotic relationship between husband and wife, or is it merely following a path of youthful passion leading to decline laid down by its predecessors?

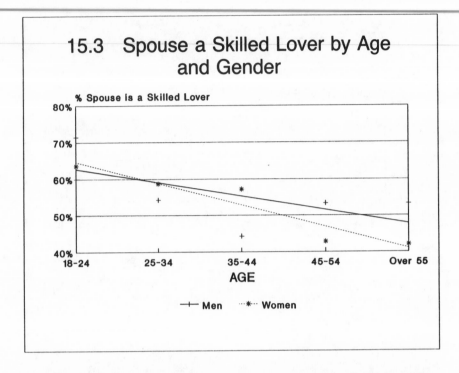

15.3   Spouse a Skilled Lover by Age and Gender

% Spouse is a Skilled Lover

(Chart: X-axis "AGE" with categories 18-24, 25-34, 35-44, 45-54, Over 55; Y-axis from 40% to 80%. Legend: —+— Men ······ Women)*

No one can at present give a confident answer to that question. In my research in the sociology of religion I have found repeatedly that the argument for age and social change, so dearly loved by European sociologists, simply washes out when one is able to study the same cohorts over time: the young are less religious because they are younger and become more religious as they grow older. They are not a revolutionary cohort.

Hence I am skeptical that the behavior of those under thirty-five (or even under fifty) in the swimming pool (or other facility), the shower, the lingerie shop, the weekend hotel, under the sky at night (or in broad daylight as far as that goes) does represent a dramatic social change. Surely the data cited before about the constant rate of sexual intercourse between husbands and wives over the last quarter century make one less than confident about an erotic revolution in marriage.

One could also be content with the observation that a substantial segment of the population at every age—perhaps even a surprisingly large segment—engages in erotic pleasures and that women, especially women over forty, find them especially im-

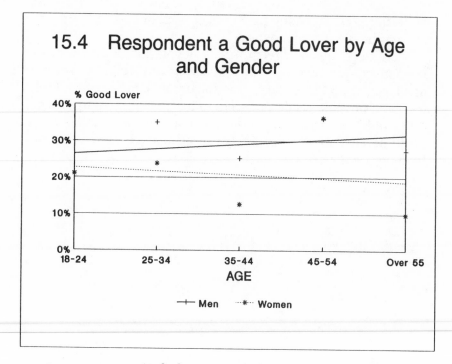

15.4 Respondent a Good Lover by Age and Gender

portant, more particularly, as I noted in Chapter 11, if they are in a condition of romantic love.

CONCLUSION

Those American marriages which escape the divorce court seem to wear rather well. Neither age nor the duration of marriage affects the fundamental happiness of the relationship. No matter what the age, the spouse is still the best friend and the choice one would make again. "Falling in love" does not become less likely with age. Women apparently become better lovers and men find them more adorable with the passage of time. The power of erotic passion declines, but fidelity does not diminish with the passage of time. The younger cohort is more given to erotic amusements and may perhaps in this matter represent some authentic social change in the relationship between husband and wife. On the other hand, those things about men which annoy women are no less important among the younger respondents than they are among the older respondents.

There does not then seem to be a revolution going on in the relationship between husbands and wives in America. The frequency of sexual intercourse has apparently not increased. Problems and possibilities do not seem to be very different from what one would expect if one considered marriage as a rather stable institution in which more variety existed across generational lines than between eras.

16. Social Class, Region, and Religion

Money can buy a little bit more marital happiness on the average, but not very much. There do not appear to be different patterns of fidelity and intimacy in the various social classes in America, not as these classes can be measured in a sample survey. Fidelity, marital satisfaction, and patterns of intimacy vary only slightly with education and income. The more affluent and the better educated are somewhat more likely to engage in erotic entertainments. Only in the West and especially the Far West does there seem to be a distinct subculture of marital intimacy.

Religion is by far the most powerful correlate of marriage attitudes and behavior we have yet discussed in this book. Although many journalists and social scientists assume that secularization is a demonstrated fact, there is no evidence to support this assumption in the United States. Moreover, there is no stronger predictor of marital happiness than religious devotion. This relationship cannot be explained as merely a simplistic and Fundamentalist approach to both religion and marriage. Finally, warmth of religious images has a powerful impact on marital satisfaction.

There are sixty-five nonwhite respondents in the samples, not a large enough number, in my judgment, to attempt an analysis of racial differences.

M A R I T A L H A P P I N E S S
A N D S O C I A L C L A S S

Money can buy a little extra bit of marital happiness. Or to put the matter more soberly, those whose families earn more than $25,000 a year are seven percentage points more likely to say that their marriage is very happy than those who do not earn that much. Those who have attended college are likewise seven percentage points more likely to say that they are very happy than those who have not. However, there is no relationship between education and income (those two standard measures of social class) on the one hand and either a statement that the spouse is also the best friend or the choice to marry the spouse again. Nor do these social-class variables affect either marital fidelity or fidelity during the past year. Finally, they have no impact on the phase of the marriage cycle: both "falling in love" and "bottoming out" are independent of income and education.

M A R I T A L R E L A T I O N S H I P
A N D S O C I A L C L A S S

Social class, however, does have an impact on the marital relationship. Those who attended college are more likely to say that the spouse respects them (by ten percentage points), and are half as likely (5% versus 11%) to say that the spouse cannot be trusted. They are also less likely to see the spouse as godlike (23% versus 32%). However, college education does not affect help with household tasks or agreement on raising children.

Income has a somewhat similar effect: the more affluent are more likely to say that the spouse respects them. They are also more likely to discuss their marriage and less likely to see their spouse as divine.

College-educated respondents are more likely to attend parties with the spouse (37% versus 24%), to swim unclad (24% versus 17%), and to engage in three or more erotic amusements (31% versus 25%).

The more affluent are also more likely to attend parties (36% versus 22%), swim in the nude (24% versus 15%), to say that they are good lovers (25% versus 17%), and to engage in erotic adventures (32% versus 25%).

Since the young are more likely to be college educated, it is possible that youth rather than education is responsible for the difference in quality of marital intimacy in different social classes. This question can be answered by a multiple regression analysis which compares the impact of age and college education net of each other on such matters as respect, nude swimming, and the propensity to see the spouse as divine.

In fact, respect from the spouse, nude swimming, and other erotic playfulness are a function of youth, not education. However, trust increases with both youthfulness and college education. The disinclination to see the spouse as godlike is a result of education and not youthfulness. Thus many of those differences which appear to be the result of social class are in fact the result of the younger age of those who have attended college.

By way of summary so far, the more affluent are more likely to say that their marriage is happier and more likely to say that their spouse respects them and merits their trust and less likely to say that their spouse reminds them of a god. The apparent relationship between social class and erotic play, however, is merely the result of greater educational attainment among the young (those under forty).

Can the greater marital happiness of the better educated and the more affluent be explained by the greater trust and respect which seems to exist in this social class between husband and wife? The answer is that yes, it can be so explained. Once greater respect and trust are taken into account, there is no relationship between either education and income on the one hand and marital happiness on the other.

Money does not buy marital happiness, then—at least not directly. Nor does education. Rather, affluence and education apparently create trust and respect between husband and wife, which make for somewhat greater happiness. Is it education or money? When the two variables are included in the multiple regression equation it becomes clear that education is the cause of respect and trust, not money. Therefore one can expect a modest increase in trust and respect in American marriages as educational attainment increases—all other things being equal. Trust and respect, however, are already strong in American marriage —68% of our respondents say the spouse respects them (and there is no correlation with gender) and over 90% say they trust the spouse (a trust which seems to be justified by the fidelity epidemic).

There may be groups at the upper or the lower end of the socioeconomic ladder which deviate from the pattern of marital intimacy reported in this chapter, but they are too small to be captured by an ordinary national sample. Fidelity, intimacy, and affection are at most only slightly affected by income and education.

I S   C A L I F O R N I A   D I F F E R E N T ?

The only variations by region in the culture of American marriage affect the West, that is, the Mountain and Pacific Coast states, and especially the Pacific Coast states.

On the Pacific Coast (California, Oregon, and Washington), spouses are less likely to help with household tasks, to talk about the marriage, and to trust the other. Indeed, while 50% of the wives in the country say that their husbands help with household tasks, only 34% of the West Coast women say the same. West Coast inhabitants are also less likely to say that the partner is good with children, but more likely (53% to 48%) to say that the partner is playful, more likely to report frequent partying (38% versus 29%), and twice as likely to report nude swimming (perhaps because of all those backyard swimming pools in California!). They are also thirteen percentage points more likely to say that they themselves are good lovers than are respondents in the rest of the country. If there is a certain "la-la land" aura to marriage on the West Coast, it must be noted that infidelity is no more common there than anywhere else in the country, although 24% of the West Coast respondents are on at least their second marriage, as opposed to 17% in the rest of the country. Nor is there any significant variation from the national rates for marital satisfaction.

REGION AND CLASS

There are no large distinct marital subcultures in America, but there are differences among various demographic and social groups—differences which follow easily predictable patterns. The young are more likely to be concerned about erotic play, women are more likely to be critical of their spouses and (perhaps less predictably) to need romantic eroticism, the better educated are likely to be happier because of enhanced respect and trust, inhabitants of the West Coast are more likely to display certain selfish traits and to swim in the nude. However, regardless of age, education, gender, and region, Americans tend to be faithful to the spouse whom they regard as their best friend and the person they would marry again if given the chance for a second time around.

RELIGIOUS DENOMINATION AND ENDOGAMY

Religious denomination—Catholic or Protestant[51]—as such has less impact on marriage than the fact of denominational difference. However, Catholics are less likely to have been faithful through the whole course of a marriage (88% versus 94% for Protestants) and through the last year of the marriage (91% versus 95% for Protestants). Catholics are also less likely to have been chaste before marriage (39% versus 46%), and this is as true of Catholics over forty as of those under forty. They are, on the other hand, ten percentage points more likely to say that the spouse helps in household tasks and that the spouse is godlike (34% versus 24%). They are also more likely to report dancing (39% versus 26%) and partying (44% versus 29%) and to say that they buy erotic underclothes (27% versus 17%).

[51]There are not enough respondents in the *Love and Marriage* survey to permit analysis of any other religious difference than that between Catholics and Protestants.

A significant correlation of .17 exists between being Catholic and a factor which is composed of joint dancing, partying, going to a hotel to be alone with each other, and exercising together.

One is reminded of the cautionary verse of Hilaire Belloc:

> Wherever the Catholic sun does shine
> There's laughter and music and good red wine,
> At least I've found it so,
> Benedicamus Dominio!

This relationship as well as the relationship with the image of the godlike spouse can be explained by the different Catholic religious imagination, one that sees God as present in the world instead of absent from it (Tracy, 1982; Greeley 1989b, 1990a).

Respondents in exogamous marriages are less likely (by seven percentage points) to say that they are happily married, and that they would marry the same spouse again (Greeley and Durkin 1990). They are more likely to say that their marriage is in the bottoming-out phase and twice as likely to say that they don't trust their spouse. They are thirteen percentage points less likely to say that the spouse is good with children and nine percentage points less likely to say that they agree on the raising of children. They are also significantly less likely to say that there is discussion about the marriage and that the spouse is kind and romantic. As Michael has pointed out, marriage can be conceptualized economically as a joint production enterprise. Shared religious values are a human resource which facilitates the effectiveness of the enterprise.

One does not conclude that all religiously mixed marriages are conflict-ridden, but only that conflict about children and other strains are more likely in such marriages and one posits that therefore the likelihood that one would choose the same spouse again declines. Indeed, when conflict over children is taken into account in a multiple regression equation, the negative relationship between exogamy and the choice of the same spouse again disappears.

PRAYER AND BIBLE

According to our respondents, 32% of American husbands and wives pray together often. Whether they pray often together or not is a very powerful correlate of marital happiness, the most powerful we have yet discovered. Seventy-five percent of those who pray say that the marriage is very happy, as opposed to 57% of those who do not pray so often. Eighty-eight percent of the prayers say that the spouse is also their best friend, as opposed to 71% of those who pray less often. Nine out of ten of the prayers say they would marry the same person again, as do four out of five of those who do not pray together so often. Furthermore, 26% say they are in the falling-in-love stage of marriage, twice the proportion of the nonprayers, and 3% say they are in the bottom phase, as opposed to 6% of those who pray less frequently.

Clearly, joint prayer is strongly related to marital happiness. Can we say that the former causes the latter? If we could, we would then be able to advise those who want to be happily married that they should pray often together with confidence that such a recipe would be very rational advice. But might it be that those who are happy together are also disposed to pray often together? Or even that both their happiness and their praying is a manifestation of rigid personalities? Might the happy prayers be in fact Fundamentalists who are revealing only their literalism and their rigidity?

I will confess that I suspected something like this at first, because those who believe in the strict literal interpretation of the Bible are in fact more likely to report frequent joint prayer than those who do not accept such a fundamentalist interpretation of the scripture (41% versus 27%). However, Biblical literalism correlates only with the falling-in-love phase of the marriage cycle, and not with the three primary measures of marital satisfaction. Moreover, in a multiple regression equation literalism does not eliminate a statistically significant relationship with "falling in love."[52]

Thus the relationship between joint prayer and happiness in a marriage is not an artifact of religious fundamentalism. It is im-

[52] Neither prayer nor literalism predicts a higher level of marital fidelity.

possible with the data presently available to us to determine the flow of influence between marital satisfaction and joint prayer. Doubtless they reinforce one another. Prayer, it is worth noting, is a much more powerful predictor of marital satisfaction than frequency of sexual intercourse—though the combination of sex and prayer correlates with very, very high levels of marital fulfillment.

The advantage to those who often pray together runs through almost every variable being analyzed in this study: respect (83% versus 62%), distrust (5% versus 9%), helping with household tasks (73% versus 61%), discussion of state of the marriage (76% versus 60%), belief that the spouse is good with children (89% versus 78%), agreement on raising children (73% versus 59%), playfulness (56% versus 45%), conviction that the spouse is a skilled lover (62% versus 49%), frequent partying (36% versus 28%). None of these relationships can be explained by Biblical literalism, which does not in general correlate with the same variables.

It may be that the prayer interlude provides husbands and wives with time away from the other responsibilities of their common and individual lives in which they can share affection and common values and thus reinforce their relationship. They would, in this model, begin to pray together because the relationship is already perceived as good; then the joint prayer would validate and improve the relationship.

Joint prayer is not a guarantee of improved marriage relationships. It may still be a rational choice, however; praying together can't hurt, and the utility, as economists would say, appears to be substantial.

C H U R C H   A T T E N D A N C E
A N D   R E T R E A T

Both regular church attendance[53] and frequent religious retreats[54] also relate positively to marital satisfaction: 76% of

---

[53] Fifty-five percent of married people go to church at least two or three times a month.
[54] Sixteen percent of the respondents make such retreats sometimes.

those who go to retreats say they are very happy in their marriage (versus 60%), and 85% say that their spouse is their best friend (versus 65%); 70% of those who attend church regularly are very happy, and 80% of them say they would marry the same person again (as compared with 57% and 75%). Thus, retreat and joint prayer are stronger predictors of satisfaction than church attendance. Eighty-nine percent of those who make the retreats say they would marry the same person again, as opposed to 72% of the nonretreatants. Both prayer together and retreats relate significantly to marital satisfaction independently of one another, though regular church attendance becomes statistically insignificant when placed in a regression equation with the other two variables.

Of those who have made retreats, 30% say they are in the falling-in-love phase, twice the proportion of those who have not; 57% say they are playful when they are alone together, as opposed to 48% of those who have not made retreats; 65% of the retreatants say that the spouse is a skilled lover, against 50% of those who do not go; and 37% report joint partying, as opposed to 28%. While the retreat does not correlate positively with erotic activities, it does not correlate negatively with them either.

Retreats can't hurt, either.

Prayer increases as men and women grow older—as do all other religious activities.[55] Unpublished work done by S. Philip Morgan and myself offers a hint that prayer increases because men and women think that prayer works—the proportion which asserts that prayers are heard increases also with age and accounts for most of the increase in prayer. To pray seems to be the pragmatic choice. There exist no data to confirm that joint prayer also increases with age because people believe it works. However, it does so increase, and the impact of joint prayer on marital happiness is higher for older respondents than it is for younger ones. Since we already know that prayer and religious devotion are life-cycle and not cohort effects—the younger generation becomes more devout as it grows older (Hout and Greeley 1987) —there is reason to believe that young people will pray more together with their spouse as the marriage grows older and that

---

[55]The low point in devotion comes when someone is twenty five years old. Then devotion begins to climb until the middle forties when it levels off again (Hout and Greeley 1987).

such prayer will relate even more strongly to marital happiness with the passage of time.

Of those under thirty-five, 19% report frequent joint prayer, as do 30% of those between thirty-five and fifty and 43% of those over fifty. Moreover, the correlation between joint prayer and marital happiness is .13 for the youngest group, .17 for the next oldest, and .22 for those over fifty. Nor is it merely prayer that correlates so strongly with marital happiness: 18% of those who do not pray every day report joint prayer as do 46% of those who pray every day. But 54% of those who themselves pray every day do not report frequent joint prayer. In a regression equation in which both variables are entered, individual prayer does relate significantly with marital happiness, but joint prayer correlates at a level twice as high: the beta—the coefficient which takes into account the influence of the other variable—is .10 for individual prayer and .20 for joint prayer.

Religious devotion, then, increases with age; this increase is the result of life cycle, not a cohort effect.[56] It is more closely related to marital satisfactions with age. Hence one might conclude speculatively that the longer a marriage endures, the more important frequent joint prayer seems to both the spouses. Moreover, since a cohort effect can be ruled out, we may say that whether the erotic amusements can or cannot be sustained in marriage as the years go on, joint prayer can not only be sustained but will increase with age. Prayer correlates more strongly with marital happiness than does frequency of sex (in the General Social Survey) and erotic amusements.

I do not wish this report to seem to be an advertisement of joint prayer as a substitute for lovemaking. I do not believe it is. The two activities complement one another instead of replacing one another. Nonetheless, it is hard to escape the conclusion that prayer is far more important in marriage than the Conventional Wisdom would have suggested.

To repeat: it can't hurt!

---

[56]That is, as the younger cohort grows older, it will follow the practices established by its parents (Hout and Greeley 1987).

THE TWO LOVES

Religion also plays another role in marriage: it relates the two loves of which St. Paul wrote, the love of husband and wife and the love of humans and God. This is an empirical and not a theological statement. Whether there be a God or not, the images humans have of Her/Him profoundly affect their marital relationships. Warm and intense images of God correlate with a warm and intense relationship with the spouse.

This is a hypothesis which I derived a number of years ago from a theory of the religious imagination (Greeley 1980, 1989a, 1990a), which argues that religion is experience, image, and story before it becomes creed, code, and cult. The latter are the necessary cognitive reflections on the former, but religion originates and derives its raw and primordial power from the former. Images of God ordinarily encode the experiences a person believes she/he has had with the Deity and explain on the symbolic and narrative level the meaning and purpose of human life.

If this be true, then it would follow that the images and stories one has about one's experience with the sacred become the paradigms and the templates around which one shapes one's life. The stories of God and the stories of one's own life should intercorrelate.

The experiences of love in one's marriage should correlate with the experiences of love one has from one's encounter with the sacred: the warmer and more passionate one's religious images, the warmer and more passionate will be one's marriage relationships, and vice versa.

The measures I normally used to portray a person's religious imagination are a series of four forced choices between God as a mother or a father, a master or a spouse, a judge or a lover, a friend or a king. For this analysis I composed a scale running from 0 to 4, the latter representing those who pictured God as a Mother, Spouse, Lover and Friend and the former those who pictured Her/Him as none of these. One point was assigned on the scale (called the "grace" scale) for each of the warm images of God.

In addition to the "grace" scale, I use a scale composed of images of the world and of human nature based on the work of

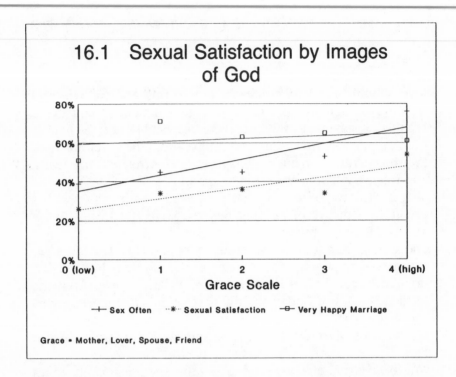

16.1   Sexual Satisfaction by Images of God

Grace Scale

—+— Sex Often   ··*·· Sexual Satisfaction   —▫— Very Happy Marriage

Grace • Mother, Lover, Spouse, Friend

theologian David Tracy (1982). In this work the scale ranges from 0 to 2, the latter score assigned to those who believe that the world is evil and human nature corrupt and the former to those who reject both positions.

My hypotheses were that the "grace" scale would correlate positively with marital happiness, sexual satisfaction, frequency of sex, sexual experimentation, sexual play, and "falling in love." In fact, five of the six hypotheses were sustained. There was a statistically significant correlation between the "grace" scale and frequency of sex, sexual satisfaction, sexual experimentation, sexual play, and "falling in love."

Of those who scored zero on the "grace" scale, more than 35% reported frequent sex (more than weekly) as opposed to over 70% who were highest on the scale (Figure 16.1). Better than 20% with a low score say that they obtained a very great deal of satisfaction from their sex life, as opposed to almost half of those who were high on the scale. The trend line indicates that both measures double as one moves up the "grace" scale. Similarly, the proportion reporting a great deal of sexual experimentation increases from a little more than 40% to almost 80%; and

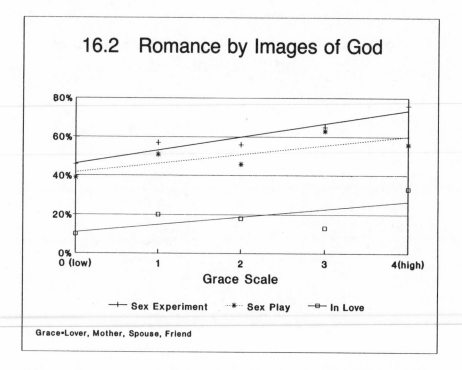

16.2   Romance by Images of God

Grace=Lover, Mother, Spouse, Friend

those engaging in sexual play (a factor made up of showers together, prolonged sex play, stripping for the spouse, and mutual undressing) rises from 40% to 60% (Figure 16.2). Finally, the proportion saying that they are in the romantic phase of a marriage doubles from 16% to 32% as the "grace" increases.

In four of the five measures, those at the top of the "grace" scale are twice as likely as those at the bottom to report intense sexual relationships, and in the fifth measure those at the top are half again as likely as those at the bottom to report such relationships.

More than 35% of the respondents who are high on the "grace" scale and see the spouse as godlike say they are in the falling-in-love phase (Figure 16.3). Indeed, such an image of the spouse increases the prospects of falling in love only for those who are not at the top of the scale (two left bars). Warm worship of God and warm worship of spouse are linked in marital romance—which is exactly what St. Paul was talking about when he wrote on the two passions.

Finally the "Tracy" scale correlates more modestly (but still

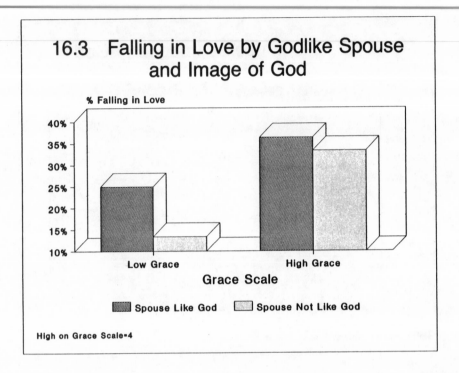

16.3 Falling in Love by Godlike Spouse and Image of God

% Falling in Love

Grace Scale

Spouse Like God   Spouse Not Like God

High on Grace Scale=4

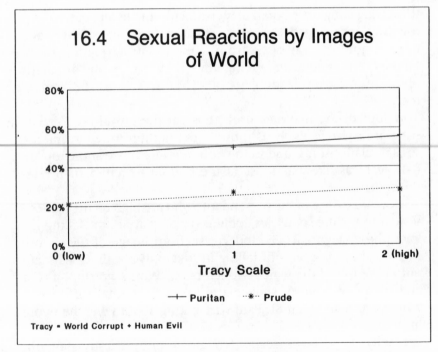

16.4 Sexual Reactions by Images of World

Tracy Scale

—— Puritan   ···*··· Prude

Tracy = World Corrupt + Human Evil

significantly) with prudish (shame) and puritanical (sex avoidance) measures. Those who think the world is evil and human nature corrupt are ten percentage points more likely also to be prudes and puritans (Figure 16.4). Certain kinds of religion do indeed cause sexual inhibitions, but other kinds of religion correlate with passion and play. The important question is, what kinds of religious experiences and templates are encoded in the religious images and stories in the human personality?

Obviously images of God and images of spouse influence one another. If God is a mother and a spouse and a friend and a lover, it is safe to be passionate with one's spouse. One can revel in the spouse and the spouse's body because God is pictured as reveling in the self. On the other hand, the passionate joy of one's encounter with the spouse may dispose one to believe (rightly or wrongly) that similar love is in charge of the cosmos.

My guess is that the images are acquired rather early in life and predispose us for subsequent relationships which reinforce them.

C O N C L U S I O N

Catholics are more likely to be unfaithful. They are also more likely to see the spouse as God and to be given to partying and dancing and suchlike. Exogamous marriages are more frustrating because of conflict over children. Fundamentalist literalism does not correlate with professed marital satisfactions. Religious retreats and frequent joint prayer relate powerfully to marital satisfaction—and both the relationship and the prayer increase with age. The warmer a person's religious images, the warmer that person's life with the spouse.

Chapters 15 and 16 have described what might broadly be called the demographic relationships that affect marital fidelity and intimacy. Briefly, women are more likely to be critical of their spouse than men. Young people are more involved in erotic amusements. Education produces somewhat more understanding and better communication in marriage. Religious devotion correlates with a wide spectrum of marital fulfillments, and its impact cannot be explained by literalist rigidity. Religious images strongly relate to sexual pleasure. The couple that plays and prays together stays together—and has a rich and rewarding sexual life, especially if its intimacy correlates with warm images of God.

17. Cohabitation, Divorce, and Premarital Sex

Sexual activity which has preceded the present marriage seems to have a negative effect on marital satisfaction, but a positive impact on erotic experimentation and frequency of sex. However, that is a function of the younger age, on the average, of those who have engaged in premarital sex. A previous marriage affects only the marital dialogue about children. But both cohabitation and premarital sex have a considerable impact on marital intimacy—there is more intimacy, but less satisfaction, in great part because of restlessness within the marriage and the willingness to cheat on the spouse. The increase in both premarital sex and cohabitation appears to be the result of a decision by younger men and women that premarital sex is not in fact immoral. Even if everyone were to engage in premarital sex (with someone other than the spouse) ''fairly often,'' the lifetime fidelity rate would decline only to 86%.

What is the impact of four "sexual revolution" variables—divorce, premarital sex, premarital cohabitation, and younger age of sexual initiation—on marriage?

A   P R E V I O U S   M A R R I A G E

There are sharp differences about children between spouses in those marriages in which the respondent has had a previous marriage. Two-thirds of the respondents who are in their first marriage say that they agree with their spouse on raising children, as opposed to half of those who are in a second[57] marriage. Similarly, 85% of those in a first marriage say that the spouse is good with children, as opposed to 68% in a second marriage. The problem is especially acute for women. Only 44% of those in a second marriage report agreement on raising children and only 58% of them think the spouse is good with children. But these are the only matters in which differences between first and second marriages can be measured by our indicators. Despite the conflict over children, respondents in second marriages are as likely to say that they are very happy in their marriage, that they would marry the same person again, that their spouse is their best friend, and that they are in the falling-in-love phase of the marriage. There is just as much trust, respect, and communication in second marriages as in the first, and the same amount of sexual experimentation. The inevitable conflicts over children may be a burden in second marriages, but they do not seem to make the marriages themselves any less satisfying than first marriages.

P R E M A R I T A L   S E X

Premarital sex has increased dramatically for women across generational lines, but not for men (Figure 17.1). Indeed, in a certain sense one can say that the "Sexual Revolution" is nothing more than women catching up with men in their premarital sexual activity, and an on-the-average three-year decline in average age of the first sexual encounter—from twenty to less than seventeen (Figure 17.2). For young women, the change seems in effect to mean that young women today have on the average one more

---

[57] "Second" is used here to indicate more than one previous marriage.

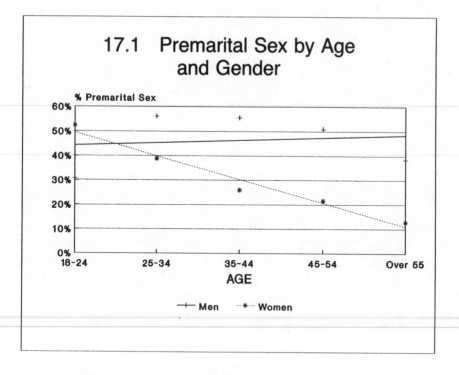

17.1 Premarital Sex by Age and Gender

sexual partner than young women did forty years ago (Figure 17.3).

Premarital sex with someone other than the intended spouse correlates with marital infidelity: 97% of those who did not engage in premarital sex with someone else have been faithful to their spouse in the course of the marriage, as opposed to 88% of those who report premarital sex "fairly often." Moreover, premarital sex also correlates significantly with extramarital sex during the past year. Obviously most of those who had premarital sexual experiences have remained faithful to the spouse after marriage. The point here is that their infidelity rate is somewhat higher than that of those who did not engage in premarital sex.

The impact of premarital sex on marital satisfaction seems strongest for men. Thus 89% of those who did not make love with other women before their marriage say that they would marry the same wife again, while 79% of those who did have premarital affairs said they would choose the same wife. There is no similar relationship for women.

Could it be that the experience of other women causes a man

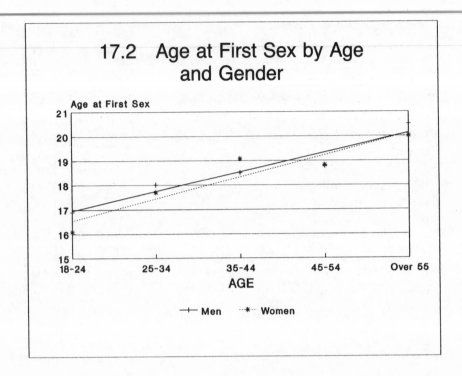

17.2   Age at First Sex by Age and Gender

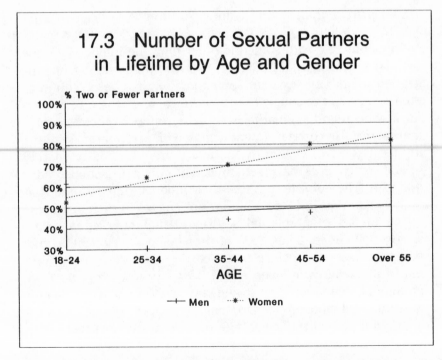

17.3   Number of Sexual Partners in Lifetime by Age and Gender

to be somewhat less enamored of his wife? Or is it rather, as seems more likely, that those who are sexually restless will be the ones more inclined toward both premarital and extramarital affairs?

Premarital sex with someone other than the eventual spouse also correlates negatively with the falling-in-love phase of the marriage cycle—21% of those who did not engage in premarital sex say that they are in the falling-in-love phase, as opposed to 14% of those who did. Those who engaged in premarital sex are not more likely to report that either they or the spouse are skilled lovers, but they are substantially more likely to report erotic play—half again as likely to score high on the erotic play scale as those who did not (36% versus 24%).

Again, I wish to emphasize that my argument is not that premarital sex causes marital restlessness (especially among men) and extramarital affairs. It is more likely that some of those who are inclined to sexual experimentation do not give up that propensity after marriage, though—and this fact cannot be emphasized too strongly—most of them do.

The relationship between premarital cohabitation with a future spouse and premarital affairs with others is not as strong as one might expect: 42% of those who did not cohabit had premarital affairs with someone else, as did 55% of those who did cohabit. Thus, even 45% of the cohabitors did not have any other premarital sexual affairs. For those under forty, there is no relationship at all between premarital sex with someone who was not a future spouse and cohabitation—only three percentage points separate the two groups. Among the young it is not merely those who already have been promiscuous who are inclined to practice for marriage with cohabitation, but also those who have been chaste: 25% of those under forty and 55% of those over forty have engaged in neither activity. Such chastity, however, does not correlate negatively with marital happiness. On the contrary, those who have been chaste are six percentage points more likely to say that they are very happy in their marriage and that they would marry the same spouse again. Chastity does not impede marital happiness, and premarital practice does not cause it.

Why has there been a decline in premarital chastity? The most simple answer is that the younger generation does not seem to think that sexual relations before marriage, either with the intended spouse or with someone else, are morally wrong. Thus, among those over forty, 70% of those who say they are very moral about sex did not engage in premarital affairs, as opposed to 53% of those who do not describe themselves as very moral; but 57% of the married people under forty engaged in premarital sex with someone other than their spouse, regardless of whether they thought they were very moral or not. The changes in attitude toward the immorality of premarital sex recorded in the annual General Social Survey statistics for the last seventeen years are thus reflections of a change, especially among younger people, in actual sexual practices. For them premarital sex may be a religious issue, but it is no longer a moral issue.

I do not argue that this is the way people ought to react, much less that moral teachers ought to change their minds because they seem to be outnumbered. I merely observe that behavior which was once considered immoral by most people is now no longer considered immoral by most. Those who wish to reassert the traditional premarital norms will accomplish nothing by denouncing premarital sex as immoral. The audience no longer agrees. They will, rather, have to begin at a much earlier state of the argument and establish that premarital sex is in fact immoral or unwise.

Is this change in moral attitudes the result of an improvement in birth control technology? Does premarital sex no longer seem sinful because the possibility of a child resulting has been minimized? I know of no direct evidence to support such a conclusion, but it does not seem unlikely.

Note well, however, that changes in attitude and behavior about premarital sex have had no impact on attitudes and behavior regarding extramarital sex. In fact, disapproval of extramarital sex has increased in recent NORC surveys (about which more in Chapter 19). Premarital sex does correlate with extramarital sex; but, even assuming that the relationship is causal and that everyone at some future date were to engage in premarital sex (besides that with an intended spouse), the fidelity rate would still be 88%—if the present relationship between premarital and extramarital sex were to remain the same!

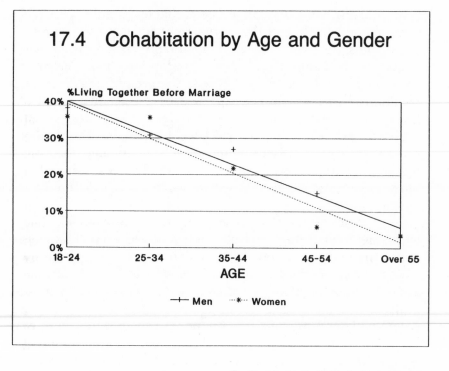

17.4   Cohabitation by Age and Gender

%Living Together Before Marriage

—┼— Men   ····*···· Women

C O H A B I T A T I O N

Cohabitation with the future spouse before a marriage seems to have the exact opposite effect of what is often stated as its goal: preparation for marriage. Cohabitation rates have increased dramatically across generational lines from less than 10% among those over sixty-five to almost 40% for those under twenty-five, with relatively little difference between the reports of men and women at every age level (Figure 17.4).

Those who have cohabited are less likely by about seven percentage points to say that their marriage is very happy and that their spouse is their best friend, though they are as likely as those who did not cohabit to say they would enter the same marriage again. The lower levels of satisfaction apply to both men and women. Those who cohabited are also six percentage points less likely to say that their spouse respects them.

If one constructs a matrix of the marital satisfaction variables used in this analysis (happy marriage, divorce, best friend, would marry again, sexual satisfaction, and sexual frequency) in the rows, and divorce, cohabitation, premarital sex, number of sexual partners, and the age of first sexual encounter in the columns, one obtains thirty cells, of which seven represent statistically significant relationships. Only one relationship is positive—between cohabitation and frequency of sex at the present time, but this relationship can be entirely explained by the relative youth of those who have cohabited. When their age is taken into account, the relationship becomes statistically insignificant. Three other relationships exist between premarital sex, cohabitation, and number of partners, on the one hand, and divorce on the other. Three more exist between the same variables and marital happiness.

All of these correlations can be accounted for by a model which takes into account only four variables: a conviction that fun goes out of the marriage as one grows older, a lack of delight in the spouse, a lack of strong positive satisfaction with one's family life, and a willingness to have an affair if one could get away with it.

Those who are more likely to have cohabited or to have been premaritally promiscuous are also more likely to think about divorce and to be unhappy in the present marriage because they are restless in that marriage and are willing to cheat on the spouse. They have, it would seem, less respect for and commitment to marriage and to the bond of sexual union.

I must quickly add that the overwhelming majority of those who have engaged in premarital sex of one sort or another are both happy in their marriages and believe that divorce is most unlikely. But there is in this segment of the population a greater restlessness and dissatisfaction on the average than there is among other married men and women. Minimally, there is no support for the folk wisdom that premarital sex of one variety or another is a preparation for marital happiness.

C O N C L U S I O N

In a second (or later) marriage, divorce affects the relationship between the husband and wife only on the subject of children. Cohabitation and premarital sex represent a major social change which results not from the abandonment of morality but from a change in moral norms, a change which has had little impact on the norms about marital fidelity. Premarital chastity among those under forty is less than half of what it was for those over forty, but it correlates positively, if moderately, with marital happiness. However, such chastity does not seem to be the result of "moral" judgments. Those under forty who consider themselves to be "very moral" about sex are no more likely to be chaste before marriage. However, as we shall see in the next chapter, religion still has a powerful impact on premarital behavior.

18. An Inhibited Society?

About two-thirds of American married men and women report that they rarely if ever abandon their sexual inhibitions. This lack of abandon does not seem to affect marital satisfaction. However, women, especially those over forty, experience an enhancement of their feelings of self-worth if they are engaged in abandon relationships, in part because the abandon contributes to their sense that they are sexual persons. Therapy, retreats, a sexually imaginative spouse, and a rejection of Biblical literalism explain in part sexual abandon. "Graceful" religious imagery more than doubles the rate of "abandonment." Since Catholics are somewhat less likely to be inhibited than Protestants, especially Fundamentalists, it is possible that in other countries there will be more abandon than in the United States.

A NATION OF INHIBITIONS?

By their own admission, married Americans are inhibited sexually. Almost half of them (46%) admit that they and their spouses never "abandon all their sexual inhibitions." Another sixth (17%) say that they rarely abandon inhibitions. A quarter say they do it sometimes, and only 7% say that do it "a lot." Thus, two-thirds rarely or never abandon their inhibitions, and only one-third do so at least sometimes.

There are no gender differences on this variable. Those under forty are more likely than those over forty to say they abandon their inhibitions at least sometimes (42% versus 33%). Those who have attended college are more likely to do so than those who have not (40% versus 32%). Catholics are more likely than Protestants (39% versus 34%). Those who hold to a literal interpretation of the Bible are less likely to do so than those who do not (26% versus 41%).

Some 16% of the variance on the sexual abandon measure can be accounted for by prolonged erotic play, mutual undressing, weekends at hotel or motel, purchase of erotic underwear, and sexual experimentation; in this instance, however, the variables ought to be thought of not as a cause of sexual abandon so much as a result of it.

Whether the persistence of sexual inhibitions after marriage for two-thirds of a population is a high or a low figure depends on what sort of a comparison is being made. Unfortunately, there are no data available either from the American past or from other countries on which to make comparative estimates. That Catholics, as compared to Fundamentalists, are more likely to say they often or sometimes abandon their inhibitions suggests that in Catholic or non-Fundamentalist Protestant countries the rates might be higher and that to some extent the level of inhibitions is a result of America's Puritan heritage.[58]

The inhibitions do not seem to stand in the way of happy marriages; nor does the absence of inhibitions seem to lead to happier marriages. There are no correlations between responses to the abandon question and the measures of marital satisfaction I have used in this study—marital fidelity, very happy, spouse is best friend, would marry the same spouse again, or falling-in-love phase of the marriage.

However, on other measures sexual abandon is not without some importance, especially for women. There is no difference between the "abandoned" men and other men in the proportion

---

[58] Half of the 28 Irish Catholics in the sample report the abandon of sexual inhibitions. The correlation of .06 is significant at the .07 level. Such a dubious correlation with a limited sample ought not to be taken too seriously. But it's fun! If we're abandoned, then what must be said of everyone else? Saints preserve us all!

saying that the spouse makes them feel important (67%) but there is a statistically significant difference for women: 70% versus 59%. This difference is especially strong for women over forty—79% versus 59%. Thus women over forty who are in sexually abandoned relationships are twenty percentage points more likely to say that their spouse makes them feel important. It may be that the attention a woman over forty receives from her husband in a situation of sexual abandon contributes powerfully to her feeling of worth, although it adds nothing to her basic satisfaction with the marriage.

Women are also more likely to disagree strongly that the fun eventually goes out of marriage if they are in abandon relationships (50% versus 39%), while there is no difference for men (44% and 44%). On this variable, however, there is not an extra effect of age.

Thus, sexual abandon seems to be considerably more important for women than for men, perhaps because the "recklessness" of such a relationship enhances their feeling of self-worth. Women are less likely than men to describe themselves as a "sexual person" (24% versus 32%) and also more likely to say that they sometimes avoid sex (39% versus 26%). However, if they are in relationships in which sexual abandon occurs, the differences between men and women vanish. Women become as likely as men to think of themselves as sexual persons and not to avoid sex.

The feeling that you are a sexual person correlates for women but not for men with the feeling that the spouse makes you feel important—66% of the men say the spouse makes them feel important regardless of their sense that they are a sexual person. But for women there is a twenty-percentage-point difference: 78% of those who think of themselves as a sexual person also say that the spouse makes them feel important, as opposed to 58% of those who do not think that they are sexual persons. It would appear that a woman's sense of herself as important to her spouse is closely related to her feeling that she is a sexual being. This relationship is especially strong among women over forty—88% of those who say that they are sexual persons also say that their husbands make them feel important, as opposed to 57% of those who do not think of themselves as sexual persons. Moreover, about a third of the correlation between abandon and the feeling of importance for women over forty can be accounted for by the enhancement of their feeling of themselves as sexual persons.

These findings may surprise many men, who would protest that while they enjoy sexual abandon, it does not seem so important to their wives, especially after a certain age has passed. Perhaps before the fact of an "abandoned" relationship, it does not seem so, but after the fact the sense of sexual abandon does indeed seem to enhance, on the average, a woman's feeling of self-worth.

Nor does the pattern reported in the previous paragraphs change when respondents over fifty are analyzed. Abandon and a feeling of importance are strongly correlated for women but not for men. So are a feeling of importance and a sense that one is a sexual person. Finally the sense that one is a sexual person explains some of the relationship between abandon and a feeling of importance.

This statistical sketch of the average impact of sexual abandon on a woman is hardly meant to be a simple recipe for enhancing the self-worth of women—especially one that will work overnight or after a weekend workshop. Yet it does point toward an important and intricate aspect of the relationship between husband and wife which requires further research.

MODELS OF ABANDON

A hint of the direction of the research can be found in the model I developed to account for the presence of sexual abandon in a marriage. I entered into a regression equation the erotic, religious, interpersonal, and demographic variables with which I had been working and told the computer to remove from the list of twenty-five predictors of abandon all that were not statistically significant.

A model including retreats together, therapy together, a spouse who is imaginative about sex, and sexual play counts for about one-seventh of the variance on the abandon measure.

However, the most powerful effect on the propensity to sexual abandon comes from religious imagery (Figure 18.1). Men at the

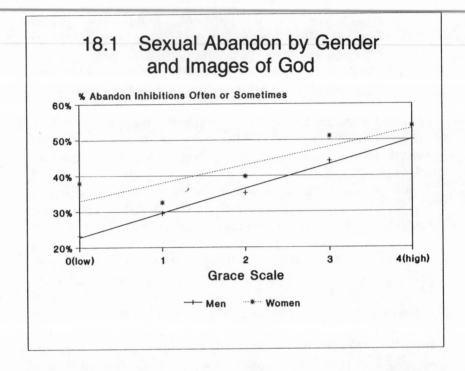

18.1 Sexual Abandon by Gender and Images of God

top of the "grace" scale (God is mother, spouse, lover, and friend) are more than twice as likely to say they abandon all their sexual inhibitions at least sometimes (50% versus 23%). For women, the increase is from 32% to 54%. In both cases the warmer and more tender the image of God, the less likely men and women are to be inhibited. If the images are very warm indeed, they have lost their inhibitions.

Abandon correlates with youth for women, but not for men. Except at the oldest age, women are more likely to report abandon (Figure 18.2).

Three out of five Americans lose their inhibitions and become abandoned on occasion under two sets of conditions. The first is that they are high on the "grace" scale and delight in the spouse, and the second is that they are high on the grace scale and think that the spouse is godlike (Figures 18.3 and 18.4). Indeed, even if they don't picture the spouse as godlike, half of them still give themselves over to abandon merely on the strength of their imagery (the far right bar in Figure 18.3).

Human intimacy and intimacy with the sacred again are closely related, in this instance to the point of erotic and religious

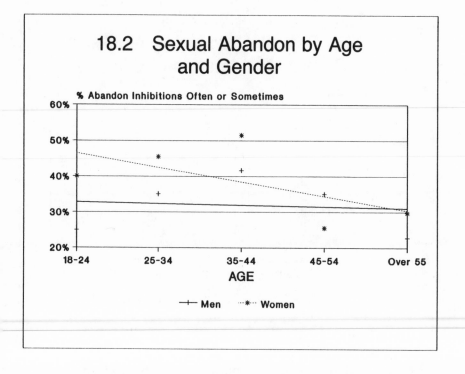

18.2 Sexual Abandon by Age and Gender

% Abandon Inhibitions Often or Sometimes

AGE

—+— Men   ···*··· Women

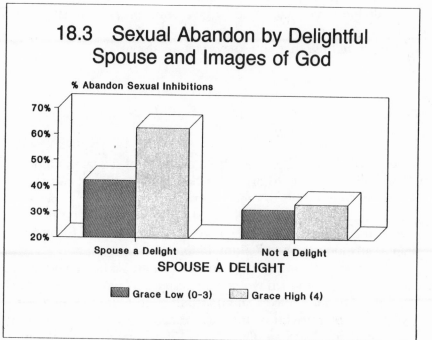

18.3 Sexual Abandon by Delightful Spouse and Images of God

% Abandon Sexual Inhibitions

SPOUSE A DELIGHT

Grace Low (0-3)   Grace High (4)

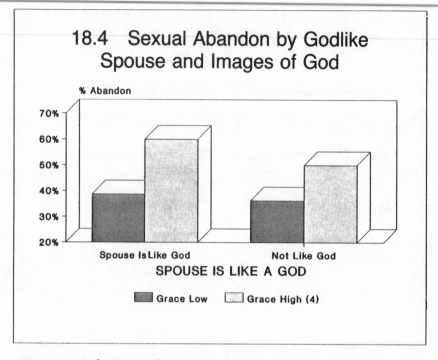

18.4 Sexual Abandon by Godlike Spouse and Images of God

ecstasy correlating with one another. If you have given yourself to a divine Lover, you tend to give yourself to a human love, and vice versa.

Go on, tell me that you knew *that* all along!

CONCLUSION

The payoff in sexual pleasure from abandon of sexual inhibitions is proved by the strong correlation between ecstatic sex and abandon. The proportion of men reporting ecstasy goes up twenty-eight percentage points (Figure 18.5) and the proportion of women goes up twenty-three percentage points from those who never abandon their sexual inhibitions.

Yet Americans apparently can do without sexual abandon in their marriages, though women and especially women over forty find that abandon makes an important contribution to their self-worth. A spouse who is imaginative about sex is crucial to the development of patterns of abandon. Erotic play is also important,

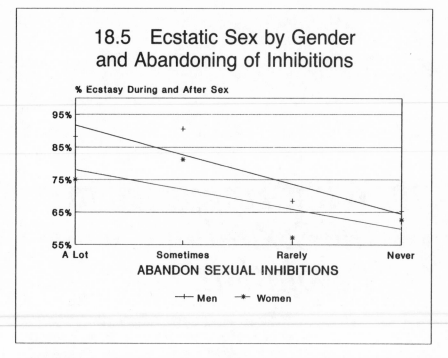

18.5 Ecstatic Sex by Gender and Abandoning of Inhibitions

% Ecstasy During and After Sex

95%

85%

75%

65%

55%

A Lot   Sometimes   Rarely   Never

ABANDON SEXUAL INHIBITIONS

—+— Men   —*— Women

especially for those over forty, perhaps more as a sign and reinforcement of abandon. Biblical literalism is a serious obstacle to
abandon, but its impact can be canceled out by either family
therapy or family retreats. The strongest predictors of abandon
are religious images, perhaps because if one abandons oneself to
God it is more easy to give up all inhibitions with one's spouse
—and/or vice versa.

Are Americans more sexually inhibited than others? To that
question we cannot give an answer. However, they are scarcely
a sybaritic people. If there has been a revolution in the sexual
relationships between husbands and wives, it still has a long way
to go to produce a population of married men and women who
are not seriously inhibited sexually.

Indeed, if one wants a sexual revolution in which abandon
replaces inhibition, perhaps the best way to achieve it is to modify
the experiences of the sacred which Americans have and thus
change the images of God which become paradigms for all intimacies in their lives.

For organized religion that should be an interesting challenge.

19. What Happened to the Sexual Revolution?

There was a contraceptive revolution in the last three decades and a divorce revolution, to use the title of Lenore Weitzman's book. There were also changes in premarital behavior, including an increase in both cohabitation and premarital sex (especially among women). There have been no changes in attitudes toward the morality of homosexuality, abortion, and pornography, though there seems to be more tolerance for these behaviors in practice. Opposition to extramarital sex has increased. Extramarital affairs still seem to be deviant behavior statistically. Marriage has endured and apparently flourishes. There have, therefore, been changes in sexual behavior and continuities. Whether revolution is the proper term for such a sober summary of what the data establish is probably a matter of personal taste.

This book will surely run up against a stone wall in the widespread conviction that a sexual revolution has occurred since the middle 1960s. Everyone knows there has been a sexual revolution, though more recently, some would say, there has been a "conservative backlash," especially because of the AIDS epidemic. If there has been a sexual revolution, why are so many people faithful to their spouses, and why does marriage seem such a stable and healthy institution?

The term *sexual revolution* is a metaphor; it compares sexual change in society to political change and asserts that the changes in sexual behavior are like the changes in political behavior when an old social order is discarded and a new one is instituted.

A metaphor is useful so long as it is understood to compare one reality to another in order to illumine the first reality. Juliet is like the sun, right? But not in all respects. She is a teenage woman, not a gaseous ball. Morals may change in some fashion the way a political regime changes, but morality and a political system are not quite the same. A metaphor describes reality vividly[59] and can be a useful device so long as it is not taken literally. Whether a metaphor is useful or not depends in part on how resistant it is to misunderstanding and distortion. A metaphor is supposed to shock, but if the shock also leads one to misinterpret what has happened, then it is something less than a useful metaphor.

If one means by the term *sexual revolution* that all traditional sexual morality has been jettisoned or that it is in the process of being jettisoned, then one has made an extravagant statement that sensible people will not take seriously. If one means that some old "taboos" have been dropped and that many others are in the process of being changed, while a few others are apparently more durable—which is what I think most people mean by the metaphor—then one has made a more moderate statement. The questions become what has changed and what has not changed, and what evidence there is to support assertions about change. Once these questions have been answered, the only issue that remains is whether the metaphor is justified by the facts—has there really been a change in sexual morality that can appropriately be called a revolution? Is it a reasonable metaphor (Juliet sheds light in darkness like the sun) or an extravagant metaphor (Juliet is like the Big Bang that launched the universe)?

The answer to such a question depends on literary tastes.

A similar metaphor in which some religious leaders have delighted during the last quarter century is "the contraceptive mentality." It implies the same sort of transformation of morals—a

[59] In Richard Wilbur's words, "Odd that a thing is most itself when likened."

collapse of all moral restraint in those people who use contraceptives.

Both metaphors involve a common assumption—that there is an integrated moral system and that if men and women reject one component of the system they will soon reject all the other components.

Doubtless moral precepts as presented in catechisms and textbooks and philosophical treatises do fit together in neat and logically coherent order. However, the logic is either derived from or imposed on the data of human experience. People discovered morality before there were ethicians. St. Thomas Aquinas, the great Catholic philosopher and theologian of the thirteenth century, realized this; he insisted that third-level natural law principles were empirical: they were to be discovered from studying the behavior of the *gens*, the "peoples." In more modern rhetoric, Aquinas was calling for anthropological research.

People may read the textbooks and listen to the catechists and even plow through Aristotle or Plato or Rawls or Nozick, but their own moral instincts are not necessarily so logical or systematic. Some "rules" may be obeyed because of fear and social pressure; others because of religious convictions that transcend mere ethics; still others because of aesthetic impulses that are difficult to articulate; and others because, quite apart from concerns of formal ethics, humans think that the proscribed behavior is wrong.

An improvement in techniques of contraception may well make it much safer to engage in premarital sex, which has never been an unpopular behavior. It does not follow, however, that all young women will become promiscuous or even that they will engage in premarital sex "with affection" but without any hope or intent of marriage. Some will and some won't. It does not follow either that later in life even those young women who have had many sexual partners before marriage will also have many or even one extramarital sexual partner. To suggest that the one follows from the other—as both our metaphors do—is to think that, because of an increase in premarital sex, the marriage bond has become less important to human beings than it used to be. Whether it has or not is an empirical question, not an a priori deduction.

It may be that the same change in contraceptive technology which has made sex safer for women before marriage will also make it easier for men and women to terminate unsatisfactory marriages. Again, it is an empirical question rather than a logical conclusion: will they also be equally prepared to violate the fidelity bonds of marriages which actually exist? One cannot conclude from changes in one form of morality that other forms of morality have also changed—rather, one must demonstrate that the changes in the other forms have actually occurred.

This discussion of "ethical systems" and ethical instincts is necessary to make explicit the assumptions which seem to support the use of the two metaphors as an assertion that sexual morality has totally changed in America.

In sober fact, some things have changed, and others have not and indeed show no sign of changing—a phenomenon which, despite the heroic oversimplifications of the mass media, pretty much typifies the human condition.

There clearly has been a dramatic change in contraceptive techniques and a willingness to accept the implications of these changes. In 1959, 73% of Americans thought that birth control information should be available to anyone who wanted it.[60] By 1975, the proportion had risen to 90%, where it remains. Note, however, that even thirty years ago almost three-quarters of the population approved of the distribution of birth control information. In 1974, 78% agreed that birth control information should be made available to teenagers; in 1983, that proportion had risen to 86%.

In 1943, 68% of Americans favored sex education in public schools. Thirty years later the proportion had risen to 79%. Now it is 85%. But even a half-century ago, two out of every three Americans favored sex education in the schools.

The General Social Survey has monitored attitudes toward premarital and extramarital sex and homosexuality since 1972. At the beginning of the period, 26% thought that premarital sex was not wrong at all. In 1988 that had risen to 40%—the change happening in the first ten years and the rate being essentially constant since then. At the beginning of the seventies, 35% thought that premarital sex was always wrong. Ten years later that rate had fallen to 28%, and there has been little shift since then. The intermediate positions "almost always wrong" and "sometimes wrong" have accounted for about a third of the re-

[60]The percentages in this and subsequent paragraphs are from Smith (1989).

spondents since the beginning of the GSS. As the divorce rates leveled off in the early eighties, so too, it seems, did attitudes toward premarital sex—perhaps for the same reasons. In Robert Michael's imagery, the impact of the Pill (and the resulting decline in the fear of pregnancy) worked its way through the system, especially in its effect on the behavior of women.

At the same time as the GSS was recording the changes in attitudes on premarital sex, it recorded a change in the opposite direction in attitudes toward extramarital sex. In 1970 and 1987 there was only a change of one percentage point in the proportion of Americans who thought "sexual relations with someone other than the marriage partner" were always wrong—and that upward, from 72% to 73%. In 1988 the rejection rate jumped to 78%. When the proportion saying that infidelity was "always wrong" and the proportion saying it was "almost always wrong" were combined, the total in 1972 was 86%. It was 85% in 1982. Since 1984 it has risen steadily until now those that say extramarital sex is always or almost always wrong is 91%—a reflection perhaps of the publicity about the AIDS epidemic. At the beginning of the period, only 2% of Americans thought it was never wrong, a proportion which is exactly the same in the most recent GSS.

The behaviors reported in this book, it hardly need be said, reflect rather precisely the mores described by Americans in eighteen years of surveys.

Nor have the attitudes of Americans on "sexual relations between two adults of the same sex" changed in the last two decades: 70% thought homosexuality was always wrong in 1973; 74% thought it was always wrong in 1988. Combining "always" wrong and "almost always wrong," the percentage was 76% in 1973 and 78% in 1988. There was a dip to 75% in the early eighties, but that was reversed in 1985, again perhaps because of the publicity about the AIDS epidemic. The proportion thinking it is never wrong was 11% in the early seventies, 14% in the middle eighties, and 12% today.

There have been some changes in other measures of attitudes toward homosexuality. In 1977, 43% of Americans thought that "homosexual relations between consenting adults should be legal." In the middle 1980s, this proportion fell to 33% and in 1989 rose to 47%, where it had been in the early eighties before the

AIDS scare began. The only decisive change in recent years is in response to the question of whether "you think homosexuals should or should not have equal rights in terms of job opportunities." In 1977 56% of Americans thought they should. In 1989 this had risen to 71%.[61]

Thus the Gay Rights movement, for all its media success and all the apparent changes in attitudes toward homosexuality, has not changed public attitudes on the wrongness of homosexual behavior, although support for equal job rights has increased. Even among those in their twenties, 78% of the respondents in the middle 1980s thought that homosexual acts were always or almost always wrong.

Smith (1989, p.189) summarizes the changes and nonchanges in attitudes toward abortion:

> Attitudes towards abortion are only somewhat related to contraceptive morality and even more remotely to sexual morality. From the start of polling on this issue in 1962 until 1974–75 approval of legalized abortions under various circumstances rose appreciably. . . . [S]upport then settled on a plateau for almost a decade. Since then approval has drifted downward but still remains well above the levels of the 1960's.

Nor have Americans grown more tolerant of pornography, although pornography is more available. In 1970, 56% of the population thought that pornography led to a breakdown of morals. In 1988 that had increased to 62%. In 1970, 49% thought that pornography led to rape. In 1988 that had risen to 56%.

Perhaps definitions of pornography have changed. Perhaps *Playboy* would not be thought pornographic anymore by many respondents. Yet the objections to pornography are as stern as ever. This is not what happens when sexual morals are undergoing a transformation all around us.

Clearly three changes have occurred:

---

[61] This paragraph is based on tabulations published in the *Gallup Report*, No. 289, October 1989.

1. Divorce rates have gone up, as Robert Michael has demonstrated, because women can control their fertility with the Pill and their economic destiny with opportunities in the job market.

2. Premarital experimentation has increased among women, again perhaps because of the Pill; however, this experimentation has hardly made young women promiscuous. More than half of the married women under thirty have had only one sexual partner in their lives.

3. Premarital cohabitation as a preparation for marriage has doubled, and disapproval of premarital sex as always wrong has diminished from 40% to 26%.

Moreover, there is a prevalence of romantic eroticism among those under forty that does not exist among those over forty. On balance it seems likely that this does represent a social change, a greater relaxation about sexual play which in turn may be linked to a greater tolerance of sexual diversity than existed in the past.

Americans may think that homosexuality is always wrong but they normally don't arrest gays or call them sodomites anymore. They may disapprove of pornography but husbands and wives may watch X-rated videos together—although 62% never do (44% of those under thirty-five). Forty-five percent of married Americans under thirty-five may have swum in the nude together at least occasionally, but only 5% say they have abandoned their sexual inhibitions a lot, and 37% say they never abandon such inhibitions.[62] A society in which a majority of married couples say they abandon their sexual inhibitions only rarely is not a society, it seems to me, for which the "sexual revolution" metaphor is all that useful.

One could argue that the birth control pill is responsible for all three changes, that the technology of contraception is the key variable in changing sexual behavior, that the changes in mores which have occurred are the result of the Pill, that a new technology has modified the culture by permitting men and women a little more freedom to do what they wanted to do all along and that this change has increased relaxation about sexual matters somewhat—but not a hell of a lot!

Moreover, while there has been a change in contraceptive mo-

---

[62] May the celibate cleric be forgiven for saying that he considers such a fact to be a shame?

rality, the "contraceptive mentality" has not led to a breakdown in marital fidelity, not even a hint of a breakdown.

Earlier I argued that a change in some components of sexual ethics did not necessarily mean a change in other components. The center of the book demonstrates that marital fidelity is high in the United States, so high that it seems most unlikely that there has been a change. I have returned to the themes of uneven change and continuity rather than change after the fact to emphasize that the findings of the present work can be integrated into a relatively uncomplicated view of human nature and human society and that they are not refuted by appeals to the "Sexual Revolution."

Practical sexual morality is not a ball of wax.

20. Winners and Losers

With some exceptions men are the winners.
With some exceptions women are the losers.
So what else is new?

Women have indeed come a long way, though not perhaps as long a way as some may think. Many women have paid a high price for their own progress or in some cases for the progress of others from which they have not benefited. The single mother of three teenagers who is unable to collect child support and must work two jobs to pay the bills might be forgiven for thinking that she is not better off than her married older sister who sits on a country veranda every afternoon sipping martinis.

The changes of the past three decades which were detailed in the last chapter have been hell for some women, purgatory for other women, and heaven for yet other women and for many men.

On balance, men seem to be the winners, as always, and women the losers.

As I mentioned earlier, I became concerned about the impact

of social change on women when I began to follow up the Glenn and Weaver (1988) report on the declining morale of women. I will now summarize that research briefly, because it is pertinent for the conclusions of this book.

In the years between the middle seventies (GSS 1972 to 1977) and the middle eighties (GSS 1982 to 1987), the proportion of men saying they were very happy declined from 32% to 30%. Among women the decline was from 36% to 32%. The former change is not statistically significant; the latter is.

Some of the decrease in the happiness of women was due to the increasing number of divorced or separated women who have not remarried. Only one-third of ever divorced or separated women have remarried, as opposed to one-half of the married men. In the eighties one-sixth (17%) of all American women were divorced and not remarried, as opposed to 12% of all American men. Their "happiness" was much lower than that of presently married women—only 18% say that they are "very happy," less than half of the proportion of married women who give such a response. (The remarried are as "happy" as the never separated or divorced, whether they be men or women.) However, only one percentage point of the decline of happiness in American women can be accounted for by the increase of divorce. The rest remains unexplained.

My guiding hypothesis as I explored these data was that pressures from the change in women's role in society might account both for the apparent drop in "happiness" among women and for the apparent drop in "happiness" among married women. The conflicts created for husband and for wife in the great historical watershed of changing role definitions might well explain the apparently increased frustrations in marriage. In addition to the "happy" variable in the GSS, four other measures are pertinent to our exploration: SATFAM, HAPMAR, SATJOB, and SATFIN. The wording of the questions is as follows:

"How much satisfaction do you get from your family life, a very great deal, a great deal, quite a bit, a fair amount, some, a little, none?"

"Taking all things together, how would you describe your marriage? Would you say that your marriage is very happy, pretty happy, or not too happy?"

"On the whole, how satisfied are you with the work you do, would you say that you are very satisfied, moderately satisfied, a little dissatisfied, or very dissatisfied?"

"So far as you and your family are concerned, would you say that you are pretty well satisfied with your present financial situation, more or less satisfied, or not satisfied at all?"

Between the seventies and the eighties there is no statistically significant change in the proportion of men or women who say that they receive a "very great deal" of satisfaction from their family life (SATFAM). On the other hand, there is a six-percentage-point drop for men in the proportion saying that they are "very happy" (HAPMAR) in their marriage (from 70% to 64%) and a four-percentage-point decline for women (from 66% to 62%). On this latter measure, unlike the measure for personal happiness, the decline is stronger for men than for women. Both changes are statistically significant.

The decline in job satisfaction (SATJOB) for both men and women, incidentally, is purely a phenomenon of age composition. As both men and women get older they become more satisfied with their jobs, in great part because there is a drop in anxiety about their financial situation (SATFIN).

As the first step in trying to unravel the complexities of the relationship between marriage and happiness, I asked if the drop in happiness among married women was related to whether they worked. Among the two groups of wives—working and nonworking—there was no difference in "happiness" in the 1970s. But in the 1980s the "happiness" of working women dropped five percentage points to 38%, still three percentage points higher than working married men, while there was no significant change in the morale of married women who do not work. They thus become the "happiest" people in America (on the country club veranda or wherever). I had located more precisely the problem of the declining morale of married women— it had occurred among married women who work. To pursue my exploration further I had to learn whether the decline was evenly distributed in the population or whether it was located in certain specific age cohorts.

The solution to the decline of happiness for married men is

easier to explain: it is entirely a function of the age composition of the population. Younger men are less satisfied with their family life, their income, and their jobs than older men. As they grow older and their jobs and income improve, they become more satisfied with family life and "happier" personally. There is no change in either the correlation or the explanation from the seventies to the eighties.

When I turned back to the more complex question of the decline of happiness among women, I observed that the only statistically significant drop in "happiness" among American women (whether married or not) takes place in the cohort born during the 1950s—the so-called Baby Boom cohort. The subsequent cohort (born in the 1960s) has the same low level of happiness (28%) in their twenties which their predecessors have in their thirties. Two questions must be asked, both involving comparisons with the crucial 1950s cohort:

1. Why have they changed in the last decade? Or to put it more concretely: How do they differ from the 1940s cohort, which occupied their age position in the population a decade ago?

2. Why is the 1960s cohort even less "happy" now than the 1950s cohort was a decade ago when the latter occupied the same age position in the population?

So I compared the fifties cohort today with the forties cohort ten years ago and the fifties cohort ten years ago with the sixties cohort today, to determine whether "pressure" and the fact of not being married might account for the differences in psychological well-being among the three cohorts.[63] "Pressure" is defined as an unwillingness to say that one's health is "excellent" and an unwillingness to express satisfaction with one's financial situation. (Fifty-two percent of the 1950s cohort score high on both these measures as opposed to 47% of the 1940s cohort.)

Using a regression model to account for the eight-percentage-points difference in "happiness" between the fifties generation

---

[63] In the 1940s cohort, 22% of the women were not married in their thirty-year-old age period (10% never married, 12% divorced or separated and not remarried); in the 1950s cohort at the same age period, 40% were not married (21% never married and 19% divorced or separated and not remarried).

today and the forties generation a decade ago—eras when both groups were in their thirties—I discovered that three percentage points of the difference are attributable to the fact that even when they are in the thirty-year-old age range, women born in the 1950s are less likely to be married than were women born in the 1940s at the same age level. Two more percentage points are explained by the "pressure" variable.

So marriage rate and "pressure" reduce to two points and statistical insignificance the difference between the two cohorts at the same state in their respective life cycles. The younger cohort is less likely to be "happy," because it is less likely to be married and more likely to be worried about health and finances.

The same model also reduces to statistical insignificance the six-percentage-point difference between two cohorts in their twenty-year-old age period—the sixties cohort today and the fifties cohort ten years ago.[64] The youngest age group's morale is lower than its predecessor at the same age because it is less likely to be married and because it is more likely to experience "pressure" as measured by concern over health and finances.

Having located the morale crisis of women among a certain group of the population (working women) and among certain cohorts (those born since 1950), I now asked where the drop is the sharpest. The answer was clear: among married women. Again, it is the two cohorts of wives born since 1950 where the problem exists. Among older groups there has been no change in the last decade. Is the conflict between home and work, reported so widely in the popular press, experienced most acutely by women today in their twenties and thirties, the cause of the apparent decline in morale?

This conflict would be, one might expect, especially powerful for women who are trying to combine occupational career and motherhood. The decline of "happiness" among mothers in their thirties today as opposed to mothers of the same age ten years ago is located most notably in those working mothers who report high "pressure." Those working mothers whose pressure level is "low" experience no such drop.

Who are the people, then, whose "happiness" has declined

---

[64] Fifty-two percent of the 1950s cohort was married during their twenties, as opposed to 37% of the sixties cohort during the same age period.

sharply in the last ten years? Women, and more especially women who work, and more especially still women who work who were born in the 1950s, and yet more especially working mothers who were born in the 1950s, and most especially of all working mothers who were born in the 1950s who report high pressure, that is, who report worries about health and finances.

That young women in their thirties who are balancing family and work are under great pressure is no secret to them or to those who know them. But the question is why they should be under more pressure today than their immediate predecessors—women born during the 1940s. One might speculate that the answer is that part of the revolution in the roles of women is a heightened expectation for what a woman must be—an expectation in herself at any rate if in no one else.

There are not yet enough young working mothers in the 1960s cohort to replicate this analysis for them, but, given the similarity in the models accounting for the drop in "happiness" among all women in this age group (as compared to their immediate predecessors), such an explanation seems very likely.

The decline in happiness for women does not seem to be a function of a drop in either job satisfaction or in occupational prestige, either absolute or relative to that of men. Indeed, at both points in time, working wives have the highest job satisfaction in the population.

Is the "happiness" problem, then, for women in their thirties and their twenties today, not the result of dissatisfaction with either their marriage or their jobs, but the pressure from two contrasting sets of demands, both of which they like? To improve my confidence about an answer to this question I looked at the pattern of their response to the HAPMAR item.

First of all, among women the only decrease reported in marital happiness is among those born before 1920 and those born in the 1950s. However, in the relative comparison that is critical—the 1940s and the 1950s cohorts when they both were in their twenty-year-old age period—there is no significant difference: approximately three-fifths say that they are very happy in their marriage. Moreover, it would appear that women in their twenties both now and ten years ago are some ten percentage points more likely to say that they are "very happy" in their marriage, thus indicating that there is a "natural" (i.e., age-related) decline to the average happiness of marriage for women from about 70% when they are in their twenties to about 60% when they are in their thirties.

The apparent drop in HAPMAR for women seems to be an age phenomenon rather than a cohort or time phenomenon. Taking age into account, women are as likely to say that they are very happy in their marriage today as they were ten years ago. There does not, then, seem to be grounds for a positive response to the Glenn-Weaver question of whether marriage as such is providing less payoff for women now than it did a decade ago. Women born since 1950 like both their jobs and their marriages and families as much as they ever did (age factors being taken into account) and as much as older women do. Their decline in "happiness" seems to be the result of the cross pressures of trying to do both tasks well, perhaps because of their own high expectations for performance, with which their mothers and their older sisters were not burdened.

The problem of increased pressure on younger working mothers and the resultant drop in their "happiness" is real enough, even if much of the pressure might come from their own expectations. But it does not result from a decline in marriage fulfillment, or in family satisfaction, or in job satisfaction.

I also discovered a paradoxical fact about married men: a real change in marital happiness has occurred not in women but in men. While there has been no change (once age is taken into account) in the proportion of men who say they are very happy personally, the proportion who say that they are very happy in their marriage has declined for all men born since 1930, significantly for those born since 1940. One is tempted to suspect that such a drop would occur among men who are committed to the old models of the proper role for women and who are therefore offended by the confusions and uncertainties generated by the new role definitions. If one were a feminist one might be inclined to say that such chauvinist men perhaps deserved to have the happiness which came from their patriarchal position diminished.

In fact, however, just the opposite seems to be the case. There is no statistically significant drop among either those born before 1940 or those born after 1940 in reported marital happiness among men who think that women should take care of the home and leave the running of the country to men. The decline, in both cohort groups, occurs among those who reject such a quintessentially chauvinist position. The men who are likely to be sympathetic to the changing of roles for women are the ones who suffer the drop in marital happiness.

However, these "pro-feminist" men, whose marital happiness has diminished, perhaps as they strive to adjust themselves to a reality supported by their convictions and perhaps even by the quality of the relationship they have with their wives, are still *more* likely than their more chauvinist counterparts to report that they are "very happy" in their marriage. One must wonder if it was precisely their greater satisfaction in marriage which caused them to be open about change, even if the change created more problems for their relationship.

In summary, a model which suggests that the gyrations of the various happiness measures during the last decade are a result of changing role expectations seems to fit the data much better than a model of a global decline in marriage. HAPMAR has declined among men who are sympathetic to feminist goals, but men's scores on "happy" have not changed, once age is taken into account. Women's HAPMAR scores have not declined once life cycle is considered, but their "happiness" has diminished—only, however, among women born since 1950 who are working mothers and find themselves caught in financial and health pressures (real or imagined or both). Finally, even working mothers are slightly more "happy" than are working men.

Three different observations might be offered about the decline in morale of working mothers born since 1950:

1. Such a drop results merely from their being more aware of the pressures which men feel routinely. They are not at any rate less "happy" than their male counterparts.

2. If a drop in morale is a necessary price to be paid as part of women's search for equality, then such a decline may be unfortunate, but no social change comes without cost.

3. Working mothers born before 1950 are as "happy" as mothers who do not work. They seem to have learned how to balance the two roles without experiencing the conflicts suffered by their daughters and younger sisters. Indeed, those born in the 1940s managed to work out this balance when they were in their thirties and their children were still young (and, on the average, the families were larger). Their de facto and pragmatic reach for equality seems to have been more successful (in terms of "happiness," at any rate) than the more fervent and ideologically based search for equality of the younger generation.

None of these speculations excludes any of the others.

There were two other conclusions that I drew from the women's morale project:

1. The delay in marriage and the increase in the number of women not married has had a negative effect on the overall "happiness" of younger women.

2. The increase in divorce and the lower rates of women's remarriage have also depressed the morale of women, as Lenore Weitzman's (1987) study of "gender-free" divorce has led me to expect.

Whatever the balances worked out by younger working mothers might be, they are still better off on the average in terms of "happiness" than their sisters who have not married or who are separated or divorced and not remarried.

With this analysis of the pressures on married women and the negative impact of divorce in mind, consider the impact on women of other changes in the sexual morality. In GSS 85 cohabitation correlated negatively with marital happiness for only one group: women under forty. Moreover, in GSS 85, among couples who were cohabiting, the personal happiness of the men was the same as that for married men, while the personal happiness of women was the same as for unmarried women—cohabiting men, in other words, were almost twice as likely to say they were "very happy" as cohabiting women.

The enhanced sexual freedom which enables young women to engage in more premarital experimentation does not seem to be as rewarding as one might have thought. Women under thirty-five have experimented more sexually and also have more regrets about such experimentation. Of the women over thirty-five, 30% regret premarital sexual encounters, as do 51% of those under thirty-five. The proportions of those who "strongly regret" their premarital sex are 12% for those over thirty-five and 20% for those under thirty-five. (Eighteen percent of men regret premarital sex, but there is no correlation with age and regret for men.)

Finally, it has been suggested by Diana Russell (1986) in her research on rape and incest that stepfather incest has increased in recent years because there are more single mothers available to be preyed upon by men who in fact desire their teenage daughters. If the results of the "Sexual Revolution" are more premarital sex for women, more divorce, more stepfather incest, and more cohabitation, the first does not seem to have improved the happiness of women and the second and the third have had clear negative consequences for them.

A long way, huh?

It must be noted, however, that while divorced women, especially if they are single mothers, are not particularly happy, they might have been more unhappy if they had remained in their marriages.

Nonetheless, to the extent that there has been a sexual revolution, men seem to be the beneficiaries:[65] women are more available for premarital sex, cohabitation is in some ways for men but not for women a satisfactory alternative to marriage, easy divorce has enabled men to leave behind family responsibilities and pursue other women with substantially fewer costs than their wives must pay, and the increase in single mothers has made their daughters more available for stepfather incest. Women, on the other hand, are more likely to be left as impoverished single mothers, to find cohabitation unsatisfactory, and to regret premarital sex. Undoubtedly, the "new" sexual and social freedom for women has been fulfilling for many women. Other women, however, must suffer loneliness, unhappiness, poverty, and guilt as a result of this "new" freedom. Perhaps they deserve more attention than they are receiving.

Do I want to turn back the clock?

I suppose I could reply that, no, I just want to report the facts. If one suggests that there are serious side effects to a social change, one cannot be legitimately charged with wanting to undo the change, save by ideological nitwits who do not want to see the dark underside of progress. It would be dishonest, irresponsible, and cowardly not to list the problems, especially since I have been

---

[65] Save for the "feminist" men described above.

influenced in my reflections on these matters by women (and feminist) scholars like Russell and Weitzman. [66]

So, no, I don't think it possible to undo the changes that have given women more control over their fertility and their lives, and even if I thought it were possible, I would not think it desirable. Rather, I want to argue that the change in the role of women, as desirable and as admirable as it may be, has been carried out with remarkable cruelty to many women—one might also say with harsh, masculine insensitivity. I contend that there is already too much masculine insensitivity in the world and we need no more of it from women who battle quite properly for the rights of women but who show (or have shown until recently) precious little sensitivity for the plight of the many women who are clear losers in the social change occurring.

Society must be restructured to protect women from the men who use the changes as a pretext and an occasion to exploit women.

It also must be restructured so that career and motherhood are not set in opposition to one another—the most inhuman of all the unnecessary dilemmas imposed on contemporary women.

You say that the dilemma is necessary?

I reply that it seems necessary only as long as men and childless women are the ones organizing society.

The two changes I proposed above are the kind of structural modifications of society for which the metaphor *revolution* would certainly not be extravagant.

For starters, what about getting the proportion of married men who help with household tasks above 50% for others besides the ones who are above the halfway mark now—the men who are falling in love with their wives!

---

[66]To those who say that only women have the right to talk about the negative effects on many women of the changes of the last three decades, I am tempted to respond scatologically.

21. Can Marriage Survive?

Yes.

While I was working on this book, *Doonesbury* presented the story of conflict between Michael and J.J. about their love life. Michael wanted to make love with her. She said that it would not be right to do so because the trend was for men and women of their age and social class to be so tired of love-making that they only engaged in it to conceive children and they didn't want a child just then, did they?

(In passing I must note that some conservative Catholic theologians would agree with her argument, as a doctrinal position, however, and not as a trend.)

Michael protested that this was nonsense.

It was not, Joanie replied hotly, it was a *published trend*.

Michael jumped out of bed and strode off to the kitchen. "I want some oat bran," he announced.

The "published trends" in human intimacy, so worshiped by

the J.J.'s of the world, have as much substance as the oat bran fad.

Yet woe to him who questions the trend.

The outcry against this report, when its preliminary results were announced, was fearsome, in great part because it was seen as denying a trend. For those who, like J.J., see the world only in trends or countertrends, in the Hegelian dialectic of the evening news or the Koppel report, the only reality would be a trend of declining marriage and then a trend of resurgent marriage. Indeed some of those who attacked this study (without reading it even in its preliminary form, of course) nervously reassured their readers that there was no promarriage trend. If married people were happier than they used to be, it was argued, the reason was that divorce was so much easier. Marriage was not back in fashion.

Some of the anger arose in defense of the paradigms with which many people respond to the confusion of the world around them. To attack the paradigm of the "declining family" was to threaten the world of such people with intellectual chaos. Some of the anger also resulted from the fact that if marriage was back in fashion, then their own decisions against it in one form or another were threatened. One can only stand by one's personal decisions, you see, if there is a conviction that these decisions represent the wave of the future.

Instead of divorcing, the *Newsweek* article that began my research in this subject proclaimed, couples are working hard at keeping their unions intact. They are taking marriage more seriously. "Despite the fact that the institution of marriage has been battered and bruised by the greater social acceptance of divorce and the easing of old legal barriers as well as the increase in cohabitation in the last twenty years, Americans haven't given up on it."

The article quotes Andrew Cherlin, a sociologist at Johns Hopkins: "'I don't think people think marriage is more fun than it used to be or somehow a more ideal form. . . . But the alternatives to marriage look less promising.'"

To explain this "change," the article cites AIDS and that mysterious force so loved by feature writers who don't know what they're talking about—"demographics." People are getting older on the average, therefore they are more likely to settle down.

Most of this is total nonsense—save for Professor Cherlin's very wise comment that the alternatives to marriage look less promising than marriage. On sober reflection, the alternatives usually do look worse, especially for women and especially for women who have children.

The picture of Americans changing their minds about marriage and divorce is not only a fiction. It is false.

What does it mean to say that a "social institution" has been battered? Does it mean anything at all, other than that more people are getting divorced? Most of them eventually remarry. Most of those who have not married will eventually marry. Cohabitation for most people is a preparation for marriage. Battered?

Does the so-called battering of a so-called social institution mean that those who remain married are less happy than they were twenty years ago or than their parents were forty years ago? Does it mean that because divorce is easier they are more likely to consider it seriously? The data suggest that the marital happiness of married women, net of age, has not declined at all, and of married men only slightly. Is divorce a serious option in most of the persisting marriages? The answer is that only 2% of the sample think that it is very likely and only 4% more think it is somewhat likely. One could say that the institution was battered not on the evidence of an increased divorce rate but only on evidence that divorce is a strong possibility for those who are still married. Yet three-quarters of them say that divorce is not at all likely (the rest say that it is not too likely).

Some battered institution!

Was there ever any evidence even in the 1970s—the "me decade"—that most Americans had given up on marriage? Was there any evidence that they were working less hard on their marriages then than they had twenty years before, or than they are now? Or is Robert Michael's model of an increase in divorce because of a technological change working through the system a much more probable explanation of what has happened than a fantastical cycle of more effort, less effort, and then more effort?

Are you, gentle and general (and arguably generous) reader, working harder at your marriage now than older friends you know did twenty years ago when they were the age you are now—those friends who did not in fact divorce? Only when we have evidence from a probability sample about such changes can we be certain that effort has really increased after a decline. Is it not more likely from what we know about human nature and the human condition that most people work at their marriages, some rather less than would be appropriate, some very hard indeed, and some (maybe most) just hard enough to keep the relationship going at a satisfactory equilibrium of happiness?

Did anyone seriously think that marriage was about to vanish from the American scene? Did anyone really believe that the "battered social institution" was about to become obsolete?

Some ideological enthusiasts, infuriated (justly enough) at the abuses of family life, were convinced that marriage "as we know it" was waning. Or at least they hoped that it was. Or at least that "traditional marriage" was in decline, whatever that meant. In fact, the history of marriage shows that it has always been a flexible relationship and that its shapes and forms have constantly changed through the years. The changes create new problems and new opportunities. The only conclusion to which one can come about future change on the basis of past change is that marriage will continue to change and that it will continue.

The monogamy rates found in British research raises the question of whether, if the *Love and Marriage* study is replicated elsewhere, similar findings about the condition of marriage will be discovered in other countries.[67]

Don't bet against it.

I trust that the reader is aware by now that this book is not reporting on a trend. It is, rather, trying to establish a benchmark against which future trends might be measured. I am not saying that there is a "trend" in favor of marriage. I am merely questioning the assertion that it is "battered" and that it is about to be replaced by something else.

Is marriage in America in a good condition or a bad condition? If the reader does not feel that he/she can find evidence for both sides in this report, then I have failed to convey the complexity of the data. Four out of five respondents would marry the same person; three out of four say that their spouse is their best friend; two out of three that their marriage is very happy; one out of three that they achieve a "very great deal" of satisfaction from their sexual life; one out of seven that they are "falling in love" with their spouse, a proportion which does not vary with age.

---

[67] A study in Ireland is currently under consideration. "What about the fidelity rates?" I asked an Irish scholar. "Ah," he said with the characteristic West-of-Ireland sigh which to the uninitiate sounds like the beginning of an acute attack of asthma. "Sure, wouldn't it be difficult for them to be much higher than in the States?"

Indeed, how do you beat 90% by much?

The working-mother phenomenon has increased strain on the working mother herself but has not on the average, as she sees it, affected her happiness in her marriage, her sexual fulfillment, or her relationship with her children. Many men and women over sixty are able to sustain an active and fulfilling sexual life, especially if they are able to continue romantic playfulness from earlier years. Women benefit especially as the years go on from such romantic play, which enhances their self-image. Most Americans paint glowing portraits of their spouses. Only one out of ten spouses has been unfaithful.

Between a fifth and a quarter of married Americans have been able to combine religious symbols and activity with sexual intimacy to achieve an intensely satisfying physical relationship.

In pondering these findings, one might well ask whether there has ever been an age in human history where there has been so high a level of marital satisfaction.

The answer is that, in the absence of previous benchmark data, we cannot be sure.

On the other side of the picture, however, a third of the respondents said that their marriage was once in serious jeopardy. A quarter do not rule out the possibility of divorce. Half admit that they are in the somewhat dull and unexciting "settling down" phase of their relationship. For perhaps a third, sexual life seems rather routine, and for another third, especially those who have grown weary with age, it is almost nonexistent. A third of American spouses are troubled by shame. A quarter say that they often avoid sex. For half, erotic play is almost nonexistent. Among the younger there is a restlessness and a willingness to cheat on the spouse (especially among those who have cohabited or have engaged in frequent premarital sex) that suggests tension and suffering in their future.

On the other hand, most of those who were in the "bottoming out" phase of marriage two or five years ago have managed to pull out of that phase and begin again. Three out of five who considered divorce in the past are now reconciled. Physical sex correlates with marital happiness, especially in crisis times, and helps husband and wife see light at the end of the tunnel of their frustration and unhappiness.

What does one make of such a mixed picture?

What one wants to make of it, I suppose. I can only say that at the end of this research I am pleasantly surprised at how much resilience and vitality there is in American marriage. Moreover I am surprised at the power and the demands of the bond between man and woman, surely the most complex, interesting, frustrating, and pleasurable relationship about which our species has yet learned.

Does this mean I am "in favor" of marriage?

To be in favor of marriage is like being in favor of the Rocky Mountains or the Pacific Ocean. All three of them are there, and none of them are likely to disappear.

The marriage bond is powerful. Is it a result of biology, culture, or social pressures? Most likely a combination of all three. When the social pressures diminish somewhat, as they have in the last three decades, the remaining social pressures and the first two energies sustain it. Most men and women want to be married, most men and women are much more likely to be happy when they are married (women more happy than when they cohabit, if not men), most men and women are reasonably satisfied with their marriages, most men and women honor the fidelity bond, and most do not want their marriages to end.

It does not follow that there are not injustices and oppressions in marriage or that all married people are ecstatic in their happiness or even that many if not most marriages could be much happier than they are. The contention here is rather the same as that expressed by Professor Cherlin: in its long history the species has not come up with any permanently appealing alternatives.

Certainly single parenthood (which usually means single and impoverished motherhood) has never been a satisfactory state, and in its recently rediscovered forms appears thoroughly unsatisfactory—though perhaps it is a more acceptable alternative to many women than the continuation of the particular marriage they were in.

The marriage bond between a man and a woman is more than a legal contract, though it may begin with a contract and involve the continuation of a contract through the life together. It is a union of minds and bodies, not union in the romantic or ideal sense, but rather as that which occurs in the hard reality of everyday life. A man and woman come together to share life and contract a union which at times seems to be more powerful than the consent that either of them has brought to it. The bond can be broken, though not as easily as it is entered, but it has, as the data in this study show, remarkable durability. Even if our respondents are exaggerating the health of their marriages, such exaggeration shows how powerfully they feel the constraint to have a healthy marriage.

All this is supposed to end because of new insights that the species acquired for the first time in 1968?

You gotta be kidding!

Yet in fact the skepticism with which this report will surely be greeted in some places and by some people is in great part based on the assumption that our generation has discovered truths that the species never knew before and that will make momentous changes in human relationships undreamed of in ages past.

Don't hold your breath.

Go to a wedding and to a wake—on the same day if you can—and witness the love at both termini of a marriage. See if you really expect marriage to vanish from the earth or to change so that it will no longer be a compelling and compulsive binding together of man and woman.

What is the nature of the bond—often called love—that holds a man and woman together and which for most men and women even in our post-everything age is an insurmountable barrier to infidelity?

To try to sort out how much of it is biological and how much of it is cultural is to try, as the angel told Augustine, to empty the sea into a hole in the sand.[68] Obviously, the marriage bond as we know it in the concrete and not in legal (civil or canonical) abstractions is an intricate combination of both. Even if it were possible, as some ideologues seem to think, to strip away all the cultural accretions and begin completely *de novo* with a man and a woman free of all the cultural constraints built up through the ages, would not a new cultural process begin to protect the union which the community and the individuals found so important at the beginning of the species and which they would almost certainly find important again?[69]

Some sociobiologists (for example, Wilson 1978) tell us that the ideal reproductive strategy for a male primate is to spread his seed into as many wombs as possible. Since they would have

---

[68] Not quite as inexplicable as the Trinity perhaps, but still unfathomable.

[69] There are debates about the effects of the attempts in the Israeli kibbutz to drastically restructure marriage—surely the most dramatic of which we know. On balance the literature on that subject, as I read it, suggests that there has been a steady development of a reestablishment of the traditional familial patterns.

more surviving descendants because of their widespread reproductive activity, evolution would select for genes which would continue such males.

A minute of serious observation and reflection would tell us that there is more happening. Most men do not and have not pursued such a strategy. It is not even clear that those who do would have all that many descendants, save in highly controlled situations such as the harem of the King Ibn Saud. More is required to bring a human fetus to maturity and its own reproductive life than merely planting seed in a fertile womb.

One wonders why the sociobiologists didn't think of that.

There is therefore a powerful propensity in the human condition to marriage and fidelity, a propensity that is resistible and has been resisted more by some than by others and more in some times and places than in others, but one that survives and flourishes in contemporary America fundamentally unaffected by recent changes in contraceptive technology.

It will not do to dismiss this propensity as nothing more than the injustice and oppression of the patriarchal legal structure (though there is often injustice and oppression and patriarchy in the way the propensity has been and is exercised). Nor will it do to say that marriage is so flawed that it must be eliminated completely and a new beginning attempted.

There is no evidence that men and women are prepared to do that. The data reported in this book strongly support the notion that, to quote Professor Cherlin again, there are no more promising alternatives.

What might one conclude from the present analysis about the condition of marriage in America today? If one accepts as an assumption the idea that an increase in divorce proves only that divorce is easier for legal and contraceptive reasons, then one cannot use an increasing divorce rate (which leveled off half a decade ago in any event) as an index of marital satisfaction, but must rather collect data from time to time on the satisfaction expressed by those who are actually married.

The present study is an establishment of criteria against which future measurements might be made. Only time can tell whether the rates of responses to the questions in the survey will go up or go down or remain stable. Surely it would he difficult for the fidelity rate to go much higher. But short of waiting for future surveys, what do I think about the portrait of American marriage painted by the respondents of the *Love and Marriage* study?

Well, to revert to Celtic indirection, couldn't the picture have been a lot worse and myself not surprised at all, at all?

Or might one ask whether, all things considered, it is unlikely that satisfaction rates have ever been as high in the whole of human history?

Well, wouldn't at the moment God be the only one who would know that, and Herself not saying?

But if She were, She might say that (*a*) yes, and (*b*) there's lots of room for improvement.

There is especially room perhaps, the celibate murmurs softly, for more romance and more abandon (a secure murmur, since he does not have to engage in either). Perhaps an increase in both will not improve the fundamental quality of American marriage. Certainly such an increase could hardly push the fidelity and monogamy rates higher.

But more romance and more abandon surely would not hurt.

Not at all, at all, at all.

References

Anzia, Joan M., and Mary G. Durkin. 1980. *Marital Intimacy*. Kansas City: Andrews and McNeil.

British Market Research Bureau Limited. 1987. *AIDS Advertising Campaign: Report on Four Surveys During the First Year of Advertising, 1986–87*. London: Her Majesty's Stationery Office.

Cherlin, Andrew J. 1981. *Marriage, Divorce, and Remarriage*. Cambridge, Mass.: Harvard University Press.

Davis, James Allan, and Tom W. Smith. 1972–1989. *General Social Survey* (machine-readable data file). Chicago: National Opinion Research Center. Distributed by The Roper Center for Public Opinion Research, University of Connecticut. Storrs, Ct. —1 data file (24,893 records) and 1 codebook (861 pp).

Demos, John. 1970. *A Little Commonwealth: Life in the Plymouth Colony*. New York: Oxford University Press.

Glenn, Norval, and N. Weaver. 1988. "The Changing Relationship of Marital Status." *Journal of Marriage and the Family*. 50: 317–324.

Greeley, Andrew. 1980. *The Young Catholic Family: Religious Images and Marriage Fulfillment*. Chicago: Thomas More Press.

Greeley, Andrew. 1989a. "The Declining Morale of Women." *Sociology and Social Research*. 73:53–58.

Greeley, Andrew. 1989b. "Protestant and Catholic—Is the Analogical Imagination Extinct?" *American Sociological Review* 54:485–502.

Greeley, Andrew. 1990. *The Catholic Myth*. New York: Scribner.

Greeley, Andrew, and Sean T. Durkin. 1990. "Dealing Rationally with the Irrational: Religion and Rational Choice." Seminar Presentation. National Opinion Research Center, Chicago.

Greeley, Andrew, Robert T. Michael, and Tom W. Smith. 1990. "A Most Monogamous People: Americans and Their Sexual Partners." *Society* 27 (July-August 1990):36–42

Hite, Shere. 1977, 1976. *The Hite Report: A Nationwide Study of Female Sexuality*. New York: Dell Publishing.

Hite, Shere. 1981. *The Hite Report on Male Sexuality*. New York: Knopf.

Hite, Shere. 1987. *The Hite Report: Women and Love: A Cultural Revolution in Progress*. New York: Knopf.

Hout, Michael, and Andrew Greeley. 1987. "The Center Does Not Hold: Church Attendance in the United States 1940–1984." *American Sociological Review*. 52:325–343

Klassen, Albert D., Colin J. Williams, and Eugene Levitt. 1989. *Sex and Morality in the United States*. Edited and with an introduction by Hubert J. O'Gorman. Middletown, CT: Wesleyan University Press.

Laslett, Peter. 1971. *The World We Have Lost*. London: Menthuen.

Laslett, Peter, ed. 1972. *Household and Family in Times Past*. New York: Oxford University Press.

Michael, Robert T. 1988. "Why Did the U.S. Divorce Rate Double Within a Decade?" *Research in Population Economics*. 6: 367–399.

Russell, Diana E.H. 1986. *The Secret Trauma: Incest in the Lives of Girls and Women*. New York: Basic Books.

Russell, Diana E.H. 1982. *Rape in Marriage*. New York: Macmillan.

Russell, Diana E.H. 1984. *Sexual Exploitation: Rape, Child Sexual*

Abuse, and Workplace Harrassment. Beverly Hills, Calif.: Sage Publications.

Shorter, Edward. 1975. *The Making of the Modern Family.* New York: Basic Books.

Smith, Tom W. 1988. "A Methodological Review of the Sexual Behavior Questions on the 1988 GSS." *GSS Methodological Report No. 58.* Chicago: National Opinion Research Center.

Smith, Tom W. 1989. "Sexual and Reproductive Morality." In *Trends in Public Opinion: A Compendium of Survey Data,* edited by Richard G. Niemi, John Mueller, and Tom W. Smith. New York: Greenwood Press.

Smith, Tom W. "Adult Sexual Behavior in 1989: Number of Partners, Frequency and Risk." Paper presented to the American Association for the Advancement of Science, New Orleans, February 1990.

Toffler, Alvin. 1971. *Future Shock.* New York: Bantam Books.

Tracy, David. 1982. *The Analogical Imagination.* New York: Seabury.

Weitzman, Lenore J. 1987. *The Divorce Revolution.* New York: Free Press.

Westoff, Leslie Aldridge, and Charles F. Westoff. 1967. *From Now to Zero: Fertility, Contraception and Abortion in America.* Boston: Little, Brown.

Willis, R.J., and Robert T. Michael. 1988. "Innovation in Family Formation: Evidence on Cohabitation in the U.S." Mimeographed paper. Chicago: National Opinion Research Center.

Wilson, Edward. 1978. *On Human Nature.* Cambridge, Mass.: Harvard University Press

Wrigley, E.A. 1969. *Population and History.* New York: McGraw-Hill.

Appendix

PSYCHOLOGY TODAY POLL
LOVE & MARRIAGE I

SEX: 1[ ] Male   2[ ] Female   INTERVIEWER'S NAME: _____

TIME STARTED: _____   INTERVIEWER'S I.D.: _____

TIME FINISHED: _____   PAGE NUMBER: _____

LENGTH: _____   REPLICATE NUMBER: _____

                                     DATE: _____

GO   89339   November 17–24, 1989

INTRODUCTION: Hello, I am _____ calling from the Gallup Organization. I'd like to ask a few questions of a married male, 18 years of age or older, who is now at home. (IF NO MARRIED MALE, ASK: May I please speak with a married female, 18 years of age or older, who is now at home?)

[IF MORE THAN ONE MARRIED MALE, TAKE THE YOUNGEST]
[IF MORE THAN ONE MARRIED FEMALE, TAKE THE OLDEST]

INTRODUCTION: We are conducting this survey with *Psychology Today* magazine and University of Chicago researchers studying family life and religion. The purpose of the survey is to learn more about attitudes of married couples toward marrige and what makes a marriage successful. Some of the questions often ask your judgment of marriage based on your own marital experience. And these questions often deal with your own personal thought and behavior. You are a totally anonymous respondent. All answers are confidential and will be used in combination with the answers of hundreds of other married individuals.

1.   Are you currently married?

   1   Yes, married male
   2   Yes, married female
   3   Not married—   TERMINATE INTERVIEW—Thank respondent, but tell them we are doing a survey of married people.

2.   How many years have you been married?

_____   _____   00   LESS THAN SIX MONTHS

3.   Is this your first marriage? [IF NO, ASK:] Is this marriage your second, third or more?

   1   Yes, first
   2   No, second
   3   No, third or more
   0   DON'T KNOW

4.   Taken all together, how would you say things are these days—would you say that you are very happy, pretty happy, or not too happy?

1 Very happy
2 Pretty happy
3 Not too happy
4 NO ANSWER
0 DON'T KNOW

5. Taking things all together, how would you describe your marriage—would you say that your marriage is very happy, pretty happy, or not too happy?

1 Very happy
2 Pretty happy
3 Not too happy
4 NO ANSWER
0 DON'T KNOW

6. Many people think that marriages go through cycles—over and over again. If the cycles are falling in love, settling down, bottoming out, and beginning again, where would you put your marriage at the present time?

1 Falling in love
2 Settling down
3 Bottoming out
4 Beginning again
0 DON'T KNOW

7. Please tell me, how often you do each of the following with your spouse—a lot, sometimes, rarely, never? [READ]

		A lot	Sometimes	Rarely	Never	Don't Know
a.	Try very hard to make your marriage better	1	2	3	4	0
b.	Go out dancing	1	2	3	4	0
c.	Go to a hotel or motel to spend time alone with each other	1	2	3	4	0
d.	Work out or play sports together	1	2	3	4	0

		A lot	Sometimes	Rarely	Never	Don't Know
e.	Talk privately and intimately	1	2	3	4	0
f.	Pray together	1	2	3	4	0
g.	Listen to music you both enjoy	1	2	3	4	0
h.	Go to parties together	1	2	3	4	0
i.	Read the same books and magazines	1	2	3	4	0
j.	Try to keep your love life romantic	1	2	3	4	0
k.	Try to improve your sex life together	1	2	3	4	0
l.	Take showers or baths together	1	2	3	4	0
m.	Give each other back rubs or massages	1	2	3	4	0

8. For each of the following statements, please tell me how well each describes your spouse. Please tell me if it strongly applies, applies somewhat, or does not apply. Would you say your spouse . . . (INSERT ITEM) [READ]

		Strongly Applies	Applies Somewhat	Does not Apply	Don't Know
a.	Is exciting	1	2	3	0
b.	Is your best friend	1	2	3	0
c.	Is good with children	1	2	3	0
d.	Is overweight	1	2	3	0

		Strongly Applies	Applies Somewhat	Does Not Apply	Don't Know
e.	Is dull	1	2	3	0
f.	Shares responsibility for household tasks	1	2	3	0
g.	Does not understand your work	1	2	3	0
h.	Does not understand your emotional needs	1	2	3	0
i.	Is physically attractive	1	2	3	0
j.	Makes you feel important	1	2	3	0
k.	Is kind and gentle	1	2	3	0
l.	Is less religious than you	1	2	3	0
m.	Has bad breath or body odor	1	2	3	0

9. For each of the following statements, please tell me if it applies to your marriage or not. Please tell me if it strongly applies, applies somewhat, or does not apply. First would you say you and your spouse . . . (INSERT ITEM)

		Strongly Applies	Applies Somewhat	Does not Apply	Don't Know
a.	Discuss your marriage with each other openly	1	2	3	0
b.	Discuss sex with each other openly	1	2	3	0
c.	Tend to like and dislike the same things	1	2	3	0

		Strongly Applies	Applies Somewhat	Does Not Apply	Don't Know
d.	Are very playful when alone together in private	1	2	3	0
e.	Generally agree on how children should be raised	1	2	3	0

10. For each of the following statements, please tell me if it applies to you or not. Please tell me if it strongly applies, applies somewhat, or does not apply. First . . . (INSERT ITEM)

		Strongly Applies	Applies Somewhat	Does not Apply	Don't Know
a.	If I had it to do all over again, I would marry the same person	1	2	3	0
b.	I wish I were a more confident lover than I am	1	2	3	0
c.	The fear of AIDS makes me more inclined to be faithful to my spouse	1	2	3	0

11. For each of the following statements about marriage, please tell me if you agree or disagree with each. Would you say you strongly agree, agree somewhat, disagree somewhat, or strongly disagree that . . . (INSERT ITEM)

		Strongly Agree	Agree Somewhat	Disagree Somewhat	Strongly Disagree	Don't Know
a.	As the years go on, much of the fun goes out of a marriage	1	2	3	4	0

		Strongly Agree	Agree Somewhat	Disagree Somewhat	Strongly Disagree	Don't Know
b.	Women work harder than men at making a marriage last	1	2	3	4	0
c.	Sex is very important in holding marriages together	1	2	3	4	0
d.	Children take the fun out of a marriage	1	2	3	4	0
e.	Most married couples are faithful to each other	1	2	3	4	0
f.	Fidelity is essential to a happy marriage	1	2	3	4	0

12. People react differently in certain circumstances. I am going to read you a list of actions a husband and wife might take if one of them were having an affair. For each action, please tell me whether or not this would apply to you and your spouse. [READ]

		Yes Applies	Does not Apply	Don't Know
a.	If my spouse had an affair with another person, I would want to know	1	2	0

	Yes Applies	Does not Apply	Don't Know
b. If I could be absolutely sure that my spouse would not find out, I would have an affair with another person	1	2	0
c. If I had an affair with another person, I would tell my spouse	1	2	0

I'd like to ask you a few questions for statistical purposes only.

13. What is your age?

    1   1
    2   2
    3   3
    4   4
    5   5
    6   6
    7   7
    8   8
    9   9
         0

14. What is the last grade or class that you completed in school? (DO NOT READ)

    1   None, or grade 1–4
    2   Grades 5, 6, or 7
    3   Grade 8
    4   High school incomplete (grades 9–11)
    5   High school graduate, grade 12
    6   Technical, trade, or business *after* high school
    7   College/university incomplete
    8   College/university graduate or more
    0   DON'T KNOW/NO ANSWER

15. What is your religious preference—Protestant, Roman Catholic, Jewish, Mormon, or an Orthodox Church such as the Greek or Russian Orthodox Church?

1 Protestant (includes Baptists, Christian Church, Episcopal, Jehovah's Witnesses, Lutheran, Methodist, Presbyterian, etc.)
2 Roman Catholic
3 Jewish
4 Orthodox Church
5 Mormon (includes the Church of Jesus Christ of Latter Day Saints)
6 Moslem
7 Hindu
8 Other
9 None
0 UNDESIGNATED

16. What is the religious preference of your spouse—Protestant, Roman Catholic, Jewish, Mormon, or an Orthodox Church such as the Greek or Russian Orthodox Church?

1 Protestant (includes Baptists, Christian Church, Episcopal, Jehovah's Witnesses, Lutheran, Methodist, Presbyterian, etc.)
2 Roman Catholic
3 Jewish
4 Orthodox Church
5 Mormon (includes the Church of Jesus Christ of Latter Day Saints)
6 Moslem
7 Hindu
8 Other
9 None
0 UNDESIGNATED

17. About how often do you pray? [READ]

1 Several times a day
2 Once a day
3 Several times a week
4 Once a week
5 Less than once a week
6 Never
7 NOT APPLICABLE (VOLUNTEERED)
8 NO ANSWER
0 DON'T KNOW

18. How often do you attend religious service? [READ]

    1 Never
    2 Less than once a year
    3 About once or twice a year
    4 Several times a year
    5 About once a month
    6 Two to three times a month
    7 Nearly every week
    8 Every week
    9 Several times a week
    0 DON'T KNOW/NO ANSWER

19. Which of the following statements comes closest to describing your feelings about the Bible? [READ]

    1 The Bible is the actual word of God and is to be taken literally, word for word
    2 The Bible is the inspired word of God but not everything in it should be taken literally, word for word
    3 The Bible is an ancient book of fables, legends, history, and moral precepts recorded by men
    0 DON'T KNOW

20. From what ethnic group or groups are you mainly descended? [DO NOT READ] [ACCEPT MULTIPLE RESPONSES]

    1 British (English, Scottish, Welsh)
    2 German
    3 Italian
    4 Polish or other Eastern European country
    5 Hispanic
    6 Irish
    7 Black
    8 Asian
    9 Other
    0 DON'T KNOW/NO ANSWER

21. About how much time each week, if any, do you spend exercising? Please don't include the time you spend getting ready to exercise or showering and changing afterward: just the actual workout time. [INTERVIEWER: ROUND THE ANSWER TO NEAREST HALF HOUR]

1 Doesn't exercise
2 ½ hour or less
3 1 hour
4 1½ hours
5 2 hours
6 2½ hours
7 3–3½ hours
8 4–4½ hours
9 5–5½ hours
0 6–6½ hours
X DON'T KNOW

22. NO QUESTION

23. NO QUESTION

24. Do your friends tell you you're attractive?

1 Yes
2 No
0 DON'T KNOW

25. Is your total annual household *income* before taxes $20,000 or more or is it less than $20,000?

1 $20,000 or more
2 Less than $20,000 —SKIP TO QUESTION **28**
0 DON'T KNOW/REFUSED —SKIP TO QUESTION **28**

26. Is it $30,000 or more, or less than $30,000?

1 $30,000 or more
2 Less than $30,000
0 DON'T KNOW/REFUSED ⎤—SKIP TO QUESTION **30**

27. Is it $50,000 or more, or less than $50,000?

1 $50,000 or more
2 Less than $50,000
0 DON'T KNOW/REFUSED ⎤—SKIP TO QUESTION **30**

28. Is it $15,000 or more, or less than $15,000?

1 $15,000 or more—SKIP TO QUESTION **30**
2 Less than $15,000
0 DON'T KNOW/REFUSED—SKIP TO QUESTION **30**

29. Is it $10,000 or more, or less than $10,000?

    1 $10,000 or more
    2 Less than $10,000
    0 DON'T KNOW/REFUSED

30. What is your race? Are you white, black, or some other?

    1 White
    2 Black
    3 Other
    0 DON'T KNOW

31. Finally, I would like to ask you some rather personal questions. Some of these questions are very sensitive. If there are any you'd rather not respond to, please say so. First, for each of the following statements, please tell me how well each describes you—very well, pretty well, not too well, or not at all?

		Very Well	Pretty Well	Not Too Well	Not at all	Don't Know
a.	Moral about sex	1	2	3	4	0
b.	Skillful lover	1	2	3	4	0
c.	A sexual person	1	2	3	4	0
d.	Avoiding sex	1	2	3	4	0

32. For each of the following statements, please tell me if you agree or disagree with each. Would you say you strongly agree, agree somewhat, disagree somewhat, or strongly disagree that . . . (INSERT ITEM)

		Strongly Agree	Agree Somewhat	Disagree Somewhat	Strongly Disagree	Don't Know
a.	The sexual revolution has affected other people a lot more than your spouse and you	1	2	3	4	0

		Strongly Agree	Agree Somewhat	Disagree Somewhat	Strongly Disagree	Don't Know
b.	Your spouse and you are more concerned with being faithful than most people	1	2	3	4	0

33. For each of the following statements, please tell me how well each describes your spouse. Please tell me if it strongly applies, applies somewhat, or does not apply. Would you say your spouse . . . (INSERT ITEM—READ)

		Strongly Applies	Applies Somewhat	Does Not Apply	Don't Know
a.	Is mysterious and intriguing	1	2	3	0
b.	Is romantic	1	2	3	0
c.	Respects your opinion	1	2	3	0
d.	Is sometimes like a god to you	1	2	3	0
e.	Does not understand your physical needs	1	2	3	0
f.	Cares more about (his/her) work than about you	1	2	3	0
g.	Cannot be trusted	1	2	3	0
h.	Has bad manners	1	2	3	0
i.	Is a skillful lover	1	2	3	0
j.	Is imaginative about sex	1	2	3	0

34. Did you and your (husband/wife) live together before you got married?

1 Yes
2 No
3 NO ANSWER
0 DON'T KNOW

35. Was there a period of time, before marriage, when you had a sexual relationship with someone of the opposite sex? [IF YES:] Did you have sexual relations fairly often, occasionally, or rarely (maybe once or twice)?

1 Fairly often
2 Occasionally
3 Rarely (maybe once or twice)
4 No, never
0 REFUSED $\left.\right\}$ SKIP TO QUESTION 37

36. Do you now feel strong regret, only some regret, or no regret at all about having this sexual relationship before being married?

1 Strong regret
2 Only some regret
3 No regret at all
4 NO ANSWER
0 DON'T KNOW

37. During the past year, how many sexual partners have you had?

_____ _____   99 REFUSED

38. During your present marriage, how many partners have you had?

_____ _____   99 REFUSED

39. How many partners have you had in your life?

_____ _____   99 REFUSED

40. We're just about to the end of the survey. Many couples are interested in trying new ideas. Please tell me how often you do each of the following with your spouse. Some of these questions are very sensitive. If there are any you'd rather not respond to, please say so. Would you say you and your

(husband/wife) do each of the following a lot, sometimes, rarely, or never . . . [READ]

		A lot	Sometimes	Rarely	Never	Refused
a.	Go to religious retreats together	1	2	3	4	0
b.	Go to marriage therapy	1	2	3	4	0
c.	Abandon all your sexual inhibitions	1	2	3	4	0
d.	Swim nude together	1	2	3	4	0
e.	Watch X-rated videos	1	2	3	4	0
f.	Buy erotic underclothes	1	2	3	4	0
g.	Make love outdoors	1	2	3	4	0
h.	Arouse each other	1	2	3	4	0
i.	Help your spouse climax before or after you do	1	2	3	4	0

41. CHECK RESPONDENT'S SEX:

    1 Male
    2 Female

42. CHECK THE DAY OF WEEK INTERVIEW WAS COMPLETED:

    1 Mon   2 Tues   3 Wed   4 Thurs   5 Fri   6 Sat   7 Sun

43. CIRCLE NUMBER OF CALL ON WHICH THIS INTERVIEW WAS COMPLETED:

    1   2   3   4

PLEASE RECORD AND VERIFY PHONE NUMBER:

| | | | – | | | | – | | | | |

AREA CODE   EXCHANGE   NUMBER

END OF INTERVIEW: THANK RESPONDENT: Thank you very much for your time. Have a nice day/evening.

I HEREBY ATTEST THAT THIS IS A TRUE AND HONEST INTERVIEW.

_____   _____

(INTERVIEWER'S SIGNATURE)   (DATE)

P S Y C H O L O G Y   T O D A Y   P O L L
L O V E   &   M A R R I A G E   II

SEX: 1[   ] Male   2[   ] Female   INTERVIEWER'S NAME: _____

TIME STARTED: _____   INTERVIEWER'S I.D.: _____

TIME FINISHED: _____   PAGE NUMBER: _____

LENGTH: _____   REPLICATE NUMBER: _____

ZEGLARSKI   DATE: _____

N = 650

GO   925049   March 1990

INTRODUCTION: Hello, I am _____ calling from the Gallup Organization. I'd like to ask a few questions of a married male, 18 years of age or older, who is now at home. (IF NO MARRIED MALE, ASK: May I please speak with a married female, 18 years of age or older, who is now at home?)

[IF MORE THAN ONE MARRIED MALE, TAKE THE YOUNGEST]
[IF MORE THAN ONE MARRIED FEMALE, TAKE THE OLDEST]

INTRODUCTION: We are conducting this survey with *Psychology Today* magazine and University of Arizona researchers studying family life and religion. The purpose of the survey is to learn more about attitudes of married couples toward marriage. Some of the questions often ask your judgment of marriage based on your own marital experience. And these questions often deal with your own personal thought and behavior. You are a totally anonymous respondent. All answers are confidential and will be used only in combination with the answers of hundreds of others married individuals.

1.   Are you currently married?

    1   Yes, married male
    2   Yes, married female
    3   Not married—TERMINATE INTERVIEW—Thank respondent, but tell them we are doing a survey of married people.

2.   How many years have you been married?

    _____ _____   00   LESS THAN SIX MONTHS
                                  99   REFUSED

3.   Is this your first marriage? [IF NO, ASK:] Is this marriage your second, third or more?

    1   Yes, first
    2   No, second
    3   No, third or more
    0   DON'T KNOW

4.   Taken all together, how would you say things are these days—would you say that you are very happy, pretty happy, or not too happy?

    1   Very happy
    2   Pretty happy
    3   Not too happy
    4   NO ANSWER
    0   DON'T KNOW

5.   Taking things all together, how would you describe your marriage—would you say that your marriage is very happy, pretty happy, or not too happy?

1 Very happy
2 Pretty happy
3 Not too happy
4 NO ANSWER
0 DON'T KNOW

6. Many people think that marriages go through cycles—over and over again. If the cycles are falling in love, settling down, bottoming out, and beginning again, [READ]

	Falling in Love	Settling Down	Bottom- ing Out	Beginning Again	Don't Know	N/A
a. Where would you put your marriage at the present time?	1	2	3	4	0	5
b. Where in the cycle would you say you were two years ago?	1	2	3	4	0	5
c. Where were you five years ago?	1	2	3	4	0	5
d. Where do you expect to be five years from now?	1	2	3	4	0	5

7. How likely do you think it is that your present marriage might end in divorce? Would you say this is . . . [READ]

1 Very likely
2 Somewhat likely
3 Not too likely
4 Not at all likely
0 DON'T KNOW

8. During the course of your marriage, did you ever think about leaving your husband/wife?

1 Yes
2 No
0 DON'T KNOW

9. As far as you know, did your husband/wife ever think about leaving you?

   1 Yes
   2 No
   0 DON'T KNOW

10. [IF YES TO EITHER 8 OR 9 ASK QUESTION 10, OTHERS SKIP TO QUESTION 11] How close did your marriage come to breaking up? Did you actually separate for a while, did you talk about separating, did you just think about separating, or didn't you ever consider separating?

    1 Actually separated
    2 Talked about separating
    3 Thought about separating
    4 Did not even consider separating
    0 DON'T KNOW

11. How much satisfaction do you get out of your family life— a very great deal, a great deal, quite a bit, a fair amount, some, a little, none?

    1 Very great deal
    2 A great deal
    3 Quite a bit
    4 Fair amount
    5 Some
    6 Little
    7 None
    0 DON'T KNOW

11a. How many children have you ever had? (including any you had from a previous marriage)

    _____ _____ 99 REFUSED
                              00 NONE—SKIP TO QUESTION 13

11b. How many are living at home now?

    _____ _____ 99 REFUSED
                              00 NONE

12. Compared to other families, would you say that your re-

lationship with your children is about average, better than average, or worse than average?

1   About average
2   Better than average
3   Worse than average
0   DON'T KNOW

13.   How would you rate your marriage in the following aspects of your relationship: very good, somewhat good, not too good, or not good at all? [READ]

		Very Good	Somewhat Good	Not Too Good	Not Good At All	Don't Know
a.	Confidence in the stability of the marriage	1	2	3	4	0
b.	Agreement on financial issues	1	2	3	4	0
c.	Ability to disagree with each other without threatening the relationship	1	2	3	4	0
d.	Sexual fulfillment	1	2	3	4	0
e.	Agreement on basic values	1	2	3	4	0
f.	Quantity and quality of lovemaking	1	2	3	4	0
g.	Agreement on religious issues	1	2	3	4	0

14.   How much satisfaction do you get out of your sexual relationship—a very great deal, a great deal, quite a bit, a fair amount, some, a little, none?

1   Very great deal
2   A great deal

3 Quite a bit
4 Fair amount
5 Some
6 Little
7 None
0 DON'T KNOW

15. Please tell me, how often you do each of the following with your spouse—a lot, sometimes, rarely, never?

		A lot	Sometimes	Rarely	Never	Don't Know
a.	Try very hard to make your marriage better	1	2	3	4	0
b.	Talk together without interruption	1	2	3	4	0
c.	Go out dancing	1	2	3	4	0
d.	Sleep in separate bedrooms	1	2	3	4	0
e.	Go to a hotel or motel to spend time alone with each other	1	2	3	4	0
f.	Pray together	1	2	3	4	0
g.	Are totally absorbed in one another	1	2	3	4	0
h.	Undress one another	1	2	3	4	0
i.	Go to parties together	1	2	3	4	0
j.	Take showers or baths together	1	2	3	4	0

		A lot	Sometimes	Rarely	Never	Don't Know
k.	Agree on how children should be raised	1	2	3	4	0
l.	Experiment with new ways of making love	1	2	3	4	0
m.	Fight with one another physically	1	2	3	4	0

16. For each of the following statements, please tell me how well each describes your spouse. Please tell me if it strongly applies, applies somewhat, or does not apply. Would you say your spouse . . . (INSERT ITEM—READ)

		Strongly Applies	Applies Somewhat	Does Not Apply	Don't Know
a.	Is exciting	1	2	3	0
b.	Is your best friend	1	2	3	0
c.	Is good with children	1	2	3	0
d.	Is dull	1	2	3	0
e.	Shares responsibility for household tasks	1	2	3	0
f.	Is physically attractive	1	2	3	0
g.	Makes you feel important	1	2	3	0
h.	Is kind and gentle	1	2	3	0
i.	Is moody	1	2	3	0
j.	Is a sharp dresser	1	2	3	0

		Strongly Applies	Applies Somewhat	Does Not Apply	Don't Know
k.	Is not to be trusted	1	2	3	0
l.	Treats you as an equal	1	2	3	0
m.	Is not responsive sexually	1	2	3	0
n.	Is secretive	1	2	3	0

17. Now, if we could ask your spouse these questions about you, how do you think she/he would respond? Please tell me if it strongly applies, applies somewhat, or does not apply. Would your spouse say you . . . (INSERT ITEM—READ)

		Strongly Applies	Applies Somewhat	Does Not Apply	Don't Know
a.	Are exciting	1	2	3	0
b.	Are his/her best friend	1	2	3	0
c.	Are good with children	1	2	3	0
d.	Are dull	1	2	3	0
e.	Share responsibility for household tasks	1	2	3	0
f.	Are physically attractive	1	2	3	0
g.	Make your spouse feel important	1	2	3	0
h.	Are kind and gentle	1	2	3	0
i.	Are moody	1	2	3	0

		Strongly Applies	Applies Somewhat	Does Not Apply	Don't Know
j.	Are a sharp dresser	1	2	3	0
k.	Are not to be trusted	1	2	3	0
l.	Treat your spouse as an equal	1	2	3	0
m.	Are not responsive sexually	1	2	3	0
n.	Are secretive	1	2	3	0

18. For each of the following statements, please tell me if it applies to you or not. Please tell me if it strongly applies, applies somewhat, or does not apply. First . . . (INSERT ITEM)

		Strongly Applies	Applies Somewhat	Does Not Apply	Don't Know
a.	If I had it to do all over again, I would marry the same person	1	2	3	0
b.	My friends tell me I'm attractive	1	2	3	0
c.	Sometimes I have fantasies about making love with someone besides my spouse	1	2	3	0
d.	Occasionally I flirt with others	1	2	3	0
e.	I am able to fight constructively with my spouse	1	2	3	0
f.	I wish there was more variety in our lovemaking	1	2	3	0

		Strongly Applies	Applies Somewhat	Does Not Apply	Don't Know
g.	If I could be absolutely sure that my spouse would not find out, I would have an affair with another person	1	2	3	0
h.	Sometimes I am ashamed to be naked in the presence of my spouse	1	2	3	0
i.	I tend to be shy with members of the opposite sex	1	2	3	0
j.	Sometimes sex embarrasses me	1	2	3	0

19. For each of the following statements about marriage, please tell me if you agree or disagree with each. Would you say you strongly agree, agree somewhat, disagree somewhat, or strongly disagree that . . . (INSERT ITEM)

		Strongly Agree	Agree Somewhat	Disagree Somewhat	Strongly Disagree	Don't Know
a.	As the years go on, much of the fun goes out of a marriage	1	2	3	4	0
b.	Most marriages are not as happy as our marriage is	1	2	3	4	0

		Strongly Agree	Agree Somewhat	Disagree Somewhat	Strongly Disagree	Don't Know
c.	Children take the fun out of a marriage	1	2	3	4	0
d.	Most married couples are faithful to each other	1	2	3	4	0
e.	Fidelity is essential to a happy marriage	1	2	3	4	0
f.	Sexual love is essential in healing the strains and tensions of life together	1	2	3	4	0

I'd like to ask you a few questions for statistical purposes only.

20.   What is your age?

```
1    1
2    2
3    3
4    4
5    5
6    6
7    7
8    8
9    9
0    0
```

21.   What is the last grade or class that you completed in school (DO NOT READ)

1   None, or grade 1–4
2   Grades 5, 6, or 7

3　Grade 8
4　High school incomplete (grades 9–11)
5　High school graduate, grade 12
6　Technical, trade, or business *after* high school
7　College/university incomplete
8　College/university graduate or more
0　DON'T KNOW/NO ANSWER

22.　Are you employed full-time, employed part-time, or are you *not* employed for pay outside of the home?

1　Full-time
2　Part-time
3　Not employed
0　DON'T KNOW

23.　Is your (husband/wife) now employed full-time, part-time, or is he/she *not* employed for pay outside of the home?

1　Full-time
2　Part-time
3　Not employed
0　NO ANSWER

24.　What is your religious preference—Protestant, Roman Catholic, Jewish, Mormon, or an Orthodox Church such as the Greek or Russian Orthodox Church?

1　Protestant (includes Baptists, Christian Church, Episcopal, Jehovah's Witnesses, Lutheran, Methodist, Presbyterian, etc.)
2　Roman Catholic
3　Jewish
4　Orthodox Church
5　Mormon (includes the Church of Jesus Christ of Latter Day Saints)
6　Moslem
7　Hindu
8　Other
9　None
0　UNDESIGNATED

25.　What is the religious preference of your spouse—Protestant, Roman Catholic, Jewish, Mormon, or an Orthodox Church such as the Greek or Russian Orthodox Church?

1 Protestant (includes Baptists, Christian Church, Episcopal, Jehovah's Witnesses, Lutheran, Methodist, Presbyterian, etc.)
2 Roman Catholic
3 Jewish
4 Orthodox Church
5 Mormon (includes the Church of Jesus Christ of Latter Day Saints)
6 Moslem
7 Hindu
8 Other
9 None
0 UNDESIGNATED

26. About how often do you pray? [READ]

1 Several times a day
2 Once a day
3 Several times a week
4 Once a week
5 Less than once a week
6 Never
7 NOT APPLICABLE (VOLUNTEERED)
8 NO ANSWER
0 DON'T KNOW

27. How often do you attend religious service? [READ]

1 Never
2 Less than once a year
3 About once or twice a year
4 Several times a year
5 About once a month
6 Two to three times a month
7 Nearly every week
8 Every week
9 Several times a week
0 DON'T KNOW/NO ANSWER

28. How often does your spouse attend religious services?

1 Never
2 Less than once a year
3 About once or twice a year

4   Several times a year
5   About once a month
6   Two to three times a month
7   Nearly every week
8   Every week
9   Several times a week
0   DON'T KNOW/NO ANSWER

29. There are many different ways of picturing God. We'd like to know the kinds of images you are most likely to associate with God. For each of the following pairs of words, please tell me which you are more likely to associate with God. First . . .

a. Do you tend to picture God more as a judge or more as a lover?

1   Judge
2   Lover
3   Neither (VOLUNTEERED)
4   Both (VOLUNTEERED)
0   DON'T KNOW

b. More as a master or more as a spouse?

1   Master
2   Spouse
3   Neither (VOLUNTEERED)
4   Both (VOLUNTEERED)
0   DON'T KNOW

c. More as a mother or more as a father?

1   Mother
2   Father
3   Neither (VOLUNTEERED)
4   Both (VOLUNTEERED)
0   DON'T KNOW

d. More as a friend or more as a king?

1   Friend
2   King
3   Neither (VOLUNTEERED)
4   Both (VOLUNTEERED)
0   DON'T KNOW

30. For each of the following statements, please tell me if you strongly agree, agree somewhat, disagree somewhat, or strongly disagree. [READ]

	Strongly Agree	Agree Somewhat	Disagree Somewhat	Strongly Disagree	Don't Know
a. The world is basically filled with evil and sin	1	2	3	4	0
b. Human nature is basically good	1	2	3	4	0
c. There is much goodness in the world	1	2	3	4	0
d. Human nature is fundamentally perverse and corrupt	1	2	3	4	0

31. Which of the following statements comes closest to describing your feelings about the Bible? [READ]

1 The Bible is the actual word of God and is to be taken literally, word for word
2 The Bible is the inspired word of God but not everything in it should be taken literally, word for word
3 The Bible is an ancient book of fables, legends, history, and moral precepts recorded by men
0 DON'T KNOW

32. From what ethnic group or groups are you mainly descended? [DO NOT READ] [ACCEPT MULTIPLE RESPONSES]

1 British (English, Scottish, Welsh)
2 German
3 Italian
4 Polish or other Eastern European country
5 Hispanic

6   Irish
7   Black
8   Asian
9   Scandinavian
0   Other
X   DON'T KNOW/NO ANSWER

33. What is your height?

_____ _____   99   REFUSED
Feet   Inches

34. What is your weight?

_____ _____ _____ Pounds   999   REFUSED

35. Is your total annual household *income* before taxes $20,000 or more or is it less than $20,000?

1   $20,000 or more
2   Less than $20,000—SKIP TO QUESTION 38
0   DON'T KNOW/REFUSED—SKIP TO QUESTION 40

36. Is it $30,000 or more, or less than $30,000?
1   $30,000 or more
2   Less than $30,000   ⎤
0   DON'T KNOW/REFUSED   ⎦—SKIP TO QUESTION 40

37. Is it $50,000 or more, or less than $50,000?
1   $50,000 or more
2   Less than $50,000   ⎤—SKIP TO QUESTION 40
0   DON'T KNOW/REFUSED   ⎦

38. Is it $15,000 or more, or less than $15,000?
1   $15,000 or more—SKIP TO QUESTION 40
2   Less than $15,000
0   DON'T KNOW/REFUSED—SKIP TO QUESTION 40

39. Is it $10,000 or more, or less than $10,000?
1   $10,000 or more
2   Less than $10,000
0   DON'T KNOW/REFUSED

40. What is your race? Are you white, black, or some other?
1   White
2   Black

3   Other
0   DON'T KNOW

41. Finally, I would like to ask you some rather personal questions. Some of these questions are very sensitive. If there are any you'd rather not respond to, please say so. First, for each of the following statements, please tell me how well each describes you—very well, pretty well, not too well, or not at all?

		Very Well	Pretty Well	Not Too Well	Not At All	Don't Know
a.	Moral about sex	1	2	3	4	0
b.	Skillful lover	1	2	3	4	0
c.	A sexual person	1	2	3	4	0
d.	Avoid sex	1	2	3	4	0
e.	Usually give in when there is an argument	1	2	3	4	0
f.	Sometimes enjoy taking off your clothes for your spouse	1	2	3	4	0

42. For each of the following statements, please tell me how well each describes your spouse. Please tell me if it strongly applies, applies somewhat, or does not apply. Would you say your spouse . . . (INSERT ITEM—READ)

		Strongly Applies	Applies Somewhat	Does Not Apply	Don't Know
a.	Is mysterious and intriguing	1	2	3	0
b.	Is romantic	1	2	3	0
c.	Is sometimes like a god to you	1	2	3	0
d.	Delights in you	1	2	3	0

		Strongly Applies	Applies Somewhat	Does not Apply	Don't Know
e.	Cares more about (his/her) work than about you	1	2	3	0
f.	Wants to make love too often	1	2	3	0
g.	Cannot be trusted	1	2	3	0
h.	Has bad manners	1	2	3	0
i.	Is a skillful lover	1	2	3	0
j.	Is imaginative about sex	1	2	3	0
k.	Drinks too much	1	2	3	0
l.	Is good at compromising	1	2	3	0

43. If we were able to ask your spouse the same questions about you, how would he or she respond? Please tell me if it strongly applies, applies somewhat, or does not apply. Would your spouse say you . . . (INSERT ITEM—READ)

		Strongly Applies	Applies Somewhat	Does Not Apply	Don't Know
a.	Are mysterious and intriguing	1	2	3	0
b.	Are romantic	1	2	3	0
c.	Are sometimes like a god to him/ her	1	2	3	0
d.	Delight in him/her	1	2	3	0
e.	Care more about your work than about him/her	1	2	3	0
f.	Want to make love too often	1	2	3	0

		Strongly Applies	Applies Somewhat	Does Not Apply	Don't Know
g.	Cannot be trusted	1	2	3	0
h.	Have bad manners	1	2	3	0
i.	Are a skillful lover	1	2	3	0
j.	Are imaginative about sex	1	2	3	0
k.	Drink too much	1	2	3	0
l.	Are good at compromising	1	2	3	0

44. Did you and your spouse live together before you got married?

1 Yes
2 No
3 NO ANSWER
0 DON'T KNOW ⎤—SKIP TO QUESTION 46

IF YES, ASK:

45. For how long?

_____ _____ Years   99 REFUSED
                                  00 LESS THAN SIX MONTHS

ASK ALL

46. Was there a period of time, before marriage, when you had a sexual experience with someone of the opposite sex other than your present spouse?

1 Yes
2 No
0 REFUSED ⎤—SKIP TO QUESTION 49

47. How many people other than your spouse?

_____ _____   99 REFUSED

48. Do you now feel strong regret, only some regret, or no regret at all about having this sexual relationship before being married?

1 Strong regret
2 Only some regret
3 No regret at all
4 NO ANSWER
0 DON'T KNOW

ASK ALL:

[FORM 1]

49. During the past year, how many sexual partners have you had, including your spouse?

		00	NONE
_____	_____	99	REFUSED

[FORM 2]

49a. During the past year, how many partners, including your spouse, did you have sexual intercourse with?

		00	NONE
_____	_____	99	REFUSED

[FORM 1]

50. During your present marriage, how many sexual partners, including your spouse, have you had?

		00	NONE
_____	_____	99	REFUSED

[FORM 2]

50a. During your present marriage, how many partners, including your spouse, did you have sexual intercourse with?

		00	NONE
_____	_____	99	REFUSED

[FORM 1]

51. How many sexual partners, including your spouse, have you had in your life?

		00	NONE
		97	97 AND OVER
		98	DON'T KNOW
_____	_____	99	REFUSED

[FORM 2]

51a. How many partners, including your spouse, did you have sexual intercourse with in your life?

                                      97   97 AND OVER

                                        98   DON'T KNOW

_____ _____ 99   REFUSED

52. How old were you the first time you had sexual intercourse?

_____ _____ Years   00   REFUSED

53. [IF MORE THAN ONE PARTNER IN QUESTION 50, ASK:] Do you now feel strong regret, only some regret, or no regret at all about the extramarital partners you've had during your marriage?

1   Strong regret
2   Only some regret
3   No regret at all
0   DON'T KNOW

[SKIP TO QUESTION 55]

54. [IF ONLY ONE PARTNER IN QUESTION 50, ASK:] If you had had other partners other than your spouse, do you think you would feel strong regret, only some regret, or no regret at all?

1   Strong regret
2   Only some regret
3   No regret at all
0   DON'T KNOW

55. We're just about to the end of the survey. Many couples are interested in trying new ideas. Please tell me how often you do each of the following with your spouse. Some of these questions are very sensitive. If there are any you'd rather not respond to, please say so. Would you say you and your (husband/wife) do each of the following a lot, sometimes, rarely, or never . . . [READ]

	A lot	Sometimes	Rarely	Never	Refused
a. Go to religious retreats together	1	2	3	4	0
b. Go to marriage therapy	1	2	3	4	0
c. Abandon all your sexual inhibitions	1	2	3	4	0
d. Swim nude together	1	2	3	4	0
e. Watch X-rated videos	1	2	3	4	0
f. Buy erotic underclothes	1	2	3	4	0
g. Make love outdoors	1	2	3	4	0
h. Play with each other intimately for a long time	1	2	3	4	0

56. Now if I had asked those same questions five years ago, how would you have answered? (IF MARRIED LESS THAN FIVE YEARS, SAY A FEW YEARS AGO.) Would you say you and your (husband/wife) did each of the following a lot, sometimes, rarely, or never . . . [READ]

	A lot	Sometimes	Rarely	Never	Refused
a. Go to religious retreats together	1	2	3	4	0
b. Go to marriage therapy	1	2	3	4	0
c. Abandon all your sexual inhibitions	1	2	3	4	0
d. Swim nude together	1	2	3	4	0
e. Watch X-rated videos	1	2	3	4	0
f. Buy erotic underclothes	1	2	3	4	0
g. Make love outdoors	1	2	3	4	0
h. Play with each other intimately for a long time	1	2	3	4	0

57. About how much time do you and your spouse talk to each other during the course of a week (in hours)?

00	NONE
98	LESS THAN ONE HOUR

_____ _____ hours   99 REFUSED

58. For each of the following statements about marriage, please tell me if you agree or disagree with each. Would you say you strongly agree, agree somewhat, disagree somewhat, or strongly disagree that . . . (INSERT ITEM)

	Strongly Agree	Agree Somewhat	Disagree Somewhat	Strongly Disagree	Don't Know
a. Your spouse and you are more concerned about being faithful than most people	1	2	3	4	0
b. Women work harder than men at making a marriage last	1	2	3	4	0
c. Lovemaking is more important to men than women	1	2	3	4	0
d. Sex is very important in holding marriages together	1	2	3	4	0

59. About how often did you have sex during the last twelve months? [READ]

1   Not at all
2   Once or twice

3   About once a month
4   Two or three times a month
5   About once a week
6   Two or three times a week
7   More than three times a week
0   REFUSED

60.   People have different feelings during and after lovemaking.
      For each, please tell me whether or not these feelings apply
      to you. [READ]

		Applies	Does Not Apply	Refused
a.	Physical satisfaction	1	2	0
b.	Delight that I have pleased my spouse	1	2	0
c.	Disappointment with myself	1	2	0
d.	Spiritual joy	1	2	0
e.	Pride in myself	1	2	0
f.	Disappointment with my spouse	1	2	0
g.	Healing of the strains and conflicts of marriage	1	2	0
h.	Embarrassment	1	2	0
i.	Ecstasy	1	2	0
j.	Boredom	1	2	0
k.	Desire for more	1	2	0
l.	Deep love	1	2	0
m.	Exhaustion, ready to go to sleep	1	2	0
n.	Shame at what I am doing	1	2	0

61. On the average, how long would you say your lovemaking lasts?

_____ _____   999 REFUSED

HOURS   MINUTES

62. Now I am going to ask you a very personal question. Have you ever been forced to have sex against your will?

    1 Yes
    2 No
    0 REFUSED

63. May I ask by whom?

    1 Other (LIST) _____
    2 Don't know
    3 Refuse
    4 Spouse
    5 Relative
    6 Friend
    7 Date
    8 Stranger
    9 Boss
    1 Doctor

64. CHECK RESPONDENT'S SEX:

    1 Male
    2 Female

65. CHECK THE DAY OF WEEK INTERVIEW WAS COMPLETED.

    1 Mon   2 Tues   3 Wed   4 Thurs   5 Fri   6 Sat   7 Sun

66. CIRCLE NUMBER OF CALL ON WHICH THIS INTERVIEW WAS COMPLETED.

    1   2   3   4

PLEASE RECORD AND VERIFY PHONE NUMBER:

| | | | – | | | | – | | | |

AREA CODE   EXCHANGE   NUMBER

END OF INTERVIEW: THANK RESPONDENT: Thank you very much for your time. Have a nice day/evening.

I HEREBY ATTEST THAT THIS IS A TRUE AND HONEST INTERVIEW.

_____   _____

(INTERVIEWER'S SIGNATURE)   (DATE)